The Bigger Book of Yes

Edited by Jon Doolan

Contents

Foreword

When the YesTribe began to assemble in June 2015, a heavy theme of adventure filled the gaps between campfire silences. Since then 'adventure' has an expanded meaning, far wealthier than a long distance journey by bike or foot or kayak.

Adventure is now a description for the new path in life. It's a school-night spent microadventuring underneath the stars or that gallant decision to quit the job and start freelancing. It's a weekend-long walk in the South Downs or a trusting leap from a plane with a glorified bedsheet folded neatly inside your backpack. Adventure is the act of doing something new and, while the occasional surprise will whisk us away on a most unsuspected pursuit, one needs to be in the right mind-set to take any given opportunity.

And this is where this big, fat YES comes in. Saying yes more is an encouraging idea, a gentle reminder that when you say "Yes!" things will happen in parallel to the gusto with which you express the word. A glum "Ok" is unlikely to become the life-long memory that an ecstatic "Hell YES!" will drive you towards. Whether you like walking or running, biking or hosting, building or creating, your idea of living a Yesful life will differ greatly to the next person.

Saying "Yes" is like having a key which opens up a door to a whole new world.

You see, it's the confidence to own a decision that counts (even if you'd said yes to something you have absolutely no experience in). Owning your decisions becomes a habitual confidence to own yourself, your identity.

Mental health and wellbeing have always been frequent factors in the YesStories shared at our monthly events. Our annual Yestival is special, not because of the variety of adventures brought to the stages, but because it's a place where everyone is accepted. It's a place where size, experience, colour, gender, sadness and hugging ability have zero bearing on whether you'll be treated with respect. Everyone, even if they turned up alone and with trepidation, leaves with new friends and a warm heart.

So read deep beneath the surface of the stories to come in this book. They're born of an attitude to live a great, useful, unique life. You'll notice the absence of comparison and (in most places) competition, for these are individual tales told because the authors found their inner strength and grew as a result of a big, healthy YES.

The writers and editors in this book follow a trend in the YesTribe of offering their time, skills and stories for free. In return, they get a value that doesn't come in paper, copper or alloy form. There is so much satisfaction in finding a way to contribute without traditional payment. I'll wager that, should they ever find themselves opposite you on a tube or bus or even somewhere in the park, the biggest reward they could ever get would be to see your smile as they read this book.

So thank you for picking it up and contributing to the wonderful work of Teddington Trust, and if the feeling takes you and a story touches you, please drop a line, a note or a tweet to the author and tell them how they made you feel. And then off you go to discover your next yes. Who knows, you might just appear in the next Even Bigger Book of Yes!

Dave Cornthwaite

Founder of SayYesMore, the YesTribe and avid sayer of Yes

Introduction

When I originally had the idea of the Big Book of Yes, all I wanted to do was showcase some of the wonderful adventure stories I'd heard from various members of the YesTribe. I had some skills in book editing and self-publishing and thought I could help these people in their first step in becoming Adventure Authors. I knew the thrill of having my own writing published. I knew the delight of holding your own book in your hand. I knew I could make a difference to these adventurers.

What I didn't know was exactly how inspiring the stories would be. I didn't realise how many people would go on to buy the book. I'll be honest, I wasn't even sure that we could pull it off.

But it was a raving success! Hundreds and hundreds of copies of the book were sold. It reached number one on eBook and print book sales charts (knocking Mark Beaumont off the podium in the process). Over a thousand pounds was raised for the Teddington Trust. It's still selling well today! I was on cloud nine!

The problem was, there were still so many stories to be told. At every YesTribe meetup or campout or YesStories, I'd hear more and more people telling me their tales of adventure.

I couldn't NOT do a second book!

So here it is. This time BIGGER and better than ever! Twenty-two incredible and inspirational stories. Each one is a celebration of the YesMoment - that instant in time when an opportunity presents itself. You've got two choices. Take the easy path, the same road you've always trodden and say "No!" Or step into the unknown, embrace the challenge and be the person who achieves their potential.

But before we even kick off with our first story, I want to say a few massive thank yous:

- The Authors – Every single one of them has donated their time and efforts into crafting amazing tales to inspire you. They don't get a penny out of this project so please, if you like what you've read, head over to their websites or social media accounts to see more of their awesomeness. You'll find these at the end of each chapter.

- The Artists – Harkiran Kalsi created another brilliant cover. Please check out more of her stunning designs at www.harkirankalsi.co.uk. Hattie Parker drew the gorgeous pictures that appear throughout the book. Just beautiful! You can find her at www.hattieparker.co.uk or on her Instagram account @hattieparkerdesign.

- The YesTribe – Dave Cornthwaite has created something really special. The YesTribe is an online and face-to-face community full of wonderful and inspiring people. All of us (authors, designers, editors and charity founders) are members of this marvellous community. If you want to SayYesMore then join the YesTribe Facebook group.

- YOU – Thank you! 100% of the royalties from the sales of this book go to Teddington Trust so you are an awesome human being just for shelling out a few quid. Well done you!! But, from the bottom of our hearts, thank you for reading our stories. We hope they inspire you to go off on your own adventures, whatever they may be.

Read, be inspired and SAYYESMORE!

Jon Doolan, July 2019

Founder of The Adventure Writers' Club

Jondoolan.com

Chapter 1

Summer of YES

by Amber Farrington

It's no secret how much I love London. I even wrote a book and created a brand about my love for it. Sure, it doesn't have the natural scenery of the Swiss Alps, or the climate of the Caribbean, but it holds a unique and beautiful charm that sets it apart from every other city in the world. There are so many things to love about it... the shops, the parks, the myriad of new restaurants and bars, the ease of transport, the bigger picture thinking, the cheap flights to anywhere in Europe and most importantly, my London friends.

I was heart-broken when I realised that my UK Visa would come to an end at the start of June. There is no black and white rule as to how soon I could re-enter on a tourist visa. It is purely up to the discretion of the immigration officer that you encounter on the day – which makes it an extremely unhelpful grey area of regulations. In any case, my research online (mostly at the highly speculative and non-admin-monitored forum of the Aussies in London Facebook group) led me to the questionable but logical conclusion that a minimum of 8 weeks out of the country should be enough to allow a smooth re-entry back into the UK.

To most people this would be brilliant. 8 weeks of uninterrupted compulsory vacation. What more could I ask for?

The obvious solution was to spend the 8 weeks travelling around Europe (you know, turning lemons into lemonade and all that!), but there was not one single part of me that was excited by this. I have travelled my whole life and loved it, but in London, I had found a place that felt like home. I was devastated at the thought of it coming to such an abrupt end. With my Visa deadline dilemma building, I felt the resistance growing within me.

So I did what all soon-to-be-exiled immigrants do... I went into denial.

As a result of my childish refusal to accept my impending exportation, I planned almost nothing for the 8 weeks I had to be away. The first 5 days were sorted but the rest I had left wide open... open for adventures, experiences and all kinds of new and exciting things!

There's no denying that this gaping hole in my travel plans was equal parts terrifying and exhilarating. Over recent years, I had gotten progressively better at taking leaps of faith and trusting that I will land on my feet. But this complete lack of plan, schedule or even knowing where my next meal would be coming from or where I'd end up sleeping? That's taking it to the next level.

More than ever before, this felt like opening my hands to the Universe and saying "Go on, then! Surprise me!"

Well, as typically happens when we say YES to something crazy or take a leap of faith into the unknown, life rewards us in ways we never could have imagined.

The trip began with a soft touch – planned, safe and in the comfort of friends. 6 of us set off together to my favourite place in Croatia... it's a beautiful part along the coastline that I discovered a few years ago (and have returned to every summer since). The beaches are pristine, there are very few tourists and it is just a beautiful, simple place to be. My mentality was a bit of, 'Fine, if I have to leave then I'm taking you lot with me!' We had an amazing time in the sunshine, soaking up the beaches, kayaking along the coast and enjoying life.

When they all left and went back to London (for their, y'know, jobs and adult lives), I felt really flat. Not only was I now on my own but I was facing the unknown. Adrift in a sea of beauty and fear.

It didn't take long for the next phase of the plan to reveal itself. The very next day I got a call from my cousin who was unexpectedly flying into Switzerland from Australia the following week and asked if I wanted to join them at their house in Interlaken.

Of course I said, "Yes!"

Interlaken is one of those places that I have always wanted to go. 15 years ago my cousin, Scott, and his now wife, Karin, got married there. My parents and brother visited for the wedding and brought back pictures and stories of adventures and magical scenery. I was unable to go to the wedding all those years ago as it was during my University exam period and I have longed to go ever since. This seemed like the perfect opportunity so I wasted no time in booking my flight to Interlaken.

It truly was more beautiful than anything I could have imagined and the scenery blew my mind. I was very fortunate to have Scott and Karin as local tour guides showing me around – by foot, bike and car.

Interlaken translates to 'between lakes' and is one of the oldest and most popular summer holiday destinations in Switzerland. It is famous for the beautiful town positioned between the two lakes (Lake Thun and Lake Brienz) and surrounding mountain peaks.

But there is one more thing that Interlaken can boast about. Apparently, this is THE place to do it – paragliding. It had been on my bucket list for as long as I'd had a bucket to write lists on.

Despite it costing over €200, I just knew this was something I had to do. One day we visited a neighbouring town (called Thun). We met up with one of my cousin's friends, Rich, who had just arrived back in Switzerland for the 3 month tourist season. He is a Paragliding instructor with over 20 years' experience. He sometimes fits in up to 12 jumps a day and so he works very hard over the season doing what he loves. But having just flown in the day before, he was looking to take someone out for a jump to blow off the cobwebs for his first jump for the season and test out his new GoPro. When he asked if I would like to be that 'someone' I actually couldn't believe my luck. I absolutely didn't mind being his paragliding GoPro guinea pig!

He took me out the next day and it truly was one of the most magical things I have ever experienced. The feeling of weightlessness that strikes you as soon as you are airborne, the sounds of the cowbells becoming a distant jingle and the simultaneous waves of adrenaline and peace that wash over you as you soar higher and higher above the trees.

Rich didn't waste time with the jokes to test my nerves pre-jump though.

"It's been a while", he said. "I can't quite remember which one ties on to where. I'm sure you'll be able to take over if anything happens mid-flight, no?"

"Sure Rich, it can't be that hard. This isn't a real job you have anyway!" I replied, trying to hide my rising fears.

"Yeah and also this is an old parachute. I save the good one for paying customers!" he said, clearly upping the ante to get some sort of reaction out of me.

I persisted acting unperturbed and responded with, "Well, if this is my last day on Earth at least I'll be going out with a bang!"

After a week in Switzerland, my cousins were ready for a change of pace and decided to head to Imperia on the Italian Riviera for a few days. I joined them and planned to continue my travels solo from there. I was feeling a pull to the Italian and French Riviera so was excited to explore these areas as the next stage of my trip.

When we arrived in Imperia, I was greeted by the impressive Marina packed with super yachts and luxury boats bigger than anything I had ever seen. "Many British millionaires keep their boats moored here because it's only an hour down the road from Monaco but less than half the cost," Scott explained as we drove in. My eyes were wide with wonder as we approached the harbour from above via the winding coastal roads. I could smell the sea before I saw it. I could almost taste the salt (and pizza) in the air. Something about this town felt very exciting.

Karin then planted the seed with, "You should get a job on one of those big boats, they are always looking for crew, wouldn't that be fun!" My mind instantly wandered into fantasyland of me on a luxury boat, rubbing shoulders with the rich and famous, getting a tan while sailing the high seas.

'Yes, let's find a way to make that happen,' I thought, with my usual naïve optimism.

Over the following days, I made enquiries with locals, joined relevant Facebook groups, holding out hope for a job opportunity to spring up… but nothing did. My cousins had to return to Switzerland leaving me solo and contemplating the unknown once again. Some days I would go down and spend hours at the Marina, letting the sun kiss my face, feeling the salty air prickling my skin and dreaming of life on board. I would admire the cool crew with their cool tans and their cool crew uniforms, loading cool supplies onto cool yachts and wondering what cool antics took place on board.

After a few days, I felt I had seen enough of Imperia and had given up hope of finding my dream boat job. I booked my train ticket to Nice with plans to set off the following day to explore France.

Later that day, just as my bags were packed and ready to go, a job appeared in the Imperia jobs noticeboard… it seemed like the one that I had been waiting for! Could it finally be?! It was for a two-week contract aboard a very big boat as a nanny for two children of a high profile VIP guest. The job left from Antibes in five days' time and returned to Nice two weeks after that on the exact date I had planned to return to the UK (and my 8-week sentence was up).

I bashed out a quick CV and sent off my application to the Chief Stewardess, Julie.

I got a call first thing the next morning – it was Julie. "Cool, so we've sent your CV to the family and they are happy. You've got the job," she said comfortably.

I paused for a second while I held back the excitable 13-year-old girl squeals that I suddenly had the urge to let out. I actually couldn't believe my luck…

"So all you need to do now is just send me your STCW certificate," she said.

"My what?"

"Your qualification that allows you to work on boats," she explained.

"Oh, err, I don't have one of those," I said, my heart sinking like an anchor. Of course it was too good to be true. Of course there would be some sort of paperwork that I'd need to work on a yacht. They wouldn't let any old riff-raff aboard these beautiful crafts.

"Okay, don't worry about it," she said breezily. "I'll chat to the captain and it'll be fine. Great, so we'll see you on the 11th!"

OH EM GEE!!! My dream of stepping foot onto one of these luxury superyachts was coming true – and even better I was going to be PAID for it! As soon as we got off the phone, I had to decide whether to prioritise letting out my 13-year-old girl squeals that I'd been supressing or calling Mum to let her know I had just hit the job jackpot.

Of course, both happened at the same time. Lucky Mum who's first response to my high pitched tones was, "Darling, are you okay? Where are you? What happened?" Poor Mumsy, let's just say this isn't the first and probably won't be the last time I shave a few years off her life.

Crew log day 1 – 11/7/18

This is it! All aboard… I have arrived in Antibes, finally found the boat. It's in a separate bay outside the main Marina because it is too big for a standard berth. I took this as a promising sign that I am in for quite a treat. Was greeted by the Chief Engineer washing the boat when I first arrived. And when I say greeted, I mean he grunted at me and then carried on cleaning. I mean, I probably did look a bit ridiculous with my huge backpack and clipped on front pack, but still a simple, "I'll get the captain for you," wouldn't have gone awry. After waiting awkwardly on the dock for someone else to appear I began to wonder if I had the wrong boat, or if this man cleaning was a subcontractor who knew nothing of my impending arrival. Luckily for me though, I would have 14 more days to learn that this was just his standard demeanour.

The Captain ran me through a lot (too many) instructions and housekeeping rules that mostly went in one ear and out the other as I was excitedly and nervously looking around at my new 'home'. He showed me to my room and I was lucky enough to be getting my own luxury room in the guest area. LUSH. The rest of the crew were squished into tiny bunks at the front of the boat whereas I felt almost guilty to get the royal treatment. Almost. Met the rest of the crew who returned to the boat in the afternoon by taxi and with what appeared to be a few thousand Euros worth of groceries. Time to crack on and help the crew with whatever needs to be done as the guests don't arrive for another couple of days now.

Crew log day 4 – 14/7/18

Hello from below deck

All guests are now on board and we are OFF and sailing! It has been a lot of hard work so far – when I'm not with the kids, I am helping the crew with jobs to be done on the interior and exterior of the boat. Turns out manual labour can actually be fun (well, when it's novel and temporary).

The 1 year old is super cute. I think I might want to keep him post-charter. Might not mention that to the parents just yet as I am getting the vibe already of Mum's reluctance to trust her bub with an almost stranger.

The 3 year old is also super cute – despite appearing to be permanently hyped up on Red Bulls, although there is none in sight. He doesn't speak English, so that makes for a fun time when trying to explain to him why he can't play with the anchor or jump on the luxurious sofas!

The chef on board is dishing up some of the tastiest food I have ever eaten. Like anywhere and like ever. He thinks I am easily pleased because I already explained to him that my cooking skills portfolio involves knowing which buttons to push on the microwave, using a can opener and scrambling eggs (which even then I sometimes don't get quite right). But what he doesn't know is that my Mum is quite the chef extraordinaire so I do know good cooking when I taste it.

I am slowly but surely getting abreast of the crew dynamics…

The Chef and Chief Stewardess appear to be an item – which doesn't seem to faze the rest of the crew as long as the job gets done.

The second Stewardess is a super hard-working smiling ball of Philippino joy who everyone can rely on to be first up and last to bed. I would say the Captain is pretty relaxed but also a bit jaded, which I find amusing. The Engineer is just plain grumpy and clearly hates life – including me as now a part of said life. I enjoy smiling extra warmly at him in the mornings.

We are currently in St Tropez – I think? Can't say for sure, as I haven't seen much sun for the past 24 hours. Heading for Sardinia tomorrow, which should be a nice long 19-hour sail into the sunset. Let's hope the kids sleep!

Captain's log day 5 – 15/7/18

(That's right I've promoted myself overnight)

We finally set sail for Olbia. One hour in and guests freaked out about the waves… in the ocean… (not sure what they were expecting?)… so we turned back…

I was blissfully unaware downstairs playing Fireman Sam with the 3 year old (away from the anchor and sans Red Bulls!). I looked up to see us docking and thought, 'Well, that was the fastest 19 hours of my life!'

So now, our slightly rattled guests are staying here for a few nights and then flying to meet us in Sardinia on Monday while we sail this bad boy off into the sunset without them.

My love of boats grows every day.

Still want to keep the baby.

I've also now well and truly earned my stripes and been let into the inner sanctum of the crew… this includes access to all angles of crew gossip.

Captain still hilarious.

Engineer still hating life... and me (because I'm still smiling at him and representing life).

Commander in Chief's Log day 6 – 16/7/18 – arrived in Sardinia!

(I'm getting properly ahead of myself now and taken the liberty of a further promotion)

Contemplating abandoning my regular life in exchange for a life at sea instead.

We had a full day of sailing with no clients on board – and this was even more blissful than I could have dreamed of.

I am now over halfway through a juicy novel, although I kept falling asleep on a sun lounger on the upper deck – disturbed only by the kitchen waftings at mealtimes and the occasional shout of "DOLPHINS!". Pinched myself a couple of times when I realised that I am actually being paid for this once in a lifetime experience. Guess now is not the time to let them know that I actually would have done this for free!

Back to work today though. I am surprisingly looking forward to them re-joining us on the boat this afternoon... even the little Dutch dynamo!

Day 7 - 17/7/18

Well, well, well... look who docked next to us today? (A boat called 'God's Own')

They are only 4 metres bigger than we are, however have an extra THREE crewmembers – which both our Chef and Stewardess agree is grossly unfair. I'm more interested in the fact that at least 2 of those 'extra 3 crew members' appear to be rather handsome and I'm starting to wonder if God has sent me a delivery of my next sea-faring boyfriend?

Guests are still not back on board. They have settled comfortably into their €2,300 a night (PER ROOM x 3 rooms) hotel Cala Di Volpe. Starting to think this boat is wasted on them...

I did get to visit said swanky hotel though... including the foyer where they filmed the James Bond movie 'The Spy Who Loved Me.' I would much prefer to be swanning by the pool as a Bond girl than clunking after a 3 year old in the Kid's Club whizzy dizz, but hey ho! For now, I'll take it!

It's a 12-minute taxi ride from the port where our boat is docked to the hotel... and the standard fare is €70. I almost fell off my seat when he told me the price. Lucky the Captain had handed me €200 on the way out and told me to get a receipt... this is clearly not his first time in Sardinia! I'm still trying to get my head around the fact that some people clearly have way too much money... and also how I can set up some sort of business to capitalise on this market next summer.

On a side note, I found out today that we have a jet ski on board... How did I miss this? I genuinely thought I'd taken a gratuitous selfie in every nook and cranny of this boat! Wondering how drunk I need to get the Captain before he lets me take it for a spin.

Day 8 - 18/7/18

The Sardinian weather gods have not been kind. We are still docked in Olbia, guests are still staying in the Bond hotel, and the weather is still too choppy to take the boat out for water sports. It's cool though. I get to spend a lot of time looking after the kids in the hotel Kids Club. At first I got excited thinking I would be able to do some up close and personal celeb spotting (Naomi Campbell is staying in the hotel, apparently), but alas the Kids Club is occupied by a lot of kids, a lot of nannies, and a distinct lack of anyone famous. I would have to get my fix of celebs in the hotel jewellery store. Speaking of which, I found the most perfect necklace – sapphire and diamond encrusted. The great news is that it only costs €1,750,000 (only need to work 874 more Charters and I'll be able to afford it!). The lady in the store politely told me to come back next year with a rich boyfriend. Perhaps it was my servant's uniform that gave me away?

Nanny log day 9 – 19/7/18

Chef and Chief Stewardess had another big fight in the kitchen today. I guess this is why they say you shouldn't mix business with pleasure. The galley (boat slang for kitchen) is not a big place and to be in close proximity with two angry lovers had me contemplating voluntarily walking the plank. Despite wanting to exit stage left, I also had the sense to know that they couldn't be trusted on their own. The volume was rising, the walls between the galley and the guests lounge are not very thick, so I took one for the team and very nobly took on the role of Mediator and Shoosher! It turns out the Chef was under the impression the guests would be eating dinner off the boat this evening, but Chief Stew had failed to communicate that they would in fact be returning to the boat shortly with very empty bellies and expecting a 3 course spread. I was more interested in maintaining professionalism around the VIP guests than getting to the bottom of 'who was right and who was wrong'. Let's just blame the grumpy Engineer and crack on with preparing dinner please! Dinner was finally served... late... very late.

Nanny log day 10/11/12/lost count but I know it's not day 14 as I'm still on board!

Boat life has now become my total reality where nothing else exists that doesn't involve crew, guests, boat, ocean and hunky South African crewmembers aboard 'God's own' (STILL docked next to us).

This afternoon I watched the hunky crew wave farewell to their charter guests and within minutes observed loud music and shirts off as party mode well and truly kicked in (must have left a hefty tip?). I paraded cute baby on upper deck, which worked a treat in grabbing attention of hunk #3. I garnered from our conversation that they collect next lot of guests tomorrow morning. Hunk #3 excitedly told me and my 'cute baby' that their next charter is 6 people – 4 guests and 2 security. Naturally I am starting to plan the surveillance… assuming if they are rolling with security then they have to be someone famous… unless the witness protection program now includes yacht charters?

I have made the rookie nanny mistake of becoming the 'cool friend from the boat' to dynamo 3 year old and also having the magic touch in getting the 1 year old to sleep. As a result, all trust issues appear to have gone out the window and I am no longer getting a spare second to myself… I guess the days of novels and dolphin spotting are on hold for now!

I have also started going for morning jogs. I've never liked running before – but put me in a marina full of super yachts and I'm suddenly inspired. Plus, they gave me a size 'small' uniform that was tight on day 1 and is not getting any looser with this chef on board. It does feel like a bit of a set up with the lack of expansion room to accommodate the holiday appetite.

Countdown to the end of the charter is now on. I overheard the guests asking the Captain if we can go to Corsica today. I wanted to chime in with, "OMG, yes! Me too! I want to see Corsica!" before reminding myself once again that I am the servant, not boss on this ship.

Day 14 – 24/7/18 we survived!

And that's a wrap. Guests have all disembarked and boarded flights back to Amsterdam. After assisting with the final clean and tidy up, I also disembarked and made my way to the airport to head back to London. It was bittersweet saying goodbye to my new friends that I had worked in such close quarters with over the past fortnight. I had grown to love them (ish…) and yep even the Engineer and I had shared moments of respect and understanding towards the end. I think it was my smiles that finally cracked him and his incessant grumpiness. The crew were preparing for their next charter where they were going to Ibiza… I kept feeling like I should be going with them as I was now part of the team, but alas there were no children needing looking after on the next Charter (although it is Ibiza so maybe a chaperone of sorts would have been useful!).

It was also bittersweet saying goodbye to the guests. They were quite lovely and I was particularly fond of the 1 year old. I was excited to be getting my sleep back though and it definitely reminded me to put plans of babies on hold for a good few more years.

I felt my nerves creeping in as I approached the front of the line at the Immigration counter of Heathrow Airport. Would they let me back in? I knew I wasn't doing anything illegal but also knew that I was in the regulatory twilight zone. I took a breath, put my trust in a higher source…

And breezed back in across the border.

It felt so good to be back on 'home soil', but within a few days of being in the confines of London, you wouldn't believe it, but I was really missing the pristine beaches of Croatia. I was missing the lakes and mountains of Interlaken. I was even missing the hard work and beautiful scenery from the boat! Had my love affair with London ended? Not exactly... we are bonded for life. One thing I had clearly seen now though is that truly everything does happen for a reason and my enforced unplanned holiday had been one of the most epic adventures and blessings of my life.

Amber Farrington is a globetrotting author and coach, based primarily in London but splitting her time between Australia and Europe. She loves traveling, yoga, anything outdoors, and nerdy puzzles. If you want to reach her, she loves swapping funny or inspiring stories.

Website: AmberFarrington.com

Facebook: amber.farrington.96

Instagram: @thelondonhustler

Twitter: @thelondonhustler

eBook: The London Hustler (available on Amazon)

Chapter 2

Pen Pusher to Pacific Rower

by Barry Hayes

The Realisation

Uncontrollably, the harsh orange glow from the street light outside seeped between the cracks in my eyelids, stabbing at my eyes, penetrating the deepest recesses of my brain, punishing me for my stupidity. As the all too familiar haze of dehydration and residual alcohol descended upon me, something felt different. Was that a pang of excitement? I couldn't understand why.

I was disorientated. I didn't know what I was doing or what day it was. Out of routine I reached for my mobile phone. Grasping blindly, I knocked over the full pint of water that 'Drunk Barry' had clearly made with the best of intentions for 'Hungover Barry' the night before. As I helplessly listened to the water spreading under my bedside table and my bed, soaking last night's shirt and the pile of dusty books that were no stranger to having bedside drinks spilt upon them, I finally located my phone dangling off the side of the bed by its charger.

10 new e-mails.

7 e-mails encouraging me to buy a variety of wares from timeshares to Viagra, 2 e-mails from long lost relatives who had, between them, seventeen billion US dollars to share with me if I invested a mere $5,000, and a final one, from a Philip Cavanagh.

Philip Cavanagh…that rings a bell.

Philip Cavanagh…

Phili…oh!!

Suddenly my struggling brain flooded with information. The realisation. What it was that had happened last night that had caused me to wake up feeling excited. The blog, the e-mail, the opportunity…saying, "Yes!"

This was the start of what would become the biggest, wildest adventure of my life so far.

The Day of Yes

Twenty-four hours previously, it was a cold February morning. The tarmac glistened and the grass was the palest of greens with the harsh frost that had settled. It was pitch dark apart from those ever-present amber streetlights which illuminated a wintry fog. It hung low in the air making it appear as if you might be in a 1980s dream sequence. I'm sure that if you took a photograph and looked at it whilst sat in a nice warm room on a weekend, you would coo and mention how beautiful it looks, perhaps using words like 'atmospheric' or 'crisp'. For me though, at five a.m. on a Wednesday morning, struggling to get out of the house to get to the first of two jobs that made up my fifteen hour workday, it was not beautiful; it was the antipathy of beautiful. It was very, very dark and very, very cold and I didn't like it one bit. I had, for the umpteenth time, slept through my alarm and so compounded the already bad situation by now being not only hungry but, much more seriously than that, caffeine-less.

Today, was not a good day.

As I blindly wrestled last night's unwashed clothes on whilst stumbling down the hall to the kitchen, I looked down. I was wearing two completely different types of shoe. It didn't seem like the day was going to get any better.

I shut my front door and shuffled across the drive, unintentionally kicking the inconveniently placed skateboard, sending it skittering across the concrete as I made my way to the car. My fingers numbed as I pulled on the car door handle, which was reluctant to open, momentarily frozen shut by nature's icebox. I pulled again on the handle, a creaking, cracking noise as the ice started to break, but still the door remained firm.

"STUPID CAR!!!" I burst out.

The door quickly opened. My unwarranted verbal assault had clearly done the trick, although I mused that shouting at a car as my first utterance of the day was perhaps not a great omen.

I bundled my gym bag, my breakfast, my lunch and my dinner into the passenger seat before clambering in and slamming the door behind me.

Breathe…

I started the engine and eased out in to the, as yet lifeless, estate before navigating my way up the hill to the main road. Eerily black trees and hedgerows accelerated past as I began to drive unnecessarily fast to ensure I made it to work for 6:25am.

Happy Tuesday

I deliver the mail. Not in the nice way where I get to drive a little red van with a black and white cat, meeting all the locals in the village and helping out with the occasional escaped sheep or needy farmer. Instead, I get to push a blue trolley with a broken wheel around a massive multinational bank, shuffling up the aisles, handing out envelopes to people that don't want envelopes. In a world of digital communications, I cater for the late adopters.

I was based in a large sprawling network of buildings made of sandstone and glass set amongst a strictly regulated landscape. From the outside it looked rather grand; large sandstone pillars either side of the main entrance situated beyond a be-fountained circular lake with three tall flag posts sporting the Union Flag, the American Flag and a flag with the company logo on. Once inside, it resembled every other large company created in the 90s. A world of grey-suited zombies fuelled by a seemingly endless supply of caffeine-based drinks. Everything was very sterile. Everything was very structured. Every day was very similar.

There were over 4,000 zombies in my office and I would watch as they patrolled the corridors, searching for new ways to satisfy their insatiable thirst for administrative duties. I would look at them, I'd shake my head and think how sad it must be to be one of them. Then I'd get my trolley of mail and shuffle off, patrolling the corridors in line with them. Same grey suit; same grey face.

Of course, the people that I refer to as zombies were actually just very nice, normal people going about their business in a normal way, earning money to support their families, to have their holidays or to invest in their hobbies. As far as office jobs go, it was and is a good environment to work in. You couldn't ask for much more from a workplace.

But I had a problem. The £5.93 per hour simply wasn't covering the basic bills for my young family during the 'double dip' recession. I was really struggling to keep my head afloat financially. I needed a second job. That was why I was on my way to work so early.

My second job was as a carer for a cerebral palsy sufferer called Lyla. When I first took the job, I didn't really know what a 'carer' did. I didn't have any experience in the caring field at all. I just needed some money and found the job whilst looking through the job centre adverts. If I could make money by helping someone in need, then that seemed like a much better option than cleaning offices or serving drunks in the evenings.

Lyla was quite a character. Flamboyant didn't cover it. Despite having almost nothing in common, she quickly became a good friend as well as my boss.

My job with Lyla would start first thing in the morning to provide any support she needed to get started with her day. Then at 07:45 I would leave her and drive over to my day job, working in the mailroom at the bank. I worked there from 08:00 until 17:00 before returning to Lyla for the evening part of my job at 17:15, which would usually last a further three hours. It is safe to say that at the end of each day after 14-16 hours at work, I was exhausted.

Today, was no different. The evening shift circulated around me scribing Lyla's university notes for the law degree she was completing. This was followed by cooking her dinner whilst being made to watch various videos on the internet that ranged from mildly amusing to completely psychotic, all of which pleased Lyla immensely but were generally beyond me.

Now, engrossed in yet another Japanese animation depicting characters with giant eyes that giggled too much, Lyla gave me my leave ten minutes early by silently gesturing with her hand in a 'shooing' motion. So, another day was over.

Once again dark, once again cold, I made my way back to the car which had once again started to frost over. I started it up and drove carefully back home, one arm out the window to keep me awake, eyes blinking with tiredness. I knew I was doing too much. I just couldn't see a way to pay the bills without having that second job.

It was also a bit of a double-edged sword. This job allowed me to pay my bills, but actually the money I earned was just a little more than I really needed. Each month I had a few hundred pounds that I could use to spend on non-essentials. Tonight my non-essential was to get to the pub to celebrate!

Now, I cannot remember exactly what it was I was celebrating. It may have been something as momentous as 'Happy Tuesday', but what I do remember was that I had a very nice time. Such a nice time that by one o'clock in the morning I was still celebrating Happy Tuesday, which at this time, simply wasn't horologically true. Thirty minutes later, I'd said my goodbyes, donned my coat, hat and gloves and I began the two mile walk home.

As I wobbled my way up the road skilfully navigating the perfectly straight pavement, occasionally stopping to cuddle the hedge, I scanned through my phone, flicking through my social media feed as is so common to do in the 21st century. As I scrolled, I came across a blog by a British adventurer that I had been following called Alastair Humphreys. Alastair explained in his blog, that an Irishman by the name of Philip Cavanagh had been in touch with him to try and persuade Alastair to join him on a big adventure that he had planned.

Philip's aim was to row across the Pacific Ocean.

'Wow!' I remember thinking. I didn't even realise that was possible to do! It sounded absolutely crazy and anyone that thought they could do such a thing must be insane.

Alastair went on to explain that he wasn't able to join Philip in his adventure but that he would put Philip's details in this blog so that any potential rowing partners could get in touch with him. Furthermore, Alastair explained that applicants did not need any rowing experience. They just needed to have the drive to learn.

I stopped staggering. I stopped being drunk. I think I stopped breathing. Here was a lunatic looking for a partner for one of the most amazing adventures on the planet... I was a lunatic; I was looking to break out of my zombie-land for an amazing adventure. All I needed to do was to say 'yes' to this opportunity. For just a very brief second, everything stopped. All noise. All movement. All light. Our two worlds were lining up, perfectly.

The Trigger

I grew up with my two younger brothers, Sam and Lewis, in a small rural village near to Chester in the North West of England. The two biggest influences in my life were my mum and my dad.

Mum taught us that we could be whoever we wanted to be... Of course, if that was a premiership footballer or professional tight rope walker then she'd be encouraging but also suggest a backup plan. You know, just in case the local ringmaster had his full quota of performers or if Liverpool FC's scouts were blind to our mad footballing skills.

My dad on the other hand, provided the adventure in our lives. Dad was in the military for 35 years so he used to go away for eight or nine months at a time. He did that for most of our lives, from before we were born until we were adults. Spending most of his time away didn't bother us growing up because that was the norm. But when he came back from being away, he would be armed with the stories of his travels. Incredible, fantastical stories about sea creatures, jungles, deserts, incredible operations, parties but also stories about the darker side; pirates, drug smugglers, the wars they had experienced.

During the Falklands war his ship was blown up by the Argentinian bombers. His story of survival fascinated me then, and fascinates me now. We all found these stories enthralling. It broadened our minds without even having to experience the adventures ourselves.

I used to tell all my friends at school about his adventures. I was, and am, incredibly proud of him.

When this same man, who had spent his life dodging bombs and bullets, ended up in a coma because of an infection, it was a difficult reality to accept. Infections are minor annoyances, not something to hinder a decorated war hero. Nevertheless, we watched as the doctors struggled to control the spread of this infection. It developed and began to poison his blood, sepsis took hold, and we were told to prepare for the worst. It was a devastating and damaging blow.

I remember sitting in the hospital whilst nurses worked around my comatose father, holding a leaflet in my hand about how to cope with loss and thinking that this was not the way he was supposed to go. Conjointly however, I found myself coming to terms with this concept; if it really was time for him to shuffle off this mortal coil, then OK. He was too young, it was not how he should have gone but what an incredible life this man had had. He had created this phenomenal legacy with a family that were incredibly proud of him. He was genuinely a hero figure to me.

As I sat there and processed this, an unpleasant realisation started to wave through my body, and it wasn't a momentary feeling. It swaddled me and stuck to me like tar; if I was in my Dad's position, right now... if I was to die tomorrow... what had I achieved? What sort of legacy had I created?

A permanently stressed out mailroom worker fighting to keep his head above the water. How on earth could my nine-year-old Jack be proud of that? I left the house before 6am and I got back at 10pm Monday to Friday. I worked Saturdays and Sundays as well. I barely even saw Jack. I used to tell all my mates at school stories about my Dad... What did Jack tell his friends about me? Did he tell them anything? How could he be proud of me?

If I externalised these thoughts, I knew people would say things like, "Don't be ridiculous Barry." "You've achieved incredible things." "You've brought up a really nice young man." "You've got a wonderful family." Blah…blah…blah.

So I didn't externalise those thoughts. I didn't want to be persuaded I'd been successful. I didn't want to be told I'd been successful in the name of pity. And I didn't want to be successful by someone else's measure. I needed to be successful in my own mind, by my own measure. I knew that I wanted to achieve something that I'd be proud of, that my family would be proud of. In a macabre way, I wanted to be clear in my mind that I'd achieved nothing in life. I didn't want to be dissuaded from that notion. It gave me the fire to do something about it.

Very quickly my mind-set changed. The more I focused on the required changes, the more my brain unlocked pathways to achieving these things. I was going to do something; I was going to be successful by my own measure. I didn't know exactly what my pathway was but I knew it began with adventure.

The big advantage my brothers and I had here over most people, and I imagine this is the same for a lot of people from a military background, is that we weren't quite as afraid of death as the next person. As overly-dramatic as that sounds, it's true. Death surrounded us. Throughout the stories of war-torn countries, of fighting, of travelling to faraway lands, of different cultures and of lost colleagues and friends; death was a part of many of those stories. It became something that we simply were not that afraid of. We numbed to it. We were matter of fact about it.

For a considerable time this manifested itself as a blatant disregard for my own safety and resulted in some questionable life choices. Now it was becoming an asset to me. It gave me the courage to do interesting things. I realised that over a 100,000 people die every day… almost all of them for some mundane reason – car accident, sickness, old age. I *am* going to join those numbers one day. It is not debateable. So if I leave this planet doing something that I believe to be amazing or incredible, after making a mark, and helping other people, then that is the best I can ask for.

But there was a twist.

Death *is* inevitable, but it wasn't my Dad's turn. After spending almost two years in various hospitals, including a portion where he escaped and flew to Spain before being brought back with a broken neck (a story for another time perhaps) he quite miraculously recovered, and is alive and well today. My only concern with him now is that there seems to be a distinct possibility that he has either sold his soul to a demon in exchange for ever lasting life, or he is a horror movie character, as he seems to consistently outmanoeuvre his appointment with Death.

Saying Yes

The world creaked back into gear and began to turn again. As I stared at this blog on my phone my brain started flashing ideas into my head way above their station. What would the boat look like? How many people would be needed for this crew? Could I physically take on something like this?

I quickened my stagger and actively reduced the amount of hedge cuddles I was having to get home as fast I possibly could. I made it home in record time and, after an altercation with my keychain, I finally fell through the door and into my hallway. Emma and Jack were sound asleep, as was pretty much everyone in the country.

Time check - Two a.m.

"Eugh!" up in three hours' time to go to work.

No matter. This was a very, very important day. I could just feel it. I fired up the computer in the spare bedroom, I relocated Philip's details and I began typing.

I read and re-read the e-mail to make sure it made sense and was not the ramblings of a drunken idiot, which of course it was. I felt it was ok and with that I pressed send. I shut the computer down, crept through to my bedroom, tip-toed across the room, and carefully slipped under the duvet next to Emma, drifting off peacefully with fanciful ideas about rowing oceans swirling around in my head.

At least that this is how it went in my head.

Emma's recollection was that I burst through the door at an 'ungodly hour', stomped through the house, had a very loud wee, interspersed with even louder farts, left my trousers in the bathroom, stomped through to the office, spent ages listening to old Nirvana songs whilst tapping away on the keyboard, made "nerr nurr nerrrrrrr" noises to the chorus of the music, clumped through to our bedroom, crashed into the wall, bounced back, landed on the bed and once lying on my back started complaining that the world was spinning too fast and kept chanting, "Ride the roller-coaster, Barry. Ride the roller-coaster." over and over before finally passing out and snoring loudly for an hour until my alarm clock went off for the next day.

Which I proceeded to ignore.

Again.

Preparations

Over the course of the next few weeks, Philip and I chatted at length about this project and before long I had flown to Dublin to meet with him. Seven pints of beer later we decided that we thought the other was 'actually quite sound' and we started plotting how we were going to put a team together to take on the Great Pacific Race.

Getting to the start line was one of the most difficult things I have ever been involved in and if there were more pages in this book then I would tell you all about it but, in short, we did eventually make it to start of this race. And it was as last minute as you can possibly imagine. It was so last minute in fact, that we met our third crew member the night before we flew to California, our fourth crew member actually in California and we didn't lay our hands on a boat (which as I understand it is a key component of a boat race) until seven days before we were due to push off.

At this stage you would have thought we would have been well trained rowing Gods and had hours upon hours of practice under our belts. Well, this summation would have been almost entirely inaccurate. In reality, before I got involved in this, I'd never really been to sea before. I'd never been on a yacht. I'd never rowed a boat, even on the river. Although some training did happen, most of it was foregone in the interests of spending time on administration trying to fund this project. The fact that we had absolutely no experience whatsoever, that we were still spannering the boat together on the morning of the race, that we'd essentially forgotten what a rowing machine looked like and that there was categorically nothing going right for us, earned us the cruel but valid nickname of 'The Jamaican Bobsled Team' of the race.

But, against all odds, on June the 9th 2014, we pushed off from mainland USA to take on this race that we had no business being in.

As we rowed out of the harbour that morning in the cool breeze, the experience was both unsettling and exciting – we knew that we were taking on the biggest challenge of our lives. We knew we were making history in the world's first race across this bit of the planet. But we also knew that there was a possibility that we might not make it across.

"Your boat is really low at the bow end!" some fishermen shouted from a nearby jetty, disturbing me from my inner turmoil.

'Annoying,' I thought, and pretended not to hear them; there was nothing we could do about it now.

We concentrated hard on trying to row in time, not for any speed or efficiency reasons, just purely so that we didn't look silly in front of the crowds that had amassed to witness us leave. As we failed at that and splashed and wobbled our way out of Monterey Harbour to the co-ordinates that marked the beginning of this race, my brain continued flashing with conflicting thoughts: This is actually happening. We're doing this. Can I do this? Will I be the weak link? Don't be the weak link. I hope I survive. I love my family. Please let's make it across. Is everyone feeling like this?

It's hard to describe the thoughts I was having; it wasn't fear, but my mind was racing with every possible outcome.

As we carried on rowing towards the official start line, things got quiet. The only noise was the catch and pull of our oars in the water. Plus Philip's swearing as he fiddled with the powerful waterproof speaker we had bought.

Everyone on all boats was immersed in their own thoughts. An uncomfortable silence had descended and the wind had stopped blowing.

Eventually this silence was broken by the distinctive horn fanfare and well-timed squealing of House of Pain's 'Jump Around' being blasted at maximum volume as Philip finally managed to connect his iPod to the speaker. We went from being quiet, calm and reflecting on our individual thoughts to suddenly being the hooligans of the race. It actually helped.

The Race

As drones whizzed overhead and news cameras rolled, a conch shell was blown from the back of a yacht to signify the start of the contest and we were off.

We immediately pulled hard on the oars, knowing full well that this pace was not achievable for very long. It almost felt like a sprint to Hawaii. As we settled into our rowing, we slowed the pace but still maintained a good speed. Long strokes moving us through the water at good pace.

"This isn't too bad," I mused.

Immediately the Pacific gave me the equivalent of hitting a dog on the nose with a newspaper in the form of a wave splashing me, soaking me, punishing me for my insolence.

As we moved out of the protection of the bay and into the unsheltered ocean, the waves were instantly larger and promptly I felt nerves coming into play.

'Are these waves enough to flip the boat over?' I thought. It looked like they were.

My body became more rigid, my rowing suffered, but despite getting pretty wet, the boat remained solid. The waves increased in size and the other racers simultaneously disappeared from view behind the various rolling crests. We wouldn't see another racer for the remainder of the crossing.

We rowed in pairs, swapping every two hours, something we would continue to do 24 hours a day for the entire crossing. As the sun dropped behind the horizon and the darkness enveloped us for the first time, I gradually felt a calmness wash over me. I had been so concerned with failing in the first few hours; being the laughingstock. I realised I had somehow got to this point with at least a small part of me still not quite believing I could do this.

The darkness signified a milestone; getting through the first day, a day that had already seen one team retire. As the night went on, I started to feel more connected with this boat and with this team I had really only just met.

The morning sun arrived, bathing the deck of the boat and bringing with it the realisation that we could no longer see land. This too was an oddly comforting experience – we've now made it so far away under our own steam that we cannot see land in any direction. This was now a proper adventure.

For the next ten days the Pacific showed us what it could do. The wind howled, thunder crashed, rain lashed our faces, waves far bigger than houses crashed over us, rolling us around the ocean, making us eternally grateful for the foul weather gear we'd managed to beg and borrow from the guys at the Monterey Peninsula Yacht Club. We lost battery power. We snapped oars. We broke our steering and our seats and our dagger-board and just about every other important piece of equipment. Our bodies became battered and broken. We suffered cuts, bruises, burns, sickness, hallucinations and by day eight we had grave concerns for the health of one of our number due to extreme dehydration.

There was a risk to life at this stage but the concept of failure did not compute. Failure was too difficult to think about. We had put every part of our lives, our money and souls into this crossing. The concept that it could be unsuccessful just couldn't form in my mind. Thankfully, after a lot of advice from doctors via the satellite phone, not to mention copious amounts of drugs, we all survived this dark period and as we broke through the ten-day barrier the boat, finally, started to level out.

In reality, the boat did not level out; it moved in the same way during the whole crossing, but our bodies slowly adjusted to it. With every day we spent aboard this vessel, we grew more connected to it. The boat became part of us and we became part of the ocean.

The sight of so much plastic then, felt devastating. It is one thing to watch a one minute video about the plastic pollution in the Pacific Ocean, or even to go to a one hour seminar about it. It is something very different to be living in it, having it polluting our home day after day for 25 days in an area of ocean that seemed to be consequently devoid of wildlife. It drilled home the fact that we are annihilating our planet with this deleterious substance and our destructive behaviours.

Eventually after 25 days, the plastic pollution eased up and on the same day, unsurprisingly, the wildlife appeared.

Crossing an ocean is challenging, and small things can make or break your day; the wildlife encounters are one of those things that make your day. So when the latter half of this crossing brought with it shoals of flying fish, pilot whales, swordfish and sea turtles, it was a very welcome change.

As we made our way across the ocean, keeping good pace, we ensured that we took the opportunity to absorb the experience as wholly as possible. Despite being in a race, if there was an opportunity to dive into the water, a thousand miles from any piece of land into ten thousand foot deep blue water, you can be sure we took it.

In spite of the hardships, we were living in a deeply beautiful world. During the day we would have the privilege of seeing the ever-changing ocean and its wildlife, the incredible sunsets and sunrises and the never-ending rainbows. At night, constant shooting stars and the milky way adorned the sky. The occasional moon bow would appear and the phosphorescence in the water created swirls of white and green that moved away from us as we rowed through the darkness.

These days spent on this ocean were powerful, formative days; they created me, and they created part of what I was now about. Experiences so deeply affective that they can never be put into words were fuelling me for the next part of my life. And as we eventually crossed the finish line forty-five days after we left California, in a race that saw most boats fail to make it across, the news that we had broken the pre-race world record by 19 days was largely irrelevant… this crossing had completely changed my life.

Reflection

I was physically the same person (save for the two and a half stone I lost in the process of the crossing), but now instead of my day dreaming being seen as a negative – it was my biggest asset. It had substance. I had proven to myself, and to anyone that cared to listen, that these daydreams could be converted to reality and that these adventures were absolutely achievable.

Have there been negatives? Unquestionably. Phenomenal debt. Enormous stress placed on the family and upon my relationships with my friends. Post adventure depression. I could go on.

But, by definition, you cannot have a positive without there being a negative. So it's a choice; you can choose to live a very comfortable life, never dealing with anything very terrible, but also never achieving anything very exciting... or, you decide today to live outside of your comfort zone, experiencing the extremes of life, good and bad. I guarantee your life will be enriched for it.

So, for anyone reading this who dreams of adventure but who feels they can't do it for reasons only known to them, consider your short time on this planet. Consider what you are here for. I implore you to try with every fibre of your being to get out there and take on that epic adventure. Please, please, please take some time to work out what your aspirations are and do one single thing today towards achieving those aspirations. Put down this book. Stop reading what I am writing and make that change today.

Do not make that change tomorrow – doing something about it tomorrow is not how you achieve your dreams. Direct, immediate action – even if it's just signing up to something on the internet, buying a pair of trainers, calling someone and telling them what you intend to do. It is so important.

Achieving your aspirations will change you; not only will you know that you can do something on this scale, other people will know, and that brings with it perhaps the most powerful part... Opportunities.

I can honestly say that I do not recall a single day since rowing the Pacific five years ago, without someone talking to me about adventure and most weeks someone will directly or indirectly provide an opportunity. I cannot always take those opportunities because of other commitments. But often I can.

Just in the last month I have rowed 800km from London to Paris, competed in a 100 mile ultra-marathon, raced in a dragon boat race, hung out with the Shaolin Monks, decided to train to swim the English Channel, been on the front page of a magazine, I'm 138 words off finishing writing this chapter, I have a meeting tonight with a guy about rowing the Atlantic in 2020, and as I'm typing this I have just been booked to speak at a dinner in New York City for a major global company. I am very proud of every one of those items but not one single event mentioned would have, or could have, happened this month if it were not for initially taking the plunge, saying yes and rowing the Pacific.

So say yes to adventure. Say yes to opportunity. Say yes to parties and journeys and volunteering and exciting things and scary things and everything in between. It will transform your life and will only lead to self-actualization. Often the only difference between someone that has achieved their aspirations and someone that hasn't is belief.

Barry Hayes is a British adventurer and motivational speaker. For further information on his talks and to keep up to date with his adventures get in touch via the following channels:

Website: theoceanrower.com

E-mail: info@theoceanrower.com

LinkedIn: linkedin.com/in/theoceanrower

Facebook: facebook.com/theoceanrower

Instagram: instagram.com/theoceanrower

Twitter: twitter.com/theoceanrower

Chapter 3

Running Across Scotland

by Becci Jewell

Once I'd declared I was going to run across Scotland, that was it, I pretty much had to. Prematurely sharing my half-baked adventure ideas ensures I at least start, if not finish, them. My Land's End to Worcester bike ride of 2015 being a good example.

"Is there a route?" my boyfriend, Jon, had asked when I brought up my running plan.

"Probably", I'd said. "Never mind a route, there'll be red squirrels bounding across our path and golden eagles soaring above the glens."

Neither squirrels nor eagles ever appeared and, for a time on our final day - by far the easiest day navigationally - we lost the route too. Standing in the pouring rain, scratched legs streaked with blood, dense vegetation, a deer fence and a precipitous garden stood in our way. This wasn't how it was supposed to be.

A grassy footpath had enticed us away from the narrow verge of the A87 where each passing lorry, bus and car dowsed us head to toe in gravelly spray. When the map confirmed that the path could save us a few miles of traffic turbulence and the threat of death by lorry, we bounded up it with squelching toes and dripping fingers. It was a few damp but happy miles later that we discovered that the map was wrong, very wrong.

"Perhaps we can freestyle it downhill through the trees until we hit the road again", I suggested breezily, trying to make it sound easy enough. Ten minutes later, as branches snagged my hair and scratched at my skin, I was quietly cursing my terrible suggestion. Jon was nowhere to be seen; only the occasional thrashing noise revealed he was still trying to bushwhack his way to freedom. The ranks of trees were so tightly packed that there was no light or life beneath their canopy, just a thick carpet of brown needles and the skeletal branches that seemed hell-bent on taking my eyes out in the gloom. My own heavy breathing and the scraping of the sharp branches clawing at my waterproofs rang loudly in my ears and I had a sudden, comical, flashback to The Blair Witch Project.

Reaching a particularly impenetrable mountain of branches and the splintered trunk of a fallen tree, I called out to Jon, "Have you gone uphill?"

No answer. Still trying to remain upbeat I called out again, "I don't reckon this path gets used very much".

Still no answer. I finally caught up with him beside the deer fence. Unsmiling and with a slightly glazed expression, he had rivulets of blood running from scratches on his legs. Looking at the garden beneath us I only managed to utter, "What if we..." before he cut me off.

"I'm not going back up there!" He was up and over the fence in a flash. With the horror of our forest descent freshly etched in my mind - and skin - I scaled the fence with the speed of someone who really, really doesn't want to be shouted at by an enraged homeowner. Not at all stealthily, we made our way downhill along the garden's ridge before dropping down into a clutch of trees, sliding from trunk to trunk, and pushing through a wall of dripping leaves and branches to emerge onto the pavement beside the road, breathing heavily and with our hair massively back-combed by the trees. There were no angry shouts or sounds of shotguns being cocked and they hadn't released the hounds. We'd got away with it.

Not wanting to loiter at the scene of the crime, we did our best nonchalant walk as we passed the house's driveway, only stopping to hoick twigs from our clothes and hair when we were a safe distance away. We didn't fully relax until reaching the café at Eilean Donan Castle where, purely for medicinal purposes, we devoured sugary drinks and slightly disappointing cake.

This was all London's fault. For the last six years, one of my hobbies has been unsuccessfully entering the ballot for the London marathon. I like to encourage my friends to enter too so we can share the mutual disappointment of not getting a place. Then two ballots ago, my good friend Carly – who, I'd like to add, had entered the ballot for the first time that year – got a place. I had assured her this would not happen and she was not impressed by her good fortune. Not wanting to run alone, Carly deferred her entry for a year but I didn't get a place in the following ballot either. The only way we'd be able to run together in 2019 was if I got a charity place.

Having volunteered as a crew member for the Royal National Lifeboat Institution (RNLI) since 2006, the charity was an easy choice. For a number of years I was the only female crew member on our inshore and all-weather lifeboats and I was often elbowed to the front of photos to show how diverse the station was becoming and maybe even to attract more females (this strategy also works on penguins, I saw it on Blue Planet Live just the other day).

After reading my persuasive spiel, the RNLI very kindly allocated me one of their marathon places and now I just had to train for the marathon and raise lots of money for them (they know where I live). I had cockily reassured them that, having survived three marathons already, I was now determined to reach beyond survival and complete marathons in a time I would be willing - happy even - to tell people about. I would train harder, eat better; I would nail this marathon malarkey.

Spending 44 days working on a ship off the coast of South America in the run up to the marathon sounded the death knell of my marathon training before it had even really begun. Yes, the ship had a treadmill on board, but there were also swarms of silky sharks that hunted flying fish around the vessel at night. Sharkcam - my GoPro attached to a long boat hook - was born and gym time was largely replaced by spending hours filming beneath the waves in the hope of capturing an award-winning National Geographic cover shot. Meanwhile eating had become something of a hobby. Ship food is extremely variable, ranging from deep-fried meat of indeterminate species to extravaganzas of fresh sushi, colourful salad bars and dishes from around the globe. And one of the main reasons I have worked offshore all these years, enduring the six-week rotations, long hours, limited communications and snug living quarters, is 3 o'clock cake. There's cake every single day. The ship I was on when I should have been running excelled at food generally but particularly at 3 o'clock cake. That's where I learnt the trick of placing an After Eight on top of each slice of chocolate brownie whilst they're still hot from the oven. It's, quite literally, the icing on the cake. Alas, an absence of training and an abundance of cake do not make for good marathon prospects.

Then, as the project was drawing to a close, in one of those life-changing moments, my most awesome Granny died. With unwavering enthusiasm for even my most hare-brained ideas, a total disregard for health and safety and a seemingly never-ending supply of chocolate hobnobs, she was one of my ultimate heroes and her rapid demise was a huge shock. Back from South America, training runs were punctuated with calls and messages as I helped to rehome my Gran's larger possessions: would her piano need retuning (absolutely), was her 50 year old wardrobe in pristine condition (nope) and could a technician from webuyanystairlift.com visit on Friday (sure, why not)? Unseasonably sunny days slipped into weeks and before I knew it, it was March. I had spent less than a week at home in Scotland all year and my marathon training and fundraising efforts were equally and dismally off-track. I needed a cunning plan. Jon (who's usually more of a cyclist) responded surprisingly positively to my declaration that I was to run across Scotland and, perhaps even more surprisingly, was willing to join me, most likely to avoid participating in the sponsored walk across hot coals that I was threatening to organise as another fundraiser. It was all coming together beautifully.

Four weeks later it was all coming together as beautifully as a March Monday morning in Inverness, in fact. Which is to say, not that beautifully. It started to rain as we jogged slowly and heavily alongside the River Ness and a cold breeze shuffled leaves around our feet. Dog walkers pulled the collars of their down jackets higher, hands tucked deeply in pockets. If spring's arrival was imminent, there was no sign of it. It was going to be a long day. We had bounced our way from Edinburgh to Inverness on the Megabus the previous day before celebrating the eve of our adventure with not just any picnic, but an M&S picnic as we watched the Antiques Roadshow from our Travelodge bed. We know how to party.

The morning dawned grey, drab and thoroughly uninviting. Uncharacteristically lacking any kind of appetite, I ate bran flakes from my camping pan as slowly as possible, twiddling my spork between my fingers. Neither of us had had much time for training and we'd only run together once although, to my relief, our pace hadn't been too different on that occasion. I had done one short training run with my backpack three days previously; Jon had only bought his backpack then and had never run with it. What could possibly go wrong? We'd done a little better with planning and had accommodation arranged for each night and, with guidance from the blog of someone who'd completed a very similar run a few years earlier, we had a good idea of what to expect along our route. From the start the stretch through Glen Affric towards Morvich had worried us, it was the bit of the plan that we lingered over, grimacing. Too much snow could block the route or simply make it too treacherous and I stalked the weather forecast nervously, also emailing local National Trust rangers for updates from the ground. Carrying thermal mats and sleeping bags would give us the option of sleeping in Camban bothy and splitting the long day in two but that would mean running with much bigger, heavier bags. Instead, we'd decided to carry an emergency mountain shelter, plenty of warm layers and a stove to heat water for hot food and drinks. Despite these precautions, we were well aware that we might have to abandon our plans of making it to Skye if the conditions weren't right on the day.

Having opted to stay in B&Bs instead of camping, our daily distances were determined by the distribution of villages and availability of accommodation. Thus our first day would take us 20 miles along the Great Glen Way, a long-distance coast-to-coast route across the Highlands, to Drumnadrochit. Frequent signposts kept us on track as we followed footpaths up and out of Inverness. It was in the woodland above the town that we began to relax, chatting away and pausing to hang like a sloth from a perfectly shaped branch. Birds flitted between the lichen-draped trees that sheltered us from the light rain and biting wind and we stopped to admire a couple of frogs in puddles on the path. We trotted along steadily, keen to make progress but also aware of the need to pace ourselves; any aches and pains we developed now would likely stick with us for the next five days. Our chatter was against a backdrop of the wind rustling the bare branches of the trees, bursts of bird song and the satisfying scrunch of our footsteps on the gravelly path. We were on our way!

This had initially been a seemingly crazy idea sown during a sleepless night in the unfamiliar quiet of my Gran's cottage where her TV no longer blared out the 10pm news and the pigeons, now shut out, could no longer coo from atop her wardrobe. Without the urgency of the London Marathon and my fundraising target looming, it may have stayed as an idea, something to do in the future. Instead, desperately craving a challenge and the vastness of the Highlands, with minimal planning and even less training, we had made it happen. It was raining, it was cold and we weren't going to be setting any new records for speed, but we had started and whatever happened from here, we'd said yes to adventure.

Emerging onto moorland we met the wind head on. Hats, gloves and buffs were readjusted and we pushed on, now with distant snow-streaked mountains egging us on. The moorland dropped down to farmland, then woodland again and soon we found ourselves at Abriachan Eco-café. Chickens and a massive black pig strolled between colourful, hand-painted signs promising soup, cake and hot drinks. Sandra soon appeared, full of warm welcomes sung in a lilting Islander accent, and we ordered everything. We were about to discover that this trip would be as much about eating as running. The off-grid café was the handiwork of Sandra and Howie, although Sandra stressed that the installation of a large mirror facing the compost loo was Howie's work alone, "So people can take a long hard look at themselves".

Toilet mirror or not, any café that serves hot chocolate with a side serving of actual chocolate gets five stars from me. Likewise, the thick ham and pea soup was accompanied by great wedges of cheese, a stack of oatcakes and a mound of tomatoes. Never mind the running, our light lunch had become an endurance event in itself and we were flagging by the time we got to the towering slice of lemon cake, also accompanied by squares of chocolate and marshmallows. It was a good few miles before we could even consider running again. When we did we were rewarded with a gently undulating path that wound through deciduous woodland, then views of Loch Ness and, as we neared Drumnadrochit, the silhouette of a tiny Urquhart Castle against the cloud-laden sky. During the afternoon, we quickly settled into a route of running punctuated with frequent stops to take photos, put woolly hats on, take woolly hats off, scoff some wine gums or cashew nuts or have a quick drink. The miles gradually passed in this manner. Just as our calf muscles were beginning to question what we were thinking, the path delivered us onto the road beside Loch Ness lifeboat station and we only had two miles left to go to Drumnadrochit!

After a solid sleep and an impressively huge cooked breakfast, we set off enthusiastically the next morning, relieved to have two shorter days of running ahead of us. From Drumnadrochit we were leaving the Great Glen Way and joining the Affric Kintail Way, a dramatic cross-country route that would take us to our next stop, Cannich, and beyond. The route immediately plunged us into a forest of gnarled, twisted old pines where the first hint of uphill reminded me of my tight calves and full stomach. I regretted having both the cereal and the cooked breakfast. Who am I kidding? And the toast. The climb was worth it for the views; looking north-east across Drumnadrochit, the deep waters of Loch Ness were steely blue and undisturbed by monsters. The sun occasionally succeeded at breaking through the clouds, affording us glimpses of the highly elusive Scottish shadow. Compared to the red squirrels, they were positively abundant and we had to strip off a layer or two as we warmed up.

Much confusion followed as we set off from the viewpoint in the wrong direction only to backtrack and find our correct route closed for forestry work. After running up and down the same stretch about four times, we were finally off, following the diversion that took us around fields, along narrow, twisting forest paths and onto wide tracks lined with neatly stacked timber. Here, an ominous growling rumble reverberated off the trees. The source - a digger - was operated by a cheery man who'd not heard of the Affric Kintail Way, a route that he was busy paving.

Again, the last few miles of the day were along the main road and we were flagging by then, my heavy legs reluctant to move. Electric shocks sporadically shot down my left arm, not exactly painful but not pleasant either, as my backpack irritated my shoulder. Welcome distractions came in the shape of a small herd of windswept and entirely disinterested Highland cows and two friendly pigs whose ears we scratched. Eventually we hobbled up the long approach to the village.

Off-season, Cannich is a funny little place with a dilapidated (and most probably haunted) hotel at its heart. The town's one restaurant only opens three nights a week over winter leaving us relying heavily on the village shop for supplies. We systematically worked through their takeaway menu with a level of dedication lacking from our training, starting with pizza, crisps and Coke before moving on to their Easter egg selection. Only the best for these pro athletes! Killing time, we even sent postcards of the wildlife we hadn't seen to reassure friends and family that we had this running thing sussed.

We struck gold with Westward B&B in Cannich, receiving a warm welcome from hosts Sue and Alastair despite arriving sweaty, muddy and earlier than expected. By mid-afternoon, showered and refreshed, I was polishing off the last of my Easter egg in front of a roaring vintage fire, watching old episodes of The A-Team and drinking gin, whilst Jon was working his way through Glen Affric Brewery's range of pale ales. Whether it was the drink or all the fresh air, we slept like babies that night.

Another routine had developed. Away from work, my computer and the multiple to do lists that constantly litter my desk, it was glorious to have our next destination as my sole focus each day. My thoughts were of the weather, our route and what food and drink we would need. Enjoying capturing our journey, I also took plenty of photos, filmed little snippets on my GoPro and wrote some brief notes each evening. That was it and I loved it. From time to time a work email would ping to my phone but it was either quickly dealt with or filed for later. I was on holiday. The simplicity of running, eating and sleeping was a welcome break. Even the aches and pains that were building were a pleasant reminder of what we had achieved. And although we often chatted as we ran, for long stretches we'd also run in comfortable silence, each thinking our own thoughts. The space was refreshing in every way.

Apocalyptic skies greeted us on the morning of day three, not much of a reward for having dragged my aching limbs from the warm and comfy king-size bed. My first steps each morning were reminiscent of a new-born giraffe, whilst my first words usually went along the lines of, "Ouch, ouchie, ouch!" One of my ankles creaked quietly. Retrieving my cardboard-stiff compression socks from the radiator, it was hard to deny that overnight the room had developed an aroma of festering cheese. I eyed Jon suspiciously.

At least 1,000 delicious calories later we were struggling uphill on a narrow lane out of the village and back into the forest, huffing, puffing and clutching our sides as we went. The rumble of heavy tree-chomping machinery echoed around us as we slowly ticked off miles on the wide forest tracks. The breeze was at its strongest and chilliest but sullen grey clouds had replaced the purple apocalyptic clouds of earlier, the threat of a downpour was less imminent. We had piled on all our layers of clothing and any breaks were spent huddled, back to the wind, rubbing our hands and trying to stay warm. A wooden signpost directing us off the fire road and into the trees was a double win - shelter from the wind and more exciting running. The narrow, twisting path zigzagged downhill and we picked up speed as we dodged tree roots that reached for our ankles, a thick cushioning layer of pine needles giving our aching knees a welcome break. Not wanting to slow down, we splashed through waterlogged sections of the path, the cold water flooding our shoes and splashing up our legs. If I have a running forté, it's definitely when gravity's on my side.

All too soon the path abruptly emerged at the car park for Dog Falls where the River Affric tumbles through a dramatic rocky gorge, the peaty brown water suddenly dazzlingly white. Exposed to the wind once again, we considered the long uphill climb ahead of us. Having neither the desire nor energy to extend our mileage, we crossed the river and started uphill leaving the falls unseen; our spheres of interest shrunken once again to wine gums and sniffing repeatedly in the snot-inducing headwind.

The dark waters of Loch Beinn a'Mheadhoin, a narrow sinuous loch to our right, were flecked with whitecaps and the ancient Caledonian pine forest swayed and creaked around us, branches knocking together in the wind. Sitting only briefly on a wooden seat overlooking the loch we mused how all that was missing was an eagle cruising overhead, scanning the landscape for its next meal. But for the quickly moving clouds, the skies were empty. Neither did squirrels retreat at our approach and I'd given up all hope of seeing a pine marten. Perhaps it was our chatting or the regular rustling of wine gum packets scaring the animals away, but this trip certainly wasn't the wildlife extravaganza I'd expected.

Before we knew it, it was day four of our run. The one that made Jon and I question whether we were up to this challenge. The one where we could really come unstuck.

All being well, we would climb up and out of Glen Affric, cross Scotland's spine and drop down into Gleann Lichd to reach Morvich at the end of the day. We had breakfast earlier than usual to give us plenty of time to cover the distance, going over the plan yet again, scrutinising the mountain weather forecast and checking we had enough water, food and phone battery to last the day.

Rough terrain, exposure to the March weather and the remoteness of the glen were on our minds as we set off but it was an excited anticipation rather than outright nausea-inducing dread. This was going to be challenging and that's exactly what I had wanted from this run. True, I was anxious that the rough terrain and remoteness would complicate things if we needed assistance but I was excited by the added onus that that placed on us to navigate properly, run carefully and manage ourselves to cope in the unforgiving environment. Extreme weather aside, how this would pan out was heavily dependent on our own actions. Dense, menacing clouds conspired with the snow-laced peaks to psyche us out as we eased ourselves into the early, easy miles on fire tracks alongside Loch Affric. Beyond the loch, we got our first views of our route. A rocky track snaked across a rolling carpet of golden, tussocky grass being buffeted by the gusts of wind blasting down the glen. Wind, by the way, that my slimline planning had ensured we were running straight into every single day. The wiry grass was largely blown and flat and the heather crouched low, anything not firmly attached to the ground was long gone.

Stormy-looking clouds scudded across the sky, skimming the higher peaks and only letting the occasional patch of sunlight illuminate distant snow-filled gullies on the mountains' flanks, and the silvery streams that crossed the track. The path became increasingly bouldery and our chatter tailed off as we concentrated on where each foot should fall to avoid turning an ankle or twisting a knee. Exposed rock faces, mounds of boulders and gullies carved by sudden mountain torrents dissected the path and we slowed to pick our way through, hands braced against thighs as we leant forward breathing heavily. We'd take off again until the next obstacle, maybe a large wind-ruffled pool of water filling the path or a stream running downhill, paying no attention to the path it crossed, the white-water fizzing across the rocks. Our shoes were soon sodden and we only broke our rhythm to bypass the deepest of the pools and streams.

Now that the conditions required tunnel-vision concentration, it was surprisingly easy for the landscape to pass us by and we stopped now and again just to look around. The land was utterly convoluted; crumpled and wild. We were here, running through Glen Affric, conquering day four. Our rudimentary planning and a measure of luck were working their magic and we began spotting landmarks that had felt fictional until now. We passed the Alltbeithe youth hostel, still closed for winter, and pushed on uphill, splashing through countless streams until the red corrugated roof of Camban bothy, our lunch stop, appeared hunched against the hillside.

Pushing open the peeling wooden door, we stepped out of the wind and into the dark corridor. Pausing as our eyes adjusted to the gloom, we lowered our hoods and shook life back into our cold hands, able to speak rather than shout again. A couple of metres along the corridor, a door on the left led into a room sparsely furnished with wooden bunks, a raised fireplace and a wobbly bench in front of the small window. My numb fingers fumbled with the clips on my backpack until I was able to wriggle free and pull on my down jacket, woolly hat and buff, before setting up my stove on the uneven paved floor. My first impressions of bothies are always heavily influenced by the tired and hungry state I inevitably arrive in. This visit was no different and, urgently in need of food, the bothy initially seemed dank and claustrophobic. A can of Coke, a hot serving of Porcini mushroom risotto (made and dehydrated by Firepot, I wouldn't know a Porcini mushroom if I saw one) and a mug of hot squash (drink of champions) later and I was in love with the bothy's panoramic glen views, the cosy interior and even the faint smell of paraffin. Needing to reach Morvich before sunset, we didn't have time to stay and explore but the bothy was clearly one to visit again. With a clatter, I pulled the wooden door shut and bolted it.

Energy levels restored, we gingerly stepped back into the wind and began the most exhilarating section of the run. The stony track wound steadily uphill between legions of snow-capped peaks and past tumbling torrents of water until suddenly we finally stood on a rise with views of Glen Affric at our backs and Gleann Lichd at our feet. With loud whoops and arms raised high we set off downhill, leaping over boulders and streams. The mountains around us were craggier now with exposed rock faces darkening their flanks. For the first time, white-water rushing over the rapids in the gorge far below was travelling in the same direction as us, towards the west coast. We'd crossed the watershed and the faster flowing streams we ran through felt even colder as they flushed through our shoes. Large slides of scree required some careful scrambling under the bored gaze of sheep with thick, tattered fleeces. Our waterproofs flapped furiously in the wind that nipped our cheeks and hands as we barrelled on, stopping only to admire the bigger waterfalls and to shout over the roar of the wind and rushing water that this running business was TOTALLY AWESOME! As we dropped lower into Gleann Lichd, eventually trip-trapping over a little wooden bridge across the river, the path flattened out and we slowed to our steady plod again, big smiles etched across our reddened, wind-chapped faces.

We always knew the last day of our run was going to be a bit pants and it was reluctantly that we left the safe haven of our B&B that morning, with its underfloor heating and three-course breakfast. Having emerged from some of the Highland's finest scenery, we had about 20 roadside miles to cover to reach the Isle of Skye. Our perpetually damp and wrinkled feet had become accustomed to pine-scented fire tracks and bouldery paths, tarmac would be drab and monotonous in comparison.

However, roads mean cafés and cafés mean cake. Plus, it was our final day; the end would quite literally be in sight. Or it would have been if the weather hadn't been horrendous. The BBC forecast had spoken of rain until 10am and a moderate breeze. Ten o'clock came and went and the rain persisted, sweeping across the glen in sheets. And there was a moderate breeze in much the same way as the hurricanes of 1987 were a bit fresh. The two combined thundered against our waterproof hoods and induced ice-cream headaches. From the B&B, we'd had less than a drizzly mile to cover before we reached the A87, our tarmac route to the Isle of Skye. "At least there's a pavement," I'd chirped, followed 200 metres later by, "At least there's a verge."

That's when we had spotted the path that soon had us scrabbling through tick-infested woodland and someone's back garden before beating a hasty retreat to the café beside Eilean Donan castle for recovery cake.

Peeling off our dripping waterproofs at our next, and final, café stop six miles later, the Isle of Skye was so close yet still so far. Rainwater pooled around our chairs as we devoured chips and hot chocolate, steaming in the warmth. Jon's very sensible desire to push on had been quietly overridden by my tendency to get hangry.

He was right. Slithering back into soaking gear and stepping back into the rain was horrible and every moving part in our legs hurt as we tried to get going again.

As luck would have it, for the next three miles an undulating off-road path above the road took us through forests of silver birch trees and onto open moorland. Harnessing my hot chocolate power, I got my second wind and, despite the aches, pains and utterly horrendous weather, I was loving it. Even from up here we only had occasional views of the Skye Bridge, our finish line, through the rain and cloud. It wasn't until the path dropped down to the Kyle of Lochalsh, bleak on such a miserable day, that the bridge finally seemed within our reach and we honed in on it, overtaking a couple of soaked tourists wheeling suitcases.

Cars swished by with headlights on and windscreen wipers at full speed. Far below us, tidal swirls and eddies stretched and crinkled the water's surface. Disappointingly, but consistently, there were no harbour porpoise to be seen.

From the bridge's peak it was all downhill to the 'Welcome to Isle of Skye' sign where we paused briefly for a soggy selfie. After 21 rain-drenched miles, having covered 88 miles since Inverness, we'd done it! With minimal planning, not quite enough training, plenty of enthusiasm for adventure and more than a pinch of good luck, we'd just run coast-to-coast across Scotland.

Five weeks later, with properly laundered but still slightly odorous running gear, the London Marathon was off the scale of incredible. It started much the same as my previous marathons: an unwholesome cocktail of tiredness from the effort of reaching the start, stomach-churning nerves, genuine concern that my mum would be lost to the crowds forever and a creeping chill from standing around in running gear. Once we were off my worries were quickly drowned out by the cacophony of noise.

It was a 26.2 mile carnival, in London, with free sweets for all. Giant Wombles, rhinos, Jesus and at least half a dozen Spidermen had all joined the party. Apparently there were elite athletes too but they were long gone. So much for taking in all the major landmarks, it wasn't until I emerged beside the Thames at mile 24, that I had any clue where I was and by then there was no time for sightseeing.

Reading names from bibs, the crowds yelled encouragement and stopping wasn't an option. Exhausted, hungry and sticky from spilt Lucozade, I wheeled right at Big Ben. Digging deep as Rhino Stacey gained on me, threatening to overtake, I shuffled along Birdcage Walk and could have cried with relief to see Buckingham Palace. Those last painful steps up The Mall, with hips and knees yelping with every movement, were over in a flash and I crossed the finish line of the London Marathon having squeezed 13 minutes from my personal best.

Whether it was the run across Scotland that helped prepare me, or the fantastically relentless encouragement of my thousands-strong cheer squad, I had made it. I hadn't even hobbled out of the finishers' area before my phone pinged to tell me the ballot had opened for next year's London marathon. What Carly uttered in response to this is, sadly, unprintable but having absolutely aced her first - and, from the sound of it, her last - marathon, her work here was done.

Did I enter the ballot for next year?

Absolutely, yes!

Becci Jewell is a massive fan of adventures (big and small), running (slowly) and eating cake (lots). When she's not working at sea, she lives in Fife where she spends her spare time volunteering on the local lifeboat crew, taking terrible wildlife photos and plotting her next escapade. This autumn she'll be cycling from Alaska to Mexico following the southward migration of gray whales (unless she has a run in with a bear in which case her journey could be much, much shorter).

www.thegraywhalecycle.com

Twitter: @jewellbecci & @graywhalecycle

Instagram: @becci_jewell & @graywhalecycle

Facebook: @thegraywhalecycle

Chapter 4

Thames Path

by Beth Goodlad

I was sitting on a train. In my rucksack was everything I would need for the next 9 days. I was trying my best to be rational, which isn't always my strong point at the best of times. Visions of axe-wielding murderers and hungry, rabid squirrels filled my head.

Worse than that. What if I 'failed'?

I was only going as far as the Cotswolds for goodness sake. Worst case scenario: someone asks me to move my tent or it's wet and miserable and I get on the train and come home.

For a long time, I had been in a bit of a destructive downward spiral. I'd come out of an emotionally abusive relationship two years ago. I was only just beginning to recognise it for what it had been. It hadn't been a failure on my part to keep the relationship together. I had struggled, and at some points failed, to keep it going.

And then I had been made redundant from my job. It felt like I'd lost a part of who I was.

And then I was asked to leave where I was living.

I had become frozen. A rabbit in the headlights. The feeling of control in my life slipping rapidly out of my grasp. I ended up living back at my parents. I was short term contracting with very little faith in myself or any real concept of who I was anymore.

I'd had several long-distance walks on my to-do list for a long time. I'd walked the Ridgeway with a group of school friends when we had left university. We had decided to cut a couple of days off the number recommended because we thought we knew better, and we'd ended up with a different limp each. For some reason, I hadn't managed to persuade any of them into doing a walk with me since.

I decided on the Thames Path on the basis of I could only take one week off work, so nine days with both weekends. All the guides I found recommended 11 days and I would need to average just over 20 miles a day while carrying whatever I was taking with me if I was going to complete it (so I obviously hadn't learnt from the Ridgeway experience). However, I was working on the basis I would be walking towards London, therefore if I wasn't going to get to the finish I could just get the train home and come back to finish it another weekend (I still like to tell myself I would have been comfortable with this scenario but, realistically, at the time I would have seen it as a failure not to complete it rather than my own adventure). The accessibility of public transport was also a big comfort blanket - if it all went wrong, I could just get on a train and come home rather than being stuck in the middle of the Scottish Highlands. I also hoped navigation will be minimal. I just needed to follow the river. What could go wrong? Finally, logic states that if I'm following a river from source to sea it will be flat, if not slightly downhill, for the entire journey so it should be easy.

With a plan and a timescale, I did try and find other people who would go with me. Some politely declined. Some declared me mad and told me that I wouldn't finish.

I booked a train ticket to Kemble station while secretly hoping that someone else would agree to come along. I think this was partly me being scared of spending that much time in my own company. It was however the first time in years I was doing something because I wanted to rather than for anyone else or trying to achieve someone else's expectation, whether perceived or real. I wasn't going to put it off into the 'later' pile because no one else would come with me.

I intended to wild camp along the way, but this was part of the trip I was terrified of (hence axe murderers and rabid squirrels). I did get concerned about the nights later in the walk as I got closer to London. I researched the closest campsite. It was still about 50 miles from the end. Wild camping meant that I had the additional weight of carrying camping gear, but it would reduce costs and meant that I didn't have to walk a pre-set distance each day to get between booked accommodation.

Day 1

So, there I was in Kemble station, which is the closest station to the source of the Thames, with a tent, a second-hand guidebook, some sachets of emergency couscous and some new walking shoes. About 20 people seemed to get off the train, which for a station that appeared to be in the middle of nowhere was quite significant. However, they seemed to disperse quickly without any indication of where they had gone. The station was quiet as I walked out to the road.

For a moment, I considered getting back on the train, going home and never talking about the week again to anyone. Then I remembered the naysayer who had told me that I wouldn't do it and decided I had better get walking

Leaving Kemble station, there is a short walk to join the Thames Path (no water) and then a short walk upstream (still no water) to the source (definitely, no water). I found myself in a field, with a carved boulder that said that this was the source of the Thames and a big tree that was mentioned in the guidebook to denote the start.

It wasn't quite as grand as I was expecting. I'd imagined water gushing from the ground, a garden of lush greenery, maybe some magical lute music playing in the background maybe with a water imp or two. It was just a rock and a tree in the middle of a field.

"Only 184 miles to go," I mused to myself as I looked at my watch. It was already lunchtime on day one. I had better get moving, while eating my lunch out of a Tupperware box.

I quickly found a man taking a photograph of a footbridge (with no water underneath it, the Thames definitely had some growing to do!). He was trying to photograph every bridge on the Thames. He told me that due to water extraction causing the drop in the water table over the years you never got water as far up as the source even when the river was in full flood. He was the first of many people who were using the river in so many different ways for their own recreation.

So off I set in the sunshine feeling rather happy with myself for the first time. I still couldn't quite believe I was here, even if the only thing telling me I'd actually found the river were the signposts with an acorn on and the occasional muddy ditch that would appear and then seem to disappear into nothing again.

I was merrily wandering through a field watching a red kite soar high above while glancing at the cows in the next field hoping there wasn't a bull when I realised that I wasn't on the path anymore. All the good feelings I'd been having quickly vanished in a moment and blind panic set in that I couldn't even see any people around. The negative voices from the train rushed back in - all I had to do was follow the river, and I couldn't even do that. I nearly sat down in the field and cried.

Forcing myself to think rationally, I had the choice of walking back the way I had come until I found the path but I didn't know how far I would need to retrace my steps or walking forward towards the road which I could see and the map suggested I would have to cross anyway had I stayed on the path. From there I could work out if I needed to go left or right to return to the Path. I chose to keep walking towards the road and in doing so felt an instant relief. Even if it was the wrong decision it felt better than the indecision and the fear that the indecision had created that I had been facing.

It turned out to be the right decision, all I had done was walk two sides of a field and not diagonally across it. I had only ever been a couple of hundred metres from where I should have been. I felt a bit sheepish at the complete panic that had consumed me moments earlier.

While I had a sit down to regroup my head that was still rushing through the panic a large tabby cat came head-butting my hand for attention. He seemed content as long as I was petting him behind the ears and the car noise from the road wasn't too loud. It seemed a very simple life and it did leave me wondering why I was so concerned with walking from A to B along a particular route. After one last ear stroke, I got back up and started walking.

Through the lakes, nature reserves and pale Cotswold-stone villages, I came to Castle Eaton where I stopped in a pub for dinner. I was a bit too nervous to talk to anyone here so I tried to read a book while I was waiting for food and eating but I couldn't really focus so watched the other people in the garden instead. From here I walked a couple of miles out of the village to find somewhere to put my tent for the night.

The first night there was a lot of reservation about finding the 'perfect' camping spot. What I was actually looking for was the most inconspicuous place possible where I had no chance of being spotted by a random passerby. Unfortunately, it's actually quite hard to look for what you can't see. If I went any further, I'd be in the next village and there definitely wouldn't be somewhere there. I couldn't keep walking all night.

Eventually, I found a spot that my current mind deemed satisfactory at best and soon had my tent up. I lay in my sleeping bag ears focused to any noise wondering if it was an angry landowner coming to tell me to get off his land or the hungry or the rabid squirrels that were coming to eat me alive. I should have been enjoying the sounds of nature but every snuffle or cracked twig set me on edge. Either way it didn't matter as I was soon fast asleep. I think it was a mixture of complete mental and physical exhaustion.

I later worked out that, in my desperation to not be found by any people in my tent, I'd actually walked about 17 miles in the right direction that day. Not bad for someone who started at lunchtime and had stopped for a paddy for what turned out to being the wrong side of a field part way through.

Day 2

Suddenly, as if without warning, the muddy trickle I had been following turned into a flowing river the next morning. I packed up quickly, still a bit worried that it was daylight, and someone would see that I had been in my clandestine camping spot. I shoved my tent in my bag and ate breakfast on the move.

I reached the village of Lechlade. This is where the waterway is considered to be navigable by boats and you would definitely call it a river. A pale stone bridge spanned the water allowing pedestrians to cross into the village. Seeing as it was too early on a Sunday for anything in the village to be open, I kept moving.

I found this a lot more enjoyable from this point on. There was always something going on with the river. It became ever changing as I watched the river grow.

There was definitely a sleepy Sunday, small village feel to every place I passed through during the day. I did get a bit concerned about my plan to buy food along the way but I survived without eating my arm or touching the emergency couscous so it couldn't have been all bad.

By the evening I had reached Newbridge where I stopped at a pub for dinner. I hadn't had a drink of alcohol for six months and I decided to have two pints of cider. I'd earned them.

After an enjoyable meal right beside the Thames I somehow managed to lose the Path. I walked backwards and forwards up a road getting photos of a lovely sunset trying to find where I'd lost it. Brambles tangled themselves around my legs while I was busy waving my camera at the sunset and before I'd realised what was happening, I had fallen over backwards with the rucksack on. Moments later I was setting up my tent with considerably less concern to its location compared to the previous day. The power of cider.

Day 3

I woke up to a misty morning, surrounded by trees to one side and meadow grass on the other. In my tipsy state I had put the tent up almost on the path itself. Hurriedly, I packed it back into my bag constantly checking over my shoulder for early morning dog walkers. I still took a moment to look at the delicate dew droplets threaded on a nearby spider web and then decided that this level of observance was obviously cider induced and rushed back to filling my rucksack.

Later in the day I came to a lock that the walking guide marked as having showers for the boaters. I asked the lockmaster and he let me use them and waived the fee because apparently the only option he had would have been to charge for a full night of camping. It was a good feeling to be clean. There are campsites at a number of locks that can be booked in advance and he did seem concerned that I wasn't sure where I was staying that night.

Later in the day I walked through Oxford. It was the summer holidays and the weather was warm. On the outskirts of Oxford, the river was being used by hundreds of children for swimming and playing in. The younger children were running around in the shallows with their parents and groups of young teenagers were jumping off of a bridge. It felt noisy and chaotic compared to the quiet countryside I had been walking through.

I also met a group of friends that were walking the Thames Path as a series of day trips, having started in London. They used it as an excuse to get together and get out walking. They reckoned they only had a trip or two left to go.

There was also a large group of open water swimmers in multi coloured swim hats and lots of neoprene on a led trip down the Thames. And Oxford Canoe club was out in force practicing on the water in the evening with juniors trying to paddle in crew boats with varying degrees of success.

By the end of the day, my legs ached, and my shoulders were getting knotted from carrying the rucksack. What I generally find doing multi-day trips is that day 3 and 4 are the days you will get muscle ache, and after that, your body gets more used to the repeated movements. I had averaged 20 miles the last two days, but there was still a lot of miles and days to go.

Day 4

I met a retired man who was walking a number of long-distance walks in stages. He was walking for 3 or 4 days on the Thames Path and then he needed to go home as his wife had an engagement for them. He was hoping to be back later in the year to do a couple more days when his wife had enough of him moping around the house getting under her feet. He seemed to have a lot of gadgets including a GPS system to locate himself which I'm sure may have been more useful on some of the other walks he described rather than this well-signposted path. He seemed to also be working his way through a route in Wales that was only available by downloading a route of GPS points to the gadget. It all seemed a bit too techy for me, but he seemed very happy if a bit too enthusiastic at waving his walking poles around while talking.

It was also the first day I met a woman who marched past me with a day sack on. The first time I saw her, she ignored my hello and then stopped about 50 meters ahead for a drink. I caught her up and she decided to talk to me. She was being dropped off by her husband in the car at the start of each day and then being collected and taken back to their holiday cottage at the end of the day. It sounded highly civilised. She announced that she was walking faster than me and had only started five days ago and then pressed me for when I had started. When I said, I was on my fourth day she announced 'Oh, well you'll be walking more hours in a day than me' and marched off in a huff. People - they're all mental!

Day 5

There were a couple of sections earlier on in the day where the path doesn't follow the river directly, and one of those was near Pangbourne. The sides of the river had become steeply banked and tree lined around here in comparison to the open fields I had seen so far. There is also a very definite uphill here as the path can't hug the bank which was a disappointment to my 'downhill all the way' route plan.

Later in the day, I came to Reading. It was an area I knew from other adventures although I haven't seen that much of it in summer with green on the trees.

The first lock below Reading is Sonning. There was a lovely café with art for sale, bunting on the lock island and homemade cake. Having mainly seen this area in February, in a kayak race while running past with a boat on my shoulder this seemed an entirely different experience. I had a nosey at the paintings but seeing as I was carrying everything in my rucksack, I definitely wasn't in the market for some artwork.

It had been a couple of days since my shower at the lock and I was thinking about where to get my next one. I was feeling rather warm and sticky. It was weird being so dirty while walking next to a whole load of water in the river especially after I had seen the open water swimmers out in force the day before. It didn't take long for me to decide to go for a dip. I don't think the teenage boy sitting at the prow of a motorboat with his dad at the back driving expected to see a woman in her underwear swimming around in the river. Well, they certainly both looked rather surprised and I waited for them to disappear upstream before getting out of the water.

I had dinner in a pub in Lower Shiplake. They did tasty food that might have come from real ingredients and they charged my phone for me, which was nice. I got chatting with the locals which is something I would normally be too reserved to do. It just seemed to happen naturally.

I walked out of the village back to the river where there were fields and brambles between the Path and river. There were, what I assumed were, fishermen's footpaths through the brambles to the river's edge. I followed the tracks and found enough space for my tent right by the water.

Day 6

I got woken in the morning to the sound of three open water swimmers who were out for a pre-work Thames swim and having a chat before they turned to go home. Up and walking to Henley, I got to watch the rowers on Henley Reach, which is a mile-long straight section of the Thames where there seem to be multiple rowing clubs out practising. The area around the river opens up into flat fields.

I did a small detour in Marlow to find lunch. Below the lock, after Marlow there were canoes, kayaks and sailing boats out from Longridge Outdoor Centre with lots of children looking like they were having tons of fun. They were certainly making a noise.

Giggles, laughter and splashing came from all the vessels.

At Cookham, the river splits into brooks, weir streams and a lock cut and the Path takes a small detour away from the water's edge to avoid the four or five channels that are here. When you join the edge of the river again the far bank is a very steep cut all the way into Maidenhead, which contrasted to the open fields on the path side. There were even more rowers out on the water in Maidenhead, where I also stopped for dinner. Beyond Maidenhead, there is a strip of trees between the path and river, and I camped in these for the night.

Day 7

I woke up to even more rowers who seemed to be out for a pre-work paddle. The Path then skirts the Olympic park at Dorney where the Olympic rowing and flat-water kayaking took place and passes the new footbridge that was constructed to provide access for the 2012 Olympics before entering Eton and crossing the bridge into Windsor.

I wandered through Windsor gawping at the crowds of tourists who were already filling the streets despite the early hour. I gave the castle a wave from the Path (I'm sure the Queen waved back!).

I found myself walking through meadows where there was a couple who were going down the banks trying to count water voles. Apparently, the water vole population in that area had been decimated in the London floods the previous winter and they hadn't found any indications that they had returned to that area yet. They were, therefore, volunteering their free time to a charity to try and monitor voles which are apparently an indicator of the biodiversity in that area.

For someone who had previously considered Windsor to be 'London' and therefore built up there was a lot of green and open areas during my walk out of the city.

I also passed the commercial campsite that was 50 miles from the finish. It was the wrong time of day for me to be stopping for the night and it looked weird to see all the tents packed closely together behind a metal linked fence, certainly not as pretty as my camping spots. As I had considered this as a potential camping location for my last night, memo to self: learn to look at distances when planning future trips.

In Shepperton, I stopped at a pub for dinner just before the foot ferry across to the south side of the river. If I didn't take the ferry, there would have been a long loop around Desborough Island. Here I got talking to a local group of friends and their friendly dog and they were telling me that this whole area had been under water in the London floods the previous winter, which was hard to imagine now.

Drops of rain fell from the sky for the first time on this trip. So, I decided to stay and have pudding. By the time I had finished it was dark, the heavens had opened, and the ferry had shut hours ago. I was busy trying to build myself up to leave the dry underneath the awning outside the pub. I could hear the rain bouncing off the cover and knew I would be drenched in seconds.

"Don't worry," said one of the people I had been talking to. "I'll drop you around at the park. There's a perfect spot for wild camping. Loads of thick trees to hide in."

A few of minutes' drive in a car that was probably worth more than I had earned in my entire life to that point (a lot of leather seats and wood dashboard), got me to the other side of the water and saved a long walk around Desborough Island. There would have been nowhere to camp on the built-up area I had been in. A quick test in speed tent erection and it was time to sleep for the night.

Day 8

I woke up and the rain from the previous night had cleared. By now my feet hurt. The rest of me felt fine but my feet were burning, and I was walking shorter distances between the points where I was stopping for a rest. Having considered Windsor yesterday as 'London' I thought that today would definitely be built up and spent a lot of the day mulling over where I was going to sleep that night and whether I should book somewhere to stay.

I went past Hampton Court Palace and spent some time with the other tourists staring through the gates that led directly down to the river. There are a lot of big metal railings to walk along with views to big gardens of lawns. Over the bridge and into the sprawl of Kingston I walked. Shoppers milled about everywhere, and I felt momentarily overwhelmed.

From Richmond/Teddington lock there is the option of two walks; one on the north side of the Thames and one on the south. Due to the fact that the Thames meanders considerably and that the path can't always stay directly on the bank of the river it means that there are significant differences in distances between the two options. I opted to stay on the south bank for the day because it seemed to have fewer detours away from the river. There was a large area of green trees around here on the map for the south bank. And the deciding factor, it was shorter in distance. My feet definitely approved my decision.

Below Teddington Lock is where the Thames becomes tidal. This means that there are considerable changes in the water level and the view throughout the day. The river is now a huge swathe of water entirely unlike to its humble beginnings.

The South Bank takes you past Kew Gardens, which I decided I would have to come back and explore when I wasn't carrying a rucksack and hadn't been sleeping in bushes for a whole week. Dinner in a pub by the river left something to be desired and I still hadn't made my choice about where I was going to sleep for the night - did I need to walk away from the river to try and find accommodation as it was getting dark?

The footpath was lined with trees along the bank, and in the end, I put my tent in the bushes next to the river across from Fulham football ground where some sort of music event seemed to be taking place. I had certainly left my concerns about trying to find the perfect camping spot from the first night behind.

Day 9

Tropical storm Bertha, who certainly didn't feel very tropical when you were out in her, hit this day. I was wandering through the streets of London completely soaked. To start with, I found this rather amusing as I had got this far with such good weather in all. But the water squelched in my shoes with every step and I wasn't feeling so benevolent towards the situation. I walked through Wandsworth Park early on in the day. I have never been there before, but it had a huge pagoda and looked like it could be nice when the sun is out.

The path took a number of detours from the riverbank due to buildings that were there long before the path was thought of, although it did remain well signposted throughout. After a long detour from the river's edge near Chelsea Bridge, I was feeling a bit miserable and soggy. That's when I first thought of a Boris Bike. I kept walking a few more miles pondering this thought. Part of my brain was telling me it was 'cheating' but the other part was telling me it was my adventure and I could do whatever I wanted to.

It was the last day, I was close enough to finish on foot if I wanted to or I could do the last few miles on a bike. Near the Millennium Wheel the second part of my brain won out. I was off on a Boris bike towards the Thames Barrier and away from the tourists buying Union Jack brollies from the street vendors.

Having spent the last week walking, the bike felt very fast and rather wobbly trying to cycle with my rucksack, but I had a huge grin on my face. I went past the Globe theatre and a burnt out Cutty Sark. The Tower of London was on the other bank and I got a bit confused with a footpath closure around the Millennium Dome (being someone who normally avoids London at all costs this was all very exciting and new) before finally reaching the Thames Barrier where the path ends. By now the river was a huge mass of moving water, so far from the dry field where it had started. It was time to just sit and watch the river for a while and think about the journey.

I then discovered that you couldn't return a Boris bike around here and aimed back towards the centre of London and off to public transport, stinking to high heaven. People avoided sitting near me on the train. It was either my pungent smell or I was being mistaken for a homeless person.

The Afterthoughts

It was my body that physically made this journey, but it was my mind that was changed. The rollercoaster of emotions throughout the trip, the fears and the anxiety, the low moments when parts of my body physically hurt and the elation in achieving what I set out to do. It was a lesson in finding joy again in the everyday. A beautiful sunset. An ancient church in the middle of nowhere. Watching red kites riding the thermals. Seeing the river grow and change. Spotting flowers in the meadows and heaths. Meeting people getting out and doing 'their thing' whatever that may be. Finding out what my body could do. Realising I could carry everything I actually needed to survive for a week on my back. It all felt so near and yet so far from my everyday life. There had been no one else to rely on and I had achieved everything myself.

I do love an adventure because life becomes a lot less complicated. You only have what you are willing to carry and your aims in a day shrink down to getting from A to B with enough food along the way. Whether your journey is walking, cycling, kayaking or whatever, the journey slows life down. I think we could all benefit from a slower pace of life from time to time.

I won't pretend that life was instantly and magically better when I returned home simply for having gone for a long walk. However, learning about myself, spending time by myself, thinking on what I wanted to do and enjoying moments within the day significantly helped me on a long path towards finding out who I was now and who I wanted to be. There were plenty of ups and downs after the journey finished and plenty more struggles to work out for myself, but it was a huge step in the right direction. I have been on other adventures on foot, by bike, in a kayak, venturing into the world of triathlon and many other things since then but I always look back on this trip both with happy memories and as a new beginning.

Beth lives about 50 miles north of London and likes to see what plants she can get to grow in the flat, playing with the cats and eating vast quantities of custard. During the day she works for a local Council where she has to remember she can't fix all of the societal ills and just do what she can. The evenings are spent kayaking, swimming, cycling or starting another craft project that won't get finished for another six months. She is currently trying to limit the number of new adventure ideas she has so that ticking things off the bucket list happens quicker than adding things to it. At the current rate she probably needs to live to about 320 years old before she sees and does everything that she wants to!

Chapter 5

My Love for the Mountains

by Callum James

My story starts many years ago. I was walking home from college with my friend, Darren, and the topic of conversation swung round again. The same topic that we'd been discussing since we'd both realised a shared unanswered call for adventure.

We were 17 or 18 years old and we were dreaming of the mountains, the challenge and the adventure. Neither of us had a car or a driving licence. It was the idle day-dream of a pair of bored teenagers.

7 years on in 2015 I got a call from Darren. "So you want to do the Snowdon hike then?" he asked. In all the years that had passed neither of us had forgotten our ambitions.

Of course I said, "Yes!"

A few weeks later, Darren, his brother Matthew and I finally got our chance. It was a mild summer's day with the wind blowing in off of the Irish sea but we made it to the top. Our ambition had been achieved.

It was so much fun that we ended up walking up again a few months later, then many more times after that. Each time we attempted a different path or a different season. Each time we loved it. We seemed to be obsessed with just climbing the same mountain. We had no hiking experience. None of us could read a map. We didn't even know how to go about starting to learn.

Fast forward to 2017 and we'd finally decided that Snowdon wasn't enough. There were hundreds of other mountains out there. So Darren and I jumped in his old Corsa and trundled up the M6 to Scotland in search of new mountains.

Our first port of call was, of course, Ben Nevis. It was the hardest climb we had ever done as the weather was atrocious. Torrential rain bombarded us like Niagara falls falling from the sky. The downpour had soaked us through our waterproofs and by the time we got to the top we were shivering. But we made it up and back in one piece with our prides intact and a sense of achievement.

We had heard of a hiking challenge named the three peaks which you are required to climb the highest peak in England, Wales and Scotland in 24 hours. After a bit of research we discovered how much group guided tours were. As a pair of skint barmen, we knew it was out of our price range. We thought about doing is ourselves but decided that it was too risky to drive such a distance and walk up three mountains unaided. Disappointed we searched around to find a new challenge.

In 1891 a founding member of the Scottish Mountaineering Club, Sir Hugh Munro, took on the task of producing a publication called Munro's table. This was a list of 282 mountains in Scotland all over 3000 feet which are known as Munros. Another list was produced by the Scottish Mountaineering Club for all the 3000-foot mountains outside Scotland in the United Kingdom, which are known as Furths meaning outside (in this case outside Scotland). There is a total of 34 Furths, 6 in England, 13 in Ireland (the list was done before Irish Independence) and 15 in Wales.

In more recent times people went out Munro bagging which is where people hike to the top of a Munro. Each summit climbed is a Munro 'bagged'. When you bagged all 282 Munros, you're considered a Munroist. Only 6000 people have climbed all Munros so it is quite an achievement.

All this made me wonder if there is such a thing as a Furthist? We lived an hour and a half drive from the Snowdonia National Park so we finally found the mountain challenge to say YES to!

Me and Matthew decided our new challenge for the summer was to walk up all 15 mountains over 3000 foot in Wales.

*

Our climbing challenge didn't start off as well as planned. We started with a trip but it wasn't quite summer yet. We headed to Glyder Fawr and there was snow and ice everywhere. Visually I prefer it. Everything looks almost mystical. However the challenge to simply walk on the icy rocky floor I definitely didn't enjoy.

We eventually got to a steep hill near the peak and, after lots of slipping and sliding, we decided it was impossible to reach the summit without the right equipment and we grumpily slogged back down.

It was like we both hadn't learnt our lesson because a few weeks later, as we enjoyed the white dramatic views, we tried walking up Carnedd Llewelyn which ended frustratingly the same way. This time we were only a few feet away from the peak.

We could have considered these two attempts as failures but I don't think we really were trying to get to the top. I think we knew that without crampons we were never going to get to the summit. We were just having fun, enjoying the views and admiring the photos opportunities.

Finally, summer started and we were straight back to climbing. We walked through the Devil's Kitchen where water flowed down the mountains through streams and waterfalls. The difference in scenery between the rocky summer mountains full of wildlife and the white, snowy, deserted peaks of winter was huge. It was like we were climbing a different mountain.

We started to walk up the steep hill that had defeated us in winter. Without its coat of ice and snow, it wasn't actually that steep at all. It felt quite good that we didn't need to crawl up this hill on our hands and knees like we had attempted before.

Not far away from this 'not so steep hill' was Glyder Fawr, the peak we'd been after all along. After another half hour walk and we were at Glyder Fach. Two peaks out of fifteen! It was great to feel the sense of accomplishment this time around. It could only get better from here!

On the way down, we went off route once again (You'd think we'd be better at this navigation lark. We were following the same route that we had used to get up). We followed a very rocky path down. We both struggled to keep our balance.

Matt slipped. A cascade of rocks tumbled down. One heavy lump smashed straight into my foot. I winced as the pain shot up my leg.

Matt stumbled down beside me. "Sorry, Callum. Are you alright?"

I looked at my foot. "I should be fine," I said through gritted teeth. "Good thing I've got these walking boots on. That would've broken my foot."

"Will you be alright to carry on?" he asked, his voice full of concern.

I nodded, and continued hobbling down the mountain.

The next morning, I lay in bed, staring at my swollen foot propped up on a pillow and strapped with frozen peas. I had to take a few days off from the mountain climbing challenge.

There are many reasons I enjoy walking. I love the smell of fresh air. It makes me feel alive. It's great to feel something real instead of sitting in your room eating rubbish and writing (like I am doing right now!).

I love the idea that, when you are walking, you get to see everything. You have enough time to see every small stream, every cave, every crevice, every bend in the mountain and how it all looks different as the sun moves across the sky. When you walk, you feel a part of the land. You feel as though each step takes you closer to the natural world we live in and closer to an understanding of your place in it.

Walking is so simple when life can be so complicated. It can clear the head of all of the inane worries of our stressful lives. It's extremely fulfilling when walking up mountains. Of course there's the satisfaction when you finally get to the top, but it's the climb that is the real reward.

*

Our next walk in the mountain was a brief getaway from real life. We decided the smallest mountain of all the Furths was the eminently achievable. The whale back-shaped ridge stands out from all the rest of the mountains. Tryfan looks tiny compared to the giants surrounding it but, despite its size, it was the most recognizable. It is the most rugged, rocky mountain and also the most dramatic. It's as if it's screaming "Climb me".

Tryfan was probably the most fun as well. Being a very rocky mountain there was lots of scrambling sections. The feeling of crumbling rocks beneath my feet as I stretch and pull myself to a secure ledge is exhilarating. I wasn't used to this kind of climbing. It was putting my body to the test. It was a great couple of hours walking and scrambling and, finally, we got to the top.

As I sat on a rock eating lunch watching the birds fly over the lake below I wished I could fly like them. My bottoms of my feet were hurting, They weren't used to walking on rocky uneven ground, but that didn't matter as I have had my lunch in worse places.

I imagined spreading my wings and soaring down the mountain, riding thermals and gliding out to the open sky.

On the way down, we seemed to find navigation a problem (again) and we ended up walking through a boggy swamp. Keeping on our feet was a challenge as we kept on tripping up on hidden burrow in the ground or falling into swampy puddles. We were covered in mud by the time we eventually got back to the car.

The next day, when I complained about my aching arms, people asked what I'd done. Saying I'd hurt them going for a walk just sounded silly. But I'd found a new love. Scramble walks feel like proper mountain climbing.

*

Our next set of mountains were Pen yr Ole Wen, Carnedd Dafydd and Carnedd Llewelyn and they are located on the Carneddau mountain range opposite Glyderau that we have previously tried to climb. The big difference between the mountain ranges is that Carneddau is more secluded. There was no one in sight, only me, Matt and our friend, Connor.

This would be the first mountain that Connor had climbed and we had picked the right day as the sun was shining in a beautiful blue sky.

At the beginning of the walk, there was a lot of scrabbling which was a hard start for a first timer like Connor. Matt's walking habit is to push himself hard for 5 or 10 minutes and build up at a good speed. I'd got used to this and normally try and keep up with him. Eventually I'd concede and drag behind.

But this time, poor Connor wasn't going to stand a chance at walking such speeds. I hung back, secretly thankful for a walking partner of a similar speed than myself. Matt, at times, did seem a bit frustrated. He would swiftly walk a section and then always sit and wait while admiring the view.

The walk on a different mountain range changed things. Everything looked different. Everything seemed more deserted. The land mass was bigger and the distance to get places was further. At points during the walk we would walk what would feel like miles without getting any higher, something that didn't seem to happen on other ranges.

As we slowly reached the summit of the last of the three mountains, the tallest on the mountain range, we slowly felt the pain. It was definitely a hard climb and all three of us were knackered.

I stood looking proudly at the top. The mix of colours and terrain were pleasing to the eyes. From rocky to grassy to bogs, the views never seemed boring. The taste of victory was satisfying even though I knew it was sweat.

On our way down we kept on losing the path (no change there then). Every few minutes I looked down at my OS map on my phone checking if we were actually going the right way. Being lost on a mountain has always been the ultimate fear of mine. With the many tales of the brutal side of the mountains and our lack of survival skills, terrible navigation and sense of direction, when we did end up being slightly lost on a mountain it made me a little nervous. But luckily there are no horror stories for today, just more time consumed searching for the path we kept on losing and finding.

Once we got down and in the car driving home I felt I was a little sunburnt on the parts that I missed with the sunscreen but it seems like I was the only one that put sunscreen on. Matt was lobster red all over. Connor was even worse. He seemed to be completely worn out with headaches, nausea and a mild case of sunstroke.

After all this, I dropped Matt off at work. His shift didn't finish until 2 in the morning. Now that is true dedication to climbing mountains!

*

The next challenge we aimed for was to climb the remaining Carneddau mountains that we hadn't reached last time. This time we had to start from the opposite side of the Carneddau close to the A55 in a place called Abergwyngregyn (You've got to love Welsh place names. Don't ask me to pronounce it!).

Each climb we did we started early in the morning because we wanted to be down before it got dark. As we are both barmen, we both would be working late, so every time we climbed, we would be climbing on limited sleep. But this time Matt and I only got 3 hours sleep between the two of us and both of us were exhausted before we had even started.

The day started off as bad as it finished, pretty awful. It began with navigation problems. We followed the map and realised we were going the wrong way after many miles. We then walked miles in the other direction and realised that we were going in the right way in the first place. Matt was very patient considering it was me doing all the navigation.

It took a very long time to get to the first peak Foel-Fras and as we were physically and emotionally spent. It took longer than it should to get to Carnedd Gwenillan and Foel Grach. When we finally got to Carnedd Llewelyn (an already walked peak), we were both knackered and we still had Yr Elen to walk up. The map made it seem very close but it really wasn't. If you are tired and hurting you really don't need a challenging climb at the end of your day. This is exactly what we got.

The walk back included the hardest downhill section I've ever done. All we wanted to do was go home to sleep. Every muscle in my body was aching, the bottoms of my feet were hard to walk on and my shoulders felt like they might fall off. We were so exhausted that if we stopped again, we would of both just fallen asleep right there on the mountain. Neither of us was talking to the other. We were both just too tired. It had been a very hard climb. I was over the moon when we finally got to back onto flat ground. Maybe we weren't as fit as we thought we were.

On days like that where you have pushed yourself too hard, you start to wonder why you are you doing this? What is it all for? Why do people obsessively go through pain and misery just to get to the top of a mountain? What is the point? Why not look at a photo of the view at home in the comfort and warmth of your living room?

When you have had a hard day in the mountains it's hard not to think negatively. It's hard to imagine yourself ever going back in the mountains.

It's strange because, after you've pushed yourself too far, you feel like mountain climbing is ridiculous, stupid and pointless. But in a week's time, you'll look back on those so-called 'bad climbing days' with fond memories. If it wasn't for the fond memories of mountains on previous walks I probably would never step foot on a mountain again!

I am not sure if it's my brain tricking me, putting myself through the same grief, or it's my brain telling me, 'You were just tired. Stop exaggerating things!' Either way, it's a good thing because I don't get to miss out on more great adventures. Life can be boring and what would be left if we didn't attempt anything that was difficult or challenging? Bland mediocrity.

Mountain climbing gets weirdly addictive. Once you get started, you begin to study maps. You trace climbing routes with your finger, imagining the peaks and valleys and tumbling mountain streams. You look at contour lines and envisage the gradient, the heights and the descents. I had imagined the whole bagging idea, where you tick off mountains you have climbed, would be the addictive part. You are ticking off your achievements one by one.

But completing one list is never enough. You begin to look at what other mountains you could climb. A lot of people that have finished walking the Munros normally have had such a passion ignited within them that they tend to move onto some of the smaller mountains like Corbetts (mountains between 2500 and 3000 feet) or Grahams (mountains between 2000 and 2500 feet). It's a never-ending adventure in the mountains.

*

The midsummer sun was already beating down on us as we prepared to return to the mountain that started it all. Snowdon. This time we were going to go up the Crib Goch route. After all the climbing we had been doing in recent times returning to the mother of them all didn't excite me as much as I thought it would. But we had to cover two of Snowdon's smaller sister mountains, Crib Goch and Garnedd Ugain.

Matt and I were smarter this time and smothered ourselves in sun cream. We set off down the popular Pyg Trail route. It was full of tourists, the complete opposite of what I had enjoyed on the other recent mountain peaks.

The sun was relentless and my eyes were burning, not from the sun but from the sun cream that has mixed in with the sweat dripping down the top of my head. At one point I had to stop as I couldn't see at all. After a few minutes of vigorous rubbing, with red raw eyes we pushed on.

Snowdonia has many stories of myths and legends that make your walk that little bit more interesting. King Arthur has many tales based in the area. Many caves across the region tell of a sleeping King Arthur who awaits the call to return to rescue Wales from future threats. Lake Llydaw, close to where we were walking, claims to contain his legendary sword, Excalibur.

Once we got onto the Crib Goch trail things got much more entertaining. If you had ever heard on the news of any climber that had been injured or died up Snowdonia, the chances are this would have occurred up Crib Goch. Crib Goch mountain is part of a very narrow ridge and I never realised how narrow it was until we got to it. The kick of adrenaline as you walk across it makes the whole trip worth it.

As I walked along, I looked down making sure my feet are placed correctly (as I imagine it would be game over if I tripped). I stared down at my feet. I could see the narrow rocky pathway where I was placing my feet and I could see the rocky drop on both sides. It was thrilling but I knew one wrong footing or trip and it was a long way down. The adrenaline pushed me on. This was truly my favourite small section of the whole Snowdonia challenge. As I walked I imagined how bad it would have been if the day wasn't as perfect. A strong gust of wind would make the walk a lot more challenging.

I took a glance back to see if Matt was loving the experience as much as I was. He wasn't. He was hanging onto anything he could, holding on for dear life. When we got to the end of the ridge Matt breathed a sigh of relief. "WOW! that was awful," he said.

Adrenaline does different things to different people. After such a stunning and fun walk the rest was pretty boring to Garnedd Ugain. From there we joined the queue up to Snowdon.

There is a story about Snowdon where King Arthur kills the mountain giant Rhitta who created a cape out of the beards of his enemies. Rhitta's corpse is apparently buried beneath a pile of huge stones at the summit of the mountain. Ordnance Survey have now used this supposed burial mound as the spot for their trig point.

Yet again on our way home, I dropped Matt off at his workplace and he worked another shift until 2 in the morning. The boy is a mad man.

Snowdonia is not just a place packed with adventure and beauty. It also has some secret gems. Things that people go out of their way to find makes it more exciting than just being at the top of a mountain.

Some people hunt out the secret pools and lakes that aren't so easy to find. The Blue Lake is a hidden, guarded by the cliffs. People find this a perfect swimming spot only accessed through a secret tunnel or by abseiling down. It was a slate quarry that opened in 1867 which eventually flooded. The area is actually private property but it doesn't seem to stop people looking for it for a bit of wild swimming.

On the way up to Snowdon on a very busy path, there is what is known as Snowdon's Secret Infinity Pool. This off-the-path pool is no longer a secret but people are going out of their way to look for it. The pool exists because of a stone wall built around a hydroelectric scheme on a mountain stream and people love the challenge of finding it. This area has now got the attention of party lovers that want to hang out and drink.

Snowdonia also had a darker side to it, there are 20 known German and British plane crash sites that happened during WW2. As a history lover, I really enjoy reading the stories of the crash sites. In October 1942 Douglas Boston Z2186 entered the cloud and was forced to navigate using their compasses. They were off course and smashed into the Carneddau Mountain range. Unfortunately, the crew members died but the pilot survived with multiple injuries. Sgt. Mervyn Sims lay close to the aircraft for two days before being discovered. He suffered from a broken leg, fractured skull, broken spine and had gangrene while recovering. Despite all of this, he made a full recovery returning to his squadron and went on to be awarded a DFC (Distinguished Flying Cross). The human body is truly amazing.

All the aircraft parts remain property of the RAF and the Military Remains Act 1986 makes it illegal for anyone to take the parts so they stay on the mountain for climbers to discover. You can't beat a bit of history during your adventures.

*

The day came for our last trail. This time we needed to get to the last 2 mountains, Elidir Fawr and Y Garn. Darren joined us. He had already walked the route before so we were better off with his navigation skills.

We followed the same route we had followed before through the Devil's Kitchen. We walked the 'steep hill' like we did when getting to Glyder Fawr. Once we got to the top we just walked the opposite way to Glyder Fawr. From here it didn't take us long to get to Y Garn.

In the far distance we could see the route to get to Elidir Fawr and we all felt pretty good about it. We were on top form and we just pushed on. It just shows that the more walking you do, the better you get.

I have always been fascinated by how the body adapts over time. The more you do something, the more your body gets used to it. My feet didn't hurt, I wasn't that tired, my shoulder felt fine despite the weight and I felt pretty good. The body is truly amazing.

It didn't look far but it took us a while to get to Elidir Fawr. Pushing on along a ridge, we finally got to our target. We stopped for food and took everything in. Below us was a massive lake. This was Marchlyn Mawr and used to be used as a high-level water source at Dinorwig Power Station.

It is said that there is a cave nearby that contains King Arthur's treasures. Strangely enough didn't feel the need to check how true this was. We were standing on the fourth largest mountain in Wales and it felt great.

We started to head back down and it took until then to actually realise that that was it. We had completed our challenge. I suddenly felt very proud that we had set out to do something and that we saw it through. It was great. It felt weird, like we had conquered the whole of Snowdonia. I felt like I could achieve anything. What mountains were next? I suddenly felt the urge to walk up everything.

The mountains fascinate me and I love being up in the mountains but I can't put my finger on why I love it up there so much. I'm not sure if I love the struggle. Pushing yourself to the max comes with a certain amount of satisfaction. The pain is normally eased by the amazing views you can admire. The challenge of it all is exciting. The uncertainty of success helps keep you buzzed like an alcoholic trying to avoid the inevitable hangover. It is very simple up in the mountains. You have all the time in the world and the only aim you have is to get to the top. There is no rush, no deadlines, no pressure. It may be a challenge but you can take your own time and take the atmosphere in. It's remarkable!

I might be obsessed with the mountains because of the peace and quiet. Unless you are walking up the tourist trails to Snowdon, you are mostly alone. Just you, the wildlife and the mountains (in my case, Matt). You have time with your thoughts which is great. You have time to sort your life out in your head (it's just a shame that everything just makes sense in your head). The only things you can hear is the wind and the tumbling of rocks and pebbles as your boots push their way up the mountain.

Occasionally you might see a stranger. Then you can either start a conversation or just a simple friendly nod as a way of saying hi. It's strange. Because you are all doing the same thing, nobody is afraid to say hi or be friendly. It's like a big community. It's the great difference between being in the mountains and being in a city.

Maybe the love of the mountains comes from the unbelievable beauty. As you stand at the bottom, the bold rugged silhouettes looming down at you, there is no way you can resist not walking up. As you start to climb and you look around at the mountains and see them covered with trees, grass, rocks, shrubs and ferns. There is just so much going on.

If the challenge ever becomes too hard you can just stop, sit down and look out to unbelievable views and beauty. You sit and start to list reasons why you shouldn't actually come back down ever again.

With such staggering scenery and surroundings why would you want to be anywhere else? It doesn't matter where you are on the mountain. You could be at the top or the bottom. Every part is stunning. When you are at the toughest point in the hike, the stunning scenery is what yells out spurring you on with thoughts of encouragement simply from its imagery. When I am here I just know it will be a good day.

Perhaps my infatuation for mountains come from the glorious feeling of achievement. When you finally get to the top and you look down on everything you have just been through you feel an enormous sense of pride. Looking down on everything and everybody, you truly feel like the king of the world. You may have struggled, you may have got close to quitting, you may have got lost, you may be hurting but none of it matters as you stand on the summit. As you look down on the rest of civilisation below, you feel like maybe you can take on the whole world. It's a feeling that isn't felt on any normal day but yet it only takes a simple 5 or 6-hour walk and it will make anyone feel amazing.

It became an addiction ticking off mountains that I have visited. It felt like I was conquering them. So what's next? Well, there are mountains everywhere. The possibilities are endless! Completing the rest of the Furth list sounds like the next challenge, perhaps trying to tick off some more of the Munros? I might look into the Yorkshire three peaks? Bob Graham round? Maybe look into learning rock climbing? Why not start hiking abroad? Iceland is pretty. Why not climb a couple of mountains or volcanoes there? The Alps? Ice climbing? Ski Mountaineering in Scandinavia? Why not throw in some of the Seven Summits? The world is my oyster and it's all very exciting!

This mountain challenge has taught me a valuable lesson. You don't have to be in some far off exotic unknown land to have an adventure. I used to feel that the UK was boring because I lived here. I used to be desperate to get on with my next adventure but always thought that could only happen by booking a plane ticket.

Adventure can happen anywhere. Just because you live on this small island doesn't mean you can't have awesome adventures.

The UK is small but is compressed with loads of beautiful scenery, loads of history and heritage, loads of hidden gems to discover and loads of potential adventures. There is so much to do and so much to see you can't possibly struggle to find adventure. Adventure is just a point of view you don't need to cycle around the world or walk a continent or row an ocean or walk up Everest to class what you are doing as an adventure. You could go for a swim in a local lake, climb a mountain, camp in your back garden, cycle to work. When I started this challenge I never considered this much of an adventure, but I was starting to discover one of the most beautiful places in the UK and I was living right on the doorstep.

It was the evening of my final walk up Eilidir Fawr. I still had the warm bubbling feeling of accomplishment fizzing in my blood as I sat at the dinner table with my parents. I boasted about my adventures. I told them the stories of the beauty and my love for the mountains. I verbally ticked off each Welsh Furth on my list. After what could have been half an hour of my adventure tales my dad stopped me in my tracks and said:

"Yeah it's great up in Snowdonia isn't it? When I was younger, I walked up all 15 in 18 hours"

I was stunned… How?… Do people actually do this?… But doing all 15 in one summer nearly killed me off. It turns out the Welsh 3000 is a challenge in itself where people walk all the Welsh fifteen 3000 foot mountains in 24 hours. It blew my mind! There's even a guy called Colin Donelly who climbed all 15 peaks in 4 hours and 19 minutes. Wow!

So maybe my achievements aren't as grand as some other adventurous souls. But that doesn't mean that my adventure wasn't perfect for me. There is always someone bigger and better.

The Welsh 3000 Challenge might have to wait for another day!

Callum is an Englishman with a Scottish name who was brought up on the Welsh border and currently lives in Ireland (very multi-cultured). He works as a barman. He is a part-time alcoholic and full-time adventure dreamer. Callum travels as much as his money allows him to, travelling all over Europe, India and Vietnam. Callum enjoys setting himself endurance based challenges, cycling through countries, walking through mountain and enjoying meeting new people.

Twitter: @TheTravelCult

           Instagram: @jmullac

Chapter 6

Travelling Under an Upside Down Sky

by Francesca Turauskis

There is a small girl in a kitchen. She wears a short bob of brown hair and a warm red jacket. Her mum's hands hold her firmly under the armpits and she balances on top of the kitchen counter so that she can stretch to see the sky outside the window. The moon is half-grown. *A 'D' for 'Developing'* her mum would say. The kitchen lights are dark, but her eyes shine. Beyond the beech tree, sparks of colour scatter the sky. With each shooting bang, the girl's body is startled. She wants to see the exploding colours, but her hands are clamped tightly over her ears, and the windows and door are shut tight to provide an auditory protection.

Her sister stands outside. Nothing but a hat covers *her* hair and ears, but her 'whoas' of delight rise above the bangs. To the girl, her sister seems so distant.

She could never do anything so brave.

*

When I stepped on the plane, I had slept for a restless few hours. Partly because of the excited insect flutters in my belly. Mostly because I had left packing until the last minute. For weeks I had been writing lists of what I wanted to take, laying out my clothes in piles, buying travel toiletries and borrowing basics. The journal I had received for Christmas the month before lay pride of place in the hand luggage pile, its leather cover hugging the black and white photograph my granddad had handed me. Tucked into the pocket made for mementos, the photo showed ferns surrounded by clear water, and a flotilla of black fish doubled in number by the shadows they cast in the bright sun. He took that photograph when he was in the RAF, on service in Rotorua. I was surprised by the revelation that he was a photographer, in his own youth.

"We caught our fish in that pool," he had told me, "and cooked them in the pool next to it."

As he talked, I tried to link his cigarette-wrinkled face with that of a young man in a contradictory land.

Like a proverbial cat, the journal and the rest of my luggage remained out of the bag. To pack it would be to finalise it. Just days before, I was working as a 'Sandwich Artist', a job I had taken purely to save money for my trip. Six months of repetitive drudgery since I left sixth form. But now, the world stood before me and New Zealand shimmered on the other side like a daydream in a film. Yet every item that I placed in the bag brought me closer to the fantasy – until I tried to fit a video camera into my pregnant-looking hand luggage.

It took many arrangements before everything was snug. I even managed to fit in my mascot, Madoc, a stuffed dragon from Porthmadog in Wales. Madoc had been on every mountain-climb with me, and now he was to fly around the world. (He would actually stay in my bag for the majority of the trip, but he was there nonetheless.)

By the time I was satisfied, the house was long asleep. I climbed up the stepladder to my bunk bed and sought sleep for myself. I would occupy many bunk beds in hostels over the next months, but it would be a long time until I slept in mine again.

*

After I dropped my newly-packed bag off at check-in, it was time for the hugs. My sister's was quick and awkward, my dad's long and breath-crushing and my mum's comfortable and lingering as I turned towards security. Turning back to wave, I could see they were upset.

"Just so we know," my dad had asked, "are you leaving because you're going towards something, or because you're running away?"

"Going towards. I would never run away."

I stepped through where they could not go and I was soon removing my boots and bag for scanning, lining up with other be-socked people to be scanned myself.

I remember sitting by Boarding Gate One. My stomach churned in knots and no book was exciting enough to distract me from my own adventure. I had been to the doctor to ask for something to help me through the flight. When I was younger, my dad had a rather joyous flight on a family holiday to New York once after taking prescribed Valium, and I secretly hoped the doctor would give me some to try.

"I'm not really happy to give you something that will put you out of it," she had said. "Not a young girl travelling by yourself."

I persuaded her for a prescription anyway, but as I sat there an hour after taking the tablet, my over-active mind decidedly lucid, I knew it was a placebo. And if you know something is a placebo, it tends to lose the effect.

'Oh my God! They just announced the start of boarding!'

Hours of waiting and that was all I managed to write, before putting the journal swiftly away. I shouldered my bag, and joined the queue onto the plane. The between world that would take me from the life I knew into something entirely new.

As the plane taxied onto the runway, the anticipation of take-off was a heavy hand on my chest. I took deep breaths, trying to dislodge it and push out the nerves. The plane sat at the start of the runway, ominously still amongst the growl of the engines. Then, slowly, it began to grumble along the tarmac. I was soon forced into my seat-back as the rumbling crescendo of the jet crammed the air. The plane rattled, the nose tipped upwards, and I closed my eyes, trying to imagine the calm grey sky in front of me rather than a metal cylinder filled with bodies. I could feel the rigid tension along my arms and hands as I gripped the seat.

As the plane began to level out, the assurance that take-off had not killed me kicked in. I could not stay scared for nine hours and after the seatbelt sign was turned off, my body relaxed slightly. On the way to my connecting flight in San Francisco, I caught snatches of sleep, watched films on the tiny screen, and inched open the window blind occasionally, only to be startled each time by the pure sunlight bouncing off the clouds. When we began to descend, I opened the blind for the umpteenth time and was rewarded for my persistence.

I saw mountains, desolate and beautiful, wearing cloaks of cloud on their shoulders. Mountains stretching higher, sharper and further than the ancient Welsh ones I knew. I longed to be a speck on that landscape.

The plane ate up the miles, and as it banked around San Francisco airport, I looked for the famous Golden Gate Bridge, but did not see it. All I managed to see of San Francisco was a few cars, a dry, dusty patch of ground outside a window, and the airport. I had to wait there for six hours. My luggage was not transferred directly to the next flight and until my check-in, I sat in the food hall opposite

'FUNG LUM, Chinese Cuisine *and* Noodles' drinking a scalding-hot hot-chocolate, and guarding the bulk of bags under my legs. I contemplated taking my video camera out to film where I was, but I still remembered the battle I had to go through to get it in the bag. I did not want to repeat that in public. Besides, it would have been mere documentation – there was nothing interesting to record.

But it *was* interesting to me. I was excited to taste the Snapple on sale at Fung Lum. I first had that drink aged fourteen whilst in New York, and it still tastes of America to me. To see it sold alongside Chinese cuisine seemed quintessentially America to me; the mixing of cultures. As I noted all this down in my travel journal, I glanced up to see one of the airport's security guards stood a few seats away. There was a handgun and a truncheon attached to his belt. As I watched him nonchalantly drinking coffee, the immensity of what I was doing hit me. The lack of sleep was catching up with me. It felt like I had stepped into a dream-sequence, the security guard seemed like an exaggerated caricature, and I found myself chuckling under my breath. I was not scared to be alone in a foreign airport, with guns nearby – I was looking forward to telling people about this small encounter. And there were far larger stories waiting for me.

*

As I looked out the window of the second plane, America faded into the sea, and the clouds sat mid-air in layers created peaks and valleys of their own. The sea and clouds seemed so close together, it was if the two were trying to touch, like two lovers separated. I mused in my journal as to whether this is why storms at sea are so powerful – the sky and sea are trying to become one.

I did not know it at the time, but the Māori of New Zealand tell a similar legend of *Ranginui*, the Sky Father, and *Papatūānuku*, the Earth Mother. When time was young, *Ranginui* and *Papatūānuku* held each other in a tight embrace. But as their first child, *Tāne Mahuta*, the great *kauri* tree, grew, he pushed them apart. The children of *Rangi* and *Papa* thanked *Tāne*, for now they had space and light. But one child, *Tāwhirimātea,* the God of Weather, was sad for his parents. Now he sends his children of wind and rain in revenge for their grief.

The plane arrived at Auckland International Airport with Hollywood timing, just as the sun was rising. Our approach above the clouds was in periwinkle twilight, but as we descended, an orange glow illuminated the window, bursting into rays as we left the cloud. I had flown from winter to summer and as I walked off the plane, the air creeping through the gap in the tunnel was cool in the early morning, but not cold. I couldn't wait to get out in it, but for now I was headed towards the depths of the airport and Customs.

New Zealand is, understandably, very concerned with its conservation. Foreign animals and plants have already created devastation in the ecosystem and Customs are keen to prevent any new introductions. Non-native seeds and vegetation are not allowed in without a licence. On the plane, we were given a thorough questionnaire to complete and I had ticked the affirmative to having 'walked across farm and/or countryside' in my walking boots in the past six months. When I reached the kiosk and handed over my answers, they took one look downwards and quickly told me to remove my shoes. As my new, but fairly muddy, boots were whisked out of sight into a backroom, my face must have registered my concern.

"Don't worry," the Customs lady smiled at me. "We'll jist clean them up a wee bit." The accent was similar to Australian, though I would never suggest that to a Kiwi. It is different in a way that is hard to pinpoint. Kiwis seem more confused when they speak, lengthening short vowels and shortening long ones. And everybody says 'wee' a lot – a testament to the strong Irish and Scottish heritage. I managed to pick up that lingual habit whilst I was out there, and still catch myself saying 'wee' instead of 'little' sometimes.

When the rest of my baggage and body had been scanned through Customs and after wandering around in socks for several minutes, I was reunited with my boots. At least, I was told they were mine. I couldn't be entirely certain. These boots looked brand new again, every speck of soil scrubbed from them. I turned them around to look at the tread. There was not even a dusting of the mud that had filled the canyons before. I laced myself back in, thinking it a bit of a shame they would not stay that pristine for long, and was free to wield my trolley up to the exit and the shuttle bus that awaited me.

*

It was seven o'clock on a Sunday morning. I stood on a deserted street in central Auckland after being deposited by the airport shuttle. By my standards, it was perfectly reasonable for everyone to be in bed, but by city standards, tourists and workers should have been dodging each other on the streets and carrying coffees. Yet, as I crossed the road on the way to my hostel, I didn't see a single person.

Even though Auckland is New Zealand's largest city, (32% of the country lives there) it seemed very small to me. It used to be the capital city of New Zealand, (after Russell, but before Wellington) and it seemed very neat and compacted, laid out in a quad with buildings that were all shiny, and new. There were a couple of taller buildings, but the only one with any force was the famous Sky Tower. You can see the Sky Tower from most places in central Auckland, so it would take some effort to get lost because you can always just head towards the Tower. Or head downhill and you'll get to the waterfront. I remember that area of the city as a palette of colours, bright in the clear air. The grey of the railing, the white of the pavement and the teal blue of the sea.

I was staying at Auckland's largest hostel, Auckland Central Backpackers or ACB. It is the first stop for many travellers when they arrive in New Zealand. Since staying there, I have heard ACB compared to a cattle station, with backpackers all herded in to one enormous building. True, it is not the most beautiful or idealistic of hostels. But it doesn't try to be a backpacker's idyll, it is just somewhere to stay, a starting point. More specifically, it was the starting point for the month-long tour I had booked myself on, so it made for an easy entry into my solo-travelling.

I found the place with ease – the forty foot high letters made it impossible not to. Large glass doors stood open to a cool atrium, its empty marble floor leading to three metal doors on the back wall that housed the lifts. These lifts would prove to be an annoyance to everyone that stayed at the hostel; slow to arrive, claustrophobic and temperamental about which floors they decided to stop at. Yet it was always a good conversation starter with fellow passengers when it took five minutes to travel to the first floor via the top.

 The doors eventually opened on an upstairs lobby. Faded, bubble-shaped seats were dotted around and there was a section for flyers and brochures to my immediate right, with titles like 'Sea Kayak Tours', 'Visit Middle Earth' and 'The World's Oldest Bungee Jump!'. The reception desk was directly in front of me, stretching across the entire back wall with a panoramic window behind it. Around the corner, there was a communal area with computers and blue and green fake-leather seats.

I remember that area so clearly because that was where I would later say goodbye to Andy and Allie, two other tour participants. Two friends from Edinburgh, Andy and Allie had the perfect double-act in name and nature. Allie, with his grey hair, large belly (probably because he really loved his drink) and kilt, was always talking. Andy, on the other hand, was quiet and did not speak unless necessary. When he did, his accent was very heavy and he would stare into your eyes in a way that could be unnerving, but seemed to be to assure himself he was understood. He often seemed quite sad. When I said goodbye to them, Allie handed me over his internet card with $15 on it. I think he gave it to me, rather than anyone else, because I was the youngest and he felt a need to look out for me.

I would meet Allie and Andy, and the others I would be spending the next twenty-six days with, the following morning when the tour started. But today I was alone and I headed through the empty lobby to the desk.

"Jist got in have you?" The lady behind the desk was perfectly cheery. "Well, unfortunately you can't get into ye room until elivin, but we can look after ye begs until then."

I left my giant rucksack there with relief and set off into the city. I wandered without aim, unless it was to acquaint myself with the area. I walked through the straight streets, wearing sunglasses to hide my red-rimmed eyes, and ended up in Victoria Park. Queen Vic got her name everywhere – but there was nothing regal about this park, just an area of browning grass with metal construction fences on one end. The site workers were the first people I had seen outside of the hostel. It was somewhat reassuring to see the city hadn't been deserted. I watched a magpie foraging amongst the dust for a while. He looked different to the shine-seekers from back home, and the saddle of white painted along his back made it look as if the artist had made a mistake.

I was soon driven away from the park by the sound of the construction. I found my way across the road to the Victoria Park Market. The building that housed the market was built in 1905, an old building by Auckland standards. It used to be a former rubbish destructor building and the orange brick chimney that used to burn refuse still seemed to glow with heat. The market was quiet, the stall battens still down, the colourful clothes in the windows still shadowed, but I found a lone cafe open and ordered myself an English breakfast and some tea to try and keep awake for that little bit longer.

It was about eight o'clock in the evening in England. I had called my parents earlier to let them know I'd arrived safely, and whilst I sat in front of the cafe, I choose another name from the phonebook.

"Hello?"

I was worried the signal would be fuzzy, but his voice was clearer than when I called him from my own house.

"Hi Granddad. It's Franny."

"Oh. Hello. You made it?"

I listened as he told me about his own travels, and said I should consider my two-day-long journey 'easy'. He told me how it had taken him weeks to fly down to Auckland, how they had stopped off in the Middle East and slept in canvas tents. I had always lived far away from my granddad, but as he talked, it was hard to believe that he was now half a world away. He had been fighting cancer for several years by that point, and I tried not to think about how difficult it would be to get home if he should lose.

I said goodnight to him, whilst he wished me good morning, then I headed back to ACB. Once there and in my empty dorm-room, I slept for a long time. When I woke up, I must have got some food and done something with my evening, but I could not tell you what. Tiredness of mind and distance of memory have rendered that invisible.

*

The next morning was the first of my twenty-six day tour. I choose the tour because it was small and informal. Our tour guide was a Kiwi named JT (a late-thirty-something surfer with sun-bleached hair, who hardly ever wore shoes) was collecting us in the reception. He seemed to have found a way to spend the majority of his adult life avoiding work. He had travelled New Zealand a hundred times and discovered he could get paid to do it if he showed some backpackers around at the same time.

"G'day folks." He glanced over us keenly. "Let's get you checked in, then meet back here. We'll head off and I'll show ya what Auckland has to offer. And bring ya togs and towels."

He was showing fourteen of us around this time – his biggest group so far, apparently. We huddled together around the desk to claim rooms. Age and gender seemed as good a determiner for room companions as anything, so I went in a four-bed with the three younger women. Carly and Fi – who hadn't arrived yet because her flight was delayed – knew each other from university. I spoke to Carly more on that first morning than any other time. She was Scottish, with fighting red hair and blue eyes and I could never quite decide if she was a quiet person or just rude to me. My other roommate, Laura, was very chatty. She had come out with a wheeled suitcase, straighteners and heels – as well as walking boots – and would throw herself off a cliff into river water, then straighten her hair as soon as possible. I call her Young Laura, yet she was a year older than me. She told us she had spent a few days with family in Auckland before meeting up for the tour, and was annoyed because she already had sunburn.

Young Laura hit it off with James straight away – perhaps because they were the two most attractive, single people on the tour. James was a dog-walker from the Isle of Wight, in his late twenties, quite good-looking, but wiry. James was in a room with Andy, Allie and a man from Yorkshire called Mike. I was very excited when we later found out that Mike and his brother had been extras in Emmerdale when he was younger.

There was one couple on tour. Tom and his girlfriend (confusingly also called Laura) had a double room to themselves that first night. We joked they were a proper WAG couple – Tom was a semi-professional footballer, Laura was a very pretty beautician with bleach-blonde hair. They had been dating for a short time before deciding to take a year off work to travel: Thailand; New Zealand; Australia; Vietnam. They were both already nicely nut-brown when we met.

I was surprised that there were no Americans on tour, but there were a couple of Canadians. Wendy and Catherine were friends from childhood who didn't get a chance to see each other much anymore, so they decided to travel around New Zealand together. Wendy was a pretty typical librarian who packed more books than clothes. Catherine, on the other hand, was wild. It was definitely *her* idea to travel. She had gotten engaged just before the tour, but I didn't hear much about her fiancé. She did not drink much, but she didn't need it. She was half Chinese and explained to me that most Chinese people living in a western country have two names – an English one and traditional one.

They were in a room with Agatha. I felt sorry for Agatha, a teacher in her late forties, who definitely wasn't expecting the tour that she got. She hated it so much that she split off at one point and met up with us later. Maybe it is true what folks joke about the German temperament, but JT's disorganised nature annoyed her. But she took some amazing photographs, which I managed to copy before we parted. One of them is still a favourite of mine. (I'm sat on a rock at a beach called Te Nikau, facing the sunset with my knees pulled up near my grinning mouth. I have my video camera with me but it is tucked away in its bag, forgotten in the moment.)

That leaves Army Steve. I don't think he was ever in the army, but he wore combats and did everything with army efficiency and seriousness. Steve was skinny and bald with big, strained eyes. None of us every really understood him. Whilst Andy seemed sad in a benign way, Steve seemed to me to be perpetually angry about something.

Ten minutes later, when we were all togged up, JT met us back in the lobby.

"Well folks, before we head off to the beach, there are a few rules..."

I may be breaking the first rule by writing this. Whilst I try to not to blow any whistles in this account, so much of our experiences travelling are about the people we meet.

"What goes on tour stays on tour. We're all here to have fun. Also, as there will be fourteen of you, we won't actually fit in my van. But for now there is just about enough room, so head on down and climb on in. Don't worry, it'll all be sweet-as for tomorrow."

We were all quite glad we wouldn't be riding around the country in JT's old bus. It looked like a once-white, old school minivan and it smelt as bad – stale water, sweat and mud, with the addition of booze. The seats were sunken and lumpy. With JT's surfboard wedged between the seats, there was already little room, even without our luggage and a fourteenth person. But we only had to travel a few miles out of Auckland to get to Muirwai Beach

Muirwai is a black sand beach, which is famous for its gannet colony and also happened to be hosting a surfing competition that day. We relaxed on the volcanic sand, marvelling at the giant boulders of volcanic rock that dotted the shore and looked like melting elephant's skin. The sand was warm like ash and was framed by crumbling cliffs topped with bright green grass and clear blue sky. The gannet colony was on top of a sea stack to the right. I could just about see the white shapes pottering about on top of the rock, or circling the air before diving into the water, arrow-precise, to rise with a glint in their beaks.

JT was out in the surf. As we watched his bright green shorts and red top ride a wave, Catherine voiced what we were all thinking.

"Do you think he brought us here just so he could surf?"

Definitely. But after a relaxed Monday afternoon, lying in the hot sand and doing not much else, we weren't complaining.

When we returned to the hostel, as soon as we walked through the lobby doors a bundle of curly blonde hair bounded into Carly, squealing – Fi had arrived. Fi was the opposite of Carly. She was one of those amazing people you can always talk to and who will talk to you. She had been stuck in Vietnam, where she had been working with orphans, and was wearing dungarees with stars and dolphins that the children had painted for her. She looked around the group with bright eyes, trying to take in the names of people she didn't know, but who already knew who she was.

Now that Fi was here, our band was complete.

That evening, we went down to the waterfront, to one of the viaduct bars. The waterfront and the bars of the viaduct basin were busy for a Monday night and not just with travellers such as us. It was Auckland Day, a public holiday for the residents of the old Auckland province. The provinces were similar to counties and based around the main cities of New Zealand. Despite the fact the provinces themselves were abolished in 1876, all the cities still seem to use the excuse of a provincial holiday to celebrate.

*

There is a young woman next to a harbour. It is January, but she is outside, her hair falling long and loose around bare shoulders. She stands with fourteen strangers and a city of people. The moon writes a 'D' in the sky, but it will be shrinking each night from here. The city lights are dark. Everyone watches as the ships in the harbour send up rockets, which scatter sparks of colour across an upside-down sky. The woman stands, far away from home and unprotected.

This is my memory. It is one of many I will collect to tell my older sister, my mum, my dad, and all those who wait for me in my distant home.

This is a beginning.

Francesca Turauskis is best described as an Adventure Advocate. Her podcast, Seize Your Adventure, ignites adventure in others and breaks down the misconceptions surrounding epilepsy. Her heart is happiest when hiking solo across mountains but she has recently discovered she also enjoys running like a wild thing on trails at the edge of suburbia. Fran's indoor alter-ego is a writer who works in the local library.

Podcast: seizeyouradventure.com/podcasts

Website: francescaturauskis.co.uk

Instagram: @frantictwalks

Facebook: @frantictwalks

Chapter 7

Trekking into the Himalayas

by Jago Hartland

The Morning

The seven o'clock sun burst through the single-glazed window and bounced off of the white walls like a disco ball. I've never particularly been the type of person to have bad mornings or have the need to rush for a cup of coffee to feel awake. Usually the excitement of the day ahead lifts me up and takes me into the kitchen on wobbly legs and with fresh eyes. I am awake before that first granule of instant hits the bottom of the coffee cup.

The brittle window in the kitchen faced the same direction as the bedroom window and the second sighting of sun felt as good as the first. For as long as I could remember, I have always been a morning person. An early start to get out before a hearty breakfast is more appealing to me than a late evening lost in a crowd.

As the kettle boiled and bubbled on my empty kitchen top, I turned around to face the open-plan kitchen and living room. Perched against the sink, I eyed up the boxes still to be unpacked, the free space to be filled and the pictures to be pinned up. It was a messy area but I didn't wish for it to be any other way. My mountain bike leant against the wall, a poster of Muhammad Ali hung above the mantel place and a bottle of champagne sat on the table with a card that read 'congratulations'.

The reason I kept having enjoyable mornings was because I was still excited to have moved into my own place. I felt a little silly having this feeling after living in my flat for over three months, and also still not being fully unpacked. My partner and I joked repeatedly about how we had time to throw away but didn't have time to hang a picture. After the first ten minutes of the typical morning routine, I put on some food and jumped into a cold shower.

When I had moved into the flat, I had a job at Cotswold Outdoor, just to cover rent. Clocking in hours at Cotswold Outdoor was never my calling but it wasn't an unenjoyable job. The team I worked alongside were like me – outdoors enthusiasts. They regularly organised dinners and climbing evenings together. I made many close friends at Cotswold Outdoor.

I changed into my cycling shorts and popped on a helmet to head off to work. The undulating ride was the perfect small sense of adventure before being 'stuck' inside for eight hours. Even though I have referred to the glorious sun as being a magic piece of my happy mornings, I am not its biggest fan. As I'm of the fair-skinned, red-headed variety, I tend to try and hide away from the burning star to avoid its energy sapping glare.

It was as I arrived at work that I felt the seven kilometres in my legs. It was a comfortable distance but it made sure I didn't get too portly for my uniform. I locked my bicycle up and entered through the staff door.

A group of team members were chatting and making coffee. We said our usual hellos and chatted about something non-work related until the manager was awake enough to address everyone and post the updates and bulletins to the cork board. It was the usual stuff. Staff hours, sales updates, key products. But every once in a while there was something a bit different.

This time it was an email, printed and pinned to the bulletin board. It wasn't very often that anything excited me enough to give it a second glance. Today was different. One photocopied scrap of paper had my full attention.

The title read: Opportunity to trek into the western Himalayas with MTV.

At first, I was confused as to why anyone would want to trek with a music TV brand. Then I read on. MTV stood for Mountain Tribal Vision. A quick five minute glance over the double-sheet spread enticed me into reading more, but it was at that moment that we were told we had to start work on the shop floor.

I must have returned back to the news bulletin five or more times that day to re-read the offer. The more I looked at it, the more I realised I was getting hooked.

A full work day went by whilst the thought of adventure niggled away at the back of my mind. With my phone camera loaded with images of the bulletin details to view later, I cycled home at the end of work, happy to be en route to a cup of Early Grey and Marmite on toast.

Worries

Most people who have taken on adventures will agree that they have faced many hurdles before they have been able to have their 'yes moment'. For me, this took two weeks just on thinking and planning alone. No annual leave was requested. No deposits were paid. Just deciding if I was logistically able to take on this adventure of a life-time was a challenge in itself.

To get a better understanding of the logistics, a usual adventure or travel trip would normally mean thinking about the financial burden, the time off work and any other commitments. For most people, fitness would be an aspect to improve on. Not everyone would have to question health before making a decision to travel.

Living with cystic fibrosis added an extra layer of complications to this already congested logistical nightmare. My diagnosis with cystic fibrosis (CF) was when I was fourteen years old. Apparently that means it was a 'late diagnosis'. I always look at my late diagnosis with a little dark humour. I was a young teenager. I had the rest of my life before me. How was this a 'late diagnosis'?

CF causes chronic chest infections and digestive problems. The signs were clear from an early age. I was born with a collapsed lung as a baby, my attendance at school averaged 60-70% due to illness and we had a history of CF in my family. Out of the six children my mother gave birth to, four were diagnosed with the condition. This is, apparently, extremely rare. The chances of having a child with CF, when both parents have the hidden gene, is one in four. My mum must have the worst luck ever.

I faced my least favourite part of the planning stage head on. Step one was shopping for travel insurance. Imagine the premiums I had to face as a young adult with CF attempting to trek above 5000m in a remote area of the Himalayas. My cheapest quote was £172!

The adventure planning continued with a pre-pack check of antibiotics and medicines and getting in touch with my hospital team at the Bristol Royal Infirmary.

Growing up in the countryside has always given my life a large sense of adventure. When I was diagnosed with CF, I knew that I didn't want to have to compromise my big adventure plans in order to always keep fit and healthy. That's why I wanted to go on this expedition more than anything.

Going through the process of getting all of my CF information in order to be able to participate on the Himalaya trek saddened me. Even though I hadn't let the condition control my life, I certainly have felt cheated and dealt an unfair hand. For someone who has dreamed of living as adventurously, being hampered by this condition is extremely frustrating.

A couple of days dragged by before my specialist team agreed I was healthy enough to join the trek. After giving the Mountain Tribal Vision manager a call to confirm and pay the deposit, I was officially secured onto the Cotswold June 2017 Himalayan team. The trek had been advertised in February 2017, which meant I had four months to prepare before I flew out to India. Unlike many of my peers in sixth form, I decided not to attend university. I wanted to work in the outdoors and you don't need a degree to do that.

I had hoped to eventually become a mountain leader. However over the fifteen months since leaving sixth form, I hadn't saved a lot of money for such an expenditure. I'd spent everything I'd earned travelling around South East Asia, Europe and on mini excursions to the mountains of Scotland and Wales. I was working numerous part time jobs, including Cotswold Outdoor, but I was only interested in zero-hour contracts to allow me to work flexible seasons. In summary, a high income wasn't my priority. How was I going to afford the trip to the Himalayas?

Saying, "Yes," to join the expedition team was the biggest and scariest thing I had ever done. I am a strong believer in the sense that things don't become less scary. You just become better prepared.

So I got myself prepared. Somehow, I managed to scrape together the funds but it wasn't easy. I had recently become an 'adult', which (others dictate) meant I had to pay bills – I was also covering the rent payments whilst I'd be away travelling. Things were going to be tight.

On top of these financial worries was the emotional concerns as departure day loomed. Myself and my partner, whom I was living with in the flat, were upset by the inevitable parting. There were restless nights and heated exchanges at a time when we were supposed to be celebrating our own big adventure – moving in together. Adventure doesn't only affect you; it affects all of those around you and even more so the ones close to you.

I was a little vexed at her for being so angry at me for going away. I had travelled before and she knew this was a big opportunity for me. No one was right or wrong yet the arguments made it upsetting nonetheless.

My money issues and the nerves of trekking into altitude for the first time were getting to me. I spent late nights counting costs in my head. I was scared to ask for help. In the years before this trip, I had travelled in lots of countries and had put myself in many risky situations. I was more nervous than ever at this point.

At the time, and reflecting on it now, I believe the decision to go on the expedition wasn't just about saying 'Yes' to the adventure. It was about saying 'No' to my recently discovered domesticated life. I guess, up until I was offered a fantastically priced expedition with work, I didn't realise how much I was falling in love with waking up to face the morning sunshine with a cup of coffee in my hand in a place I could call 'mine'. I should have known, and I believe I may have, that leaving that day would change my life forever.

India

A feeling of being hit by the thick dusty warm air of Delhi is something most people never forget. It is like being covered all over your body in an unwashed duvet. You sweat from the moment you step off the plane until you return to depart on your way home. I will always associate that feeling with adventure. Stepping off that plane and being punched through my body with adrenaline and excitement. It's why I enjoy it so much.

Alongside the two other team members from Cotswold Outdoor, I met Tanzin, the trip organiser, at the airport. We all crammed into a taxi to head to our hotel for the night before a fifteen hour car journey the next day. The first couple of days were a blur due to the excitement, jetlag and the pure madness of Indian roads.

We travelled far up into Northern India and entered Manali in the foothills of the Himalayas. Manali is the place of dreams, with a large river running through the valley and houses built up on either side in between the cedar trees. Old town Manali was bustling with life. Florescent colours, street food and the mountains that surrounded the area gave a sense of vulnerability and spiritualism.

My nerves had settled over the first four days of travel and I returned to my confident, larger-than -life personality. Meeting Tanzin's affectionate family and our head Sherpa, Namgyual, had relaxed me a lot. It turned out that our Sherpa, chef and horseman were all of Tibetan heritage and I quickly came to learn that all the rumours of Tibetan hospitality were true. Tibetan culture is similar to arriving for tea at your grandmother's – a delicious array of cakes present themselves before you have a change to say, "No, thank you."

On the first evening of rest in Manali, I felt a little more short of breath than usual. There are staircases covering the town and hidden passageways that climb off in all directions. Relief flooded over me to see that the other two members of the team had also found the environment more challenging for walking. It was later stated by Tanzin that Manali was based 2000m above sea level and we have already started our gradual climb into the mountains. '2000m!' I thought. I couldn't help but think, 'How on Earth am I going to be able to cope above 5000m?'

The slight stress elevated my heart rate. I started to notice my irregular breathing. My oxygen regulation throughout my body was out of sync.

The vicious cycle repeated itself. Increased heart rate. Sharper breaths. Muscle fatigue.

Just the thought of the altitude had awoken my pre-departure stresses. My heart thumped hard in my chest as I took deep breaths to try to regulate my breathing.

Our next night's accommodation was at the Kolong Retreat, which was a further eight hour car journey into the Himalayas. During one of those hours, we only managed to cover a distance of twelve kilometres due to the roads into the mountains. I would say they were badly maintained but, quite frankly, there wasn't very much to maintain.

After eight hours of head-butting each other, the doors and the roof of our little van, we were thankful to arrive at our cabin.

Our log cabin was luxurious and perched on the side of a mountain facing across the valley to the most striking mountain range I had ever seen. Small ice shelves hung high above us. Grand patches of snow, larger than the village we stayed in, covered the hillsides.

As night approached, I walked out alone onto the balcony near the dining room. The sky was lit with the brightest stars and it reflected off of the snow on the mountains. The snow absorbed the light and became its own lantern. I could've stood in the cool air all night and not noticed the passage of time.

The thought that I could be staring in the direction of a snow leopard excited me. But there was no detail on the mountains that night. The prayer flags above my head were distraught as they whipped about in the icy wind. I still felt the chill in my bright orange down jacket and woolly hat. Only my face was exposed, the tip of my nose going numb in the cold.

In that moment, I felt overwhelmed at the volume of the environment surrounding me. Just the huge enormity of the mountains and the sky was awe-inspiring. A sense of pride in chasing my dreams after facing so many obstacles rushed through my veins. The silence was deafening. I could have quite easily shed a tear of pure joy. My heart was full of the sensation of life fulfilment.

In such a moment, worries of home are lifted away with the wind. Life's stresses disappear into the night's sky like forgotten wraiths. If it wasn't for Namgyual arriving outside to call me for dinner, the evening could have been lost to that cold wind and my preoccupying thoughts.

Sickness

It was more vivid than anything I had previously experienced. I couldn't stand up but I heard all of my friends' and families' voices surrounding me. It was just as though I was in normal conversation but I had an image of the wooden slat floor ingrained in my mind.

The same thoughts kept racing through my mind. 'Where is everyone? Why can't I look up from the floor? Where am I?' After the image of the floor left my mind, I could only imagine the walls breathing, as if they were being drawn into the room and then expanding the room back out to its original size.

I awoke wet in my sweat and feeling nauseous. My eyes felt as if they had just exited a roller coaster and were beginning to re-orientate themselves. Before I could completely regain my sense of self, I was being stared back at in the mirror by a young man who resembled me, although he looked as though he had just finished a ten mile run and applied a light blue lipstick to finish.

My fear had begun: my first experience of altitude sickness.

The following hour was composed of a brisk shower, drinking a litre of water and eating an energy bar to ensure I had enough calories. Once again, I felt stronger and more at ease, enough to make the decision not to wake Namgyual at five o'clock in the morning to inform him in the morning instead.

We were now just over 3000m above sea level. I couldn't help but wonder how the others were feeling and whether I would feel better and strong enough for the 5000m push. As I rested my head back down to sleep, my mind was full of constant reminders of my bed in my flat, my missing company back home and my CF. It was as if it was laughing at me for believing I was strong enough to take on this challenge. I felt as if I was mocking myself from within. The collective genes of my condition were holding me back and taking pleasure in scaring me. It's crazy how the mind works.

We had a full day's rest that included a leisurely four hour hike to help us acclimatise. I awoke early the following day and helped with the packing of the vehicle with the support team. I was really enjoying their company – a little more than the other two members of our team. By this time it was becoming quite normal for me to spend a few hours a day talking with Namgyual about all matters from home and about his family. I felt an immediate connection with him and his endearing smile only grew on me – he even laughed at my rather foolish humour and terrible English jokes.

We were now on our route higher into the mountain and towards our first camping spot. Camp One was positioned at 4000m and we didn't need to do any walking, which was quite the relief. The previous day's hike and today's car journey had reassured me once again that I was feeling more confident about getting some good walking mileage in. My mind was overflowing with the experience and the beautiful scenery and I had little time to think about altitude sickness.

Our team were merely a speck of khaki colours positioned on the side of a jagged mountainous canvas. The height of the opposing mountains was daunting. Then it occurred to me – we were completely alone out there.

Once we had discovered our camp spot on a small patch of track, the team set up a mess tent and cook's tent within the hour. We had hours to rest and relax before supper and then even more leisure time before getting an early night in preparation for an early morning's pack up. I decided to rest in my tent after taking a few small video diaries and enjoying the landscape. No matter which way I looked, I couldn't spot any distinct tracks through the mountains. Other than the baby blue sky above, the only view all around was rock and snow.

The 3mm blow-up roll mat felt surprisingly comfortable to lay back on. The previous five days of travel and extreme change in weather made me feel exhausted quite often – I later realised it was also due to bad altitude sickness. My one man tent was spacious and the top of the tent was a clear two feet from my head. I laid there enjoying the ten degree temperature as the sun warmed the tent.

Sickness Returns

Imagine you are fully asleep. Then suddenly you fall and wake up. Your heartbeat is racing. Within seconds your body is flushed with heat. Your breathing is rapid and shallow.

This is what I felt as I crawled to the suddenly very small doorway of my tent. I pushed my boots to the side and held myself up by my hands over the sharp stony path. With another rush of painful heat coursing through my body I began to vomit. A blurry few seconds later, I noticed that Namgyual was rushing straight towards me.

"Are you okay Jargo?" he said, concern etched on his hard features.

I was surprised to feel in higher spirits than my last experience in the cabin.

"Not too bad thanks, Mr Namgyual." I tried to grin at him.

If I had known how painful the following three days were to be, my spirits would have dampened a lot faster. The incident in my tent meant that I spent the rest of the evening in the dining mess tent laid beside the table and resting while Namgyual tested my oxygen levels to see if I was stable. I didn't feel overly unwell.

It was probably my stubbornness and self-confidence that pushed me on the next morning. It certainly took the pressure off of the other two in the team after I had to be given supplementary oxygen within the first night of camping. Good job Jago!

In the morning I was feeling strong and well rested. That was a very good sign seeing as today was the day we were going above 5000m. Namgyual had told us that we had been slightly unlucky with the weather as the Western Himalayas had an unusually large amount of snowfall for June. This meant difficult hiking for us. He reassured us many times, two hours walking to the top followed by four hours walking back down the other side of the mountain to a 4200m campsite. Just an easy 1000m elevation gain between us and another delicious mess tent dinner.

The Summit

Walking began easily. Namgyual was at the front, me in second place and the other two members of the team following behind. We were covering the distance at a good pace. One hour went by with three rest breaks for food and water, and yet I was feeling quietly buoyant. It turned out that we had to slow a little for the other two team members to catch up. I didn't want to push them but it was reassuring to feel I was setting a fast pace. I had a sense of contentment as if I was back home and training with the running club or with friends.

In the months before this trip, I had completed the National Three Peaks Challenge in less than twenty-four hours and had run two running events: in one ten-mile trail run, I came first in my category. I have always joked with others about how I start out as the fittest on my trips and always end up the most ill. Because of my CF, my body technically 'deteriorates' four times faster than the average person's due to my immune system not working as efficiently, food not digesting properly and growing chronic chest infections.

When returning home from my first trip to Vietnam in 2016, my lung function had dropped from a previous 96% to a very sad 62% as I grew one of the worst types of infections: pseudomonas. The following three months consisted of heavy antibiotics to kill the infection. At this point in my life, I was consuming: six pills a day, four nebulisers, an inhaler for in-between, four powder drinks and something not so pleasant. I have always been extremely grateful that my CF condition isn't worse than it is as I have known many others to take a lot more medication on a daily basis. Even though that is the case, it still irritates me that I get fatigued faster and more seriously than any of my peers or team members. I usually train multiple hours a day before an expedition only to have to begin back at the start when I arrive home after the trip.

When I have spoken to people about why I challenge myself in difficult environments, I explain to them that the feeling of power and vulnerability I get when facing the mountains is something I can't replicate anywhere else.

The snow-covered top was in sight. With prayer flags darting in every direction, their ends buried under the snow, it was a sight to remember. There was a large concrete base holding up a tall sign with Tibetan writing on it along with the height, '5200m Above Sea Level'.

As I dragged my sorry body puffing and panting the last few big steps to the sign, I was in shock. We were now above 5000m. Dropping myself down against that sign and sipping from my apple juice cartoon felt amazing. The ten minutes that we were up there was a relaxing break with snacks and fluids to try and make ourselves feel a little more alive.

At this point, my body wasn't screaming at me anymore – I felt more like there was a rush of endorphins making me feel weightless and entranced with the snow. We stayed sat there as Namgyual was testing our oxygen and I was last to be tested. Before I could notice the small device was on my finger, Namgyual had yanked it off and held it tight in his hands. He blew softly onto it and placed it onto his own, read the reading and then popped it back onto my finger. "How are you feeling, Jargo?" he asked.

Certainly feeling a tad less confident, I replied with honesty and said I was feeling fine.

The following few hours of downhill walking gave us a better view out of the clouds. Getting down to our camp was becoming more difficult as the time went on. I was very thankful to have made it within a couple of kilometres of camp before I was beginning to feel at my worst again. My glasses, hat, gloves, two jackets, boots and over trousers were starting to feel much too constraining. Having altitude sickness has been the only time in my life I have felt claustrophobic in my own clothing. I was gripping onto my rucksack straps with white knuckles to take my mind away from the headache that thumped between my temples.

Over the next small contour, we spotted the camp and I picked up my pace to get there. The last muddy hundred metres to the small stone building was proving too challenging. I noticed that Namgyual had been keeping a close eye on me as I slipped and waded all the way into the building.

There was no grace in what happened next. All three of us, exhausted and hurting, plonked ourselves down and within minutes we were laying on our sides on the stone benches flat out asleep.

I awoke a few times in the next hour and half to see Namgyual checking on us and placing a rugged horse blanket on top of me to keep warm. I can still see that moment as clear in my mind as this morning. A picture of stone walls and strong winds pushing dirty grey clouds across the sky. It was disorientating to the eyes. I was unbalanced and scared. The altitude and fatigue placed me into a demented, fearful state. There are few moments in my life when I question what had just happened – this was one of those moments.

It was finally time to get up and head over to the mess tent for food. When we arose, I was unclear what I was doing and once again vomited twice on my way to the dining tent. Namgyual, my chaperone, held me up. Terror contorted his face as he watched the pure red liquid of my vomit hitting the snow. Then his features eased with relief as he realised we'd had tomato soup earlier in the day.

Supper that night was hard to swallow but still delightful. I truthfully hit my roll mat like a sack of potatoes that night.

The next two days climbing further down to a height of 3000m made me feel human once again.

There are many mountaineers that sum up the emotional experience of altitude sickness very well. It isn't just about the pain or about a strong absence of loved ones that makes you emotional. The lack of oxygen in your body and brain makes you extra sensitive and a lot of people justly become big babies, as I did. I cried each day over the following three days thinking about home and what I had just pushed myself through.

When I was rested at 3200m in the home village of Namgyual, I laughed hysterically and wondered what had just happened. The experience was surely terrifying and surreal, but I was bewildered at my emotional reaction to it. That night, sitting around the campfire with a glass of Cheung, (a Tibetan homebrew, which tastes like the bottom of a ten year old barrel of cider) we laughed hard, played music and had a beautiful night under the stars. I was cheerful and happy to be alive. What an incredible contrast compared to the tearful nights before.

The trek lasted for twelve days hiking further into the mountains and then backtracking close to our original route on the way to our pickup spot. In that time, we had played a large amount of card games, drank a great amount of Chai tea, we all had become sick at different stages and we had grown together as team.

One night, Namgyual and I were full of energy, more so than the others. We decided to run over the top of an unnamed monastery built into the caves. As we reached the top, I had been jerked to one side by a strong grasp to my top. Namgyual pointed 200m across the mountain. A fully-grown snow fox darted in the opposite direction. Its white, fluffy build stood out against the rocky terrain and we could see him for a short while before the master of disguise disappeared.

We were standing at the furthest point in the Himalayas we were to discover, gazing towards the horizon. What an amazing way to finish the expedition.

Returning to Civilisation

Getting back to Manali was something we had all looked forward to. But for me at least, when we arrived back to our guest house with showers and toilets and Wi-Fi, I wanted nothing more than to be back in the mountains without a care in the world.

Before this trip, I thought I had experienced enough difficult challenges to be fully prepared both physically and mentally. I have come to learn that every experience is different. The twelve days spent in the mountains had been unlike anything I had been through before. The mental impact has stayed with me forever. The cocktail of snow and rock, culture and kindness, pain and appreciation made me grow stronger as a person. I left a part of myself in the mountains and returned a new person.

I walked down from my upstairs room to join Tanzin and Namgyual sitting outside in the sunlit courtyard for a cup of tea and a chat. Tanzin was previously very concerned about my altitude sickness and remarked how I was one of the worst cases the team had experienced before. To his delight, Namgyual had told him I was a fantastic patient. More specifically, he said I kept walking and I continued the vicious cycle of eating after vomiting only to bring it up once again. Keeping calories up and fluids in is fundamentally important in altitude. When you have sickness, there is no argument; you have to compensate for it as much as you can.

Tanzin went on to offer me a job working in the UK for Mountain Tribal Vision. With my shocked expression, I told him I would have to think on it. In reality I already knew my answer.

Of course I said, "Yes!"

Facebook: facebook.com/My65Roses

Instagram: @my65roses_jagohartland

Chapter 8

A Bumpy Ride

by Jen Williams

We're lost. It's dark. We are cycling up a huge hill in the driving rain and we don't even know if we're going in the right direction. We're meant to be on a gravel cycle path but a wrong turn has spat us out on to a busy highway with lorries hurtling past at 90km/h far too close for comfort. I'm in tears. My legs are aching and I can hardly breathe. I'm four months pregnant. And our toddler, sat in a bike seat behind my husband covered in a waterproof poncho, is singing the Paw Patrol theme tune at the top of his lungs.

"What are we doing?" I scream at my husband. "I'm a terrible mother. We're terrible parents. This is selfish. This isn't safe." I am exhausted, starving, at the mercy of pregnancy hormones and, at this moment, close to having a panic attack. I throw a full on toddler tantrum and announce that I cannot continue, waiting for a gap between lorries before dismounting my bike and climbing over the metal crash barrier into a pitch black, muddy field. The thick brown paste clings to my trainers and icy brown water seeps into my socks, making me immediately regret my decision.

We stand there for five minutes imagining hopelessly that the situation might change – surely it will stop raining? Maybe a lorry will find a way to stop and offer us a lift? Perhaps we'll find a cycle path somewhere in this mud bath of a field? Perhaps the hill is about to end?

It feels like an impossible dilemma to us – we carry on in the torrential rain along this pitch black road, the procession of car headlights reflected in the puddles as they hurtle past. Or we stop here in a muddy field at the side of the road, without a tent, for the entire night. Neither seems that safe or appealing with a toddler and a growing bump but, sense finally kicks in after a couple of bars of chocolate are consumed, and we agree to continue. I look at Sam, my two year old, grinning from ear to ear, delighted with his chocolate snack, the Thomas the Tank Engine train he is holding and his red poncho, and I take a deep breath. He's not scared. He's not stressed. He's not cold. He actually appears to be still having fun. Well, then, so can we. I clamber back on to my bike, tip my head down against the driving rain and push on up the hill trying to stay in as straight a line as possible so as not to veer into the path of an HGV and, as I do so, we all belt out the words in our most tuneful singing voices, "Paw Patrol, Paw Patrol, whenever you're in trouble. Paw Patrol, Paw Patrol, we'll be there on the double!" And I smile.

Overwhelmed

Two years and two months earlier, I am overwhelmed.

I am lying on a wheeled hospital bed in an, actually very nice, birthing suite in West Middlesex Hospital with lilac walls and stencilled inspirational quotes dotted around. I am exhausted, bleeding heavily and am aching all over.

It was a 'natural' birth – the holy grail according to all of the midwives and birthing classes we dutifully took ourselves to in the lead up to the big day. I was later to be praised and envied by my various baby club friends for toughing it out without painkillers and not 'resorting' to morphine or epidurals. The truth is though, if

I could have had painkillers, I honestly would have. 1000 times. My baby boy was the wrong way round you see. His spine was meant to be against the front of my tummy but was, in fact, pushing the other way against my spine. When the overwhelming sharp, spasms of contractions arrived, the pain was felt down my entire spine and into my coccyx in a way that was completely unexpected and unmanageable. The midwife recognised this and went off to get painkillers to my delight but, by the time she had returned, I had experienced the sudden, overwhelming, physical urge to push, an urge that you have absolutely no choice but to go with, and suddenly it was too late for painkillers and I had to get this baby out all on my own.

So I pushed, and I pushed, and I pushed, and I pushed. I went into a birthing pool and out again; into stirrups; on a stool. I passed out and had to be revived. I had nothing left to give. Senior midwives were summoned. Doctors were told to be on stand by for a C section. I wept and screamed and wept some more. Finally, after three hours (the average length of pushing is about 45 minutes I now know), a fierce looking midwife dressed in navy blue looked at me sternly and almost shouted, "This is your last chance or we're going to surgery. Two more pushes."

And I did it. He was out! Immediate relief. Screaming filled the air. A blood and gunk covered skinny little bundle of an alien looking baby boy! I simultaneously wanted to both hold him and go immediately to sleep, the maternal instinct luckily kicking in so that I chose the first with the second shortly after.

And now, here I am, a mother. I'm so incredibly lucky and brimming over with such an intense love. There's an actual human being relying on me for its survival. I have to grow up, be responsible, be selfless. I'm so happy. But I'm also completely overwhelmed. Within a few hours of birth, I already feel like I've lost my identity. Like I'm more distant from my friends. Like I have to be super human. And like I'm somehow more alone.

Motherhood

It's common knowledge that the first few months of parenthood are the hardest – 'the hundred days of hell' as they're known. I think everyone walks around in a little bit of a fog, in shock at the new level of responsibility, exhausted by the sleepless nights and secretly frustrated that none of the routines or magic solutions are working for them as yet.

For the first few months of my pregnancy, I suffered with quite intense pre-natal anxiety, a condition which is rarely talked about but that is similar to post-natal depression/anxiety that sets in during pregnancy rather than after the baby is born. I was quite unwell and saw a mental health midwife for a while but, as my hormones settled and the monumental change in my life ahead became slightly less terrifying, I was lucky enough to recover significantly. Hence, when I look at the period post-birth, I wouldn't describe myself as having post-natal depression because I was so much better than I had been in those first few months of pregnancy. However, what I will say is that this period for me was perhaps a bit more 'foggy' than I had expected.

Samuel, my baby boy, had what I now know is called 'silent reflux' and hence breastfeeding was a huge, all consuming challenge. In fact, he refused completely. However, indoctrinated by all of the benefits of breastfeeding thrown my way almost every day by well-meaning friends, relatives and midwives, I persevered for far longer than I should have. The thought of letting him down or that people might judge me for not 'trying hard enough' kept me going and prevented me from seeing sense for several months. I felt like I wasn't a good enough mother. I was intensely jealous of all of my new mum friends who were just happily popping their baby on to their breast in various cafes, music classes and parks, and I kept trying to copy them, kept trying to fit in and do as good a job as they were. But I just couldn't. I stopped going out to cafes and stopped meeting up with friends. I stopped picking up friend's calls because I felt like such a failure. I started spending a lot of time in bed. And Sam started to lose weight and the words 'failure to thrive' started being bandied around.

Finally, after trying four different reflux medications and various different breastfeeding techniques, we finally had Sam referred to a lovely paediatrician who, to our great relief, told us, "I don't think breastfeeding is going to get any easier. His reflux is too severe. I suggest starting weaning early and moving to bottles." I nearly kissed him. I still want to. From that moment, everything changed. I stopped beating myself up. I stopped obsessing and I stopped apologising. A doctor had told me it was ok to put an end to both mine and Sam's daily distress. I started feeding my son. I started enjoying being a mum.

From then on, things continued to become easier and motherhood became increasingly enjoyable. I went back to work, Sam started nursery, I began to see my friends more for meals and drinks out, we managed to take ourselves on a few holidays. Sam thrived and we absolutely adored watching him grow and develop.

Despite this, both myself and my husband still felt like we'd lost ourselves a little and the anxiety and panic of those early days of motherhood continued, although to a lesser extent, for me. Before having a kid, we'd been a pretty adventurous pair. We've lived and worked in Uganda, climbed the 'Three Peaks' (the three highest points in England, Wales and Scotland) to make a music video for Rob's band, cycled on a tandem from London to Berlin to then run the Berlin marathon, and backpacked around the world – and we had been absolutely sure that this would continue when parenthood arrived.

However, despite our best intentions, things had started to gradually change. We became bogged down in a world of baby classes, play dates and trips to Ikea on a Sunday. The pressure of making new 'mum friends' and trying to fit in in the suburbs had resulted in my social anxiety increasing immensely and the politics of the incredibly cliquey baby groups made every play date, party and baby class a huge mental challenge, and dramatically decreased my self-confidence. I had lost the outgoing, joyous, slightly eccentric person I had been for the past 36 years and started to question everything I did, everything I said and every parenting decision I made. However, Sam loved going to nursery and loved his little friends and I suddenly started feeling like routine was more important than it actually is. Compared to many of our friends, we were still seen as a bit 'crazy' and 'hard to keep up with' but, measuring against our own values, life had become too small. I have to emphasise that there is absolutely nothing wrong with a life like this. It just is not who I am or who I had strived to be up until the day my baby boy arrived on the planet. Going in that direction had started to make me feel lost, anxious and like a shadow of my former self. I had stopped recognising the harassed, exhausted, self-conscious mother looking back at me from the mirror, stressed because I hadn't got my child to bed on time, put the laundry in, finished the online shop or said the wrong thing on a mothers' WhatsApp group. Stressed about things that honestly don't really matter.

I'm wise enough to know that children need safety and security and that I can't just continue completely as I did before having a child. But isn't there a middle ground? One in which we could have some adventures, say yes to some new challenges, and actually have some fun with our eccentric, happy, extrovert of a two year old? I started sitting in the evening with my husband cradling a glass of wine on our big brown sofa in front of the TV in our little terraced house in the Hertfordshire suburbs, reminiscing wistfully about the time six years previously when we'd jumped on a tandem bike and ridden the 700 miles from London to Berlin before immediately running the Berlin marathon. We talked about the adrenalin rush, the joy at waking up every day not knowing what lay ahead, the tiffs about routes and timings, the daily exhaustion and painful bums, the evening pint to celebrate the successful end of yet another leg on the journey, and the overwhelming pride, relief and satisfaction when we crossed that finish line into the arms of our parents and friends on a bright, sunny day in one of our favourite cities in the world. That moment of feeling completely and utterly happy and alive.

As we remembered, I almost shook with excitement and pride whilst simultaneously feeling sick to the pit of my stomach that these adventures were a thing of the past.

"But do they really have to be? Is it really all over?" I said to my husband after a couple of glasses of wine. "Can't we still be adventurous people? Can't we still do challenges like that with a kid?"

"Maybe we can," said Rob absentmindedly. "Maybe we could cycle from Paris to Amsterdam or something. I don't think that's too far." Then he went to bed and thought nothing else of it.

The YesGrant

You would think after 11 years together that my husband would have known. Put a slight idea absentmindedly into my head and it will grow exponentially into a full blown obsession within 24 hours. Never ever suggest anything to me if you don't want it to become all I think about!

So, whilst he continued with his life obliviously, I started to dream. On the crowded, sweaty Thameslink train commute to work, on the stuffy, noisy tube that followed, sat at my computer in my artificially lit office in Clapham Junction, lying in bed at night debating whether to comfort or leave the crying baby in the room across our tiny landing. I just kept wondering. Could we do another long distance cycle?

So, my excitement ignited when, scrolling through Facebook on the miserable train from Vauxhall to Clapham Junction (the third leg in my joyous commute) in December 2017, I spotted a post from the YesTribe, *'Get cooking on a plan for early 2018. We've partnered up with Berghaus and on Monday we'll be launching a #yesgrant as a little helping hand for one of you to take on a project.'*

A project? Could a cycle from Amsterdam to Paris with a two year old be classed as a project? Could we use the cycle as a way to demonstrate to parents everywhere that adventures can still continue once you have kids? That life can be exciting?

I couldn't get this 'YesGrant' out of my head. Finances were pretty tight since Sam came along with the mortgage on our little terraced house, extortionate nursery fees and changes to happier but less well paid jobs. To do this cycle, we'd have to buy or rent decent bikes, get a child bike seat, panniers, maps, pay for Eurostar tickets etc. etc. This grant could really help to make this happen.

And then there was the other element, if we won the YesGrant, we'd have to do it, right? No more excuses. No more worrying. No more, "Maybe when he's a bit older. Maybe when we have a bit more money. Maybe someday… one day… in the future." Life is now, to be lived now. Not one day, some day, maybe. I didn't want to think about all the reasons 'why not' anymore and I knew that if I discussed the idea any more with my husband, I just might. So, I didn't talk to him and made a conscious decision not to stop and think about the practicalities of such a challenge because I knew the anxieties would take over.

I sent the application and thought no more about it, getting consumed with Christmas and New Year and general day to day life. Until, in early January, I got an email from Emma and Dave at the YesTribe asking if they could call us for an interview to talk about our proposed challenge, how we were going to make it happen and why they should choose us. At this point, I thought I better tell my husband.

"So it seems we have an interview tomorrow for a grant so that we can do that cycle from Paris to Amsterdam that we talked about."

"What cycle that we talked about?" he says.

"You know, you suggested that maybe we could cycle from Paris to Amsterdam with Sam so that we could do a challenge again?"

"But I don't even know if there are cycle paths. I don't even know how long it is. I haven't done any research. I just said that in passing, I didn't think we'd actually agreed to anything."

"Oh well, we have the interview now so we may as well do that and see what happens. We probably won't win anyway."

And so, the next evening, we sat in our kitchen on our high stools at our wooden breakfast bar, opened our laptop and nervously prepared for our big Skype interview. Sam was on our laps, squirming away but we were determined that he would be part of the conversation – he's very cute, maybe it might sway the decision!

Three smiley faces filled the bright screen, I gulped, nervous about the questions ahead, anxious about how we might come across. Then Emma said with a grin "we'd just like to say congratulations, you're our YesGrant winners!"

Oh my word. It was all a trick! There was no interview. We'd won!

The rest of the conversation was a blur but, when we got off the call, Rob and I were virtually jumping up and down with joy. We'd just won a grant from the YesTribe to do a long distance cycle! We were adventurers again! The buzz of feeling like someone who was going to do something different, who was going to take on a challenge, who was going to chase an adventure, gave me butterflies of nerves and excitement that I hadn't felt in years. We messaged our friends and family, so proud of ourselves and ready to show that we could do it.

Soon after, not unexpectedly, the anxiety and fear creeped in. We hadn't researched the route at all before applying and were particularly worried that the whole cycle would end up being along busy roads, making it feel pretty unsafe for our two year old. We didn't know what bikes we needed and how much they would cost second hand and we weren't sure how we could possibly carry all of our stuff, including toys, a toddler bed, nappies and possibly a high chair booster, on two bikes. However, despite this, we both had a spring in our step and were absolutely determined that we would manage it at some point in 2018. Probably Autumn.

The News

Fast forward two days and I'm in a dark, dreary hotel room on the first floor of a budget business hotel in rainy Brussels on a work trip. I'm sitting on the grey, faded flowery carpeted floor, leaning against the double bed, staring into space and trying not to look at the white plastic stick in front of me on the floor. The stick on which gradually a faint blue cross is appearing in the little white window!

Pregnant. Well, that's unexpected. I am genuinely absolutely delighted. Delighted and a bit shocked. I had completely assumed the test would be negative. I'd just bought it because I had a tiny niggle and wanted to make sure I could drink that night at dinner. Yet, here I am. There's a tiny bean growing inside of me. We're having another baby!

I call my husband who is equally shocked and delighted. We, as natural worriers, immediately talk about money, jobs, maternity leave, and how we're going to manage all of this. It isn't until the next day though that we suddenly remember the cycle.

Cue Google!

We type in *'can you do a long distance cycle whilst pregnant?'* *'Is it safe to cycle whilst pregnant?'* *'Miscarriages caused from cycling whilst pregnant.'* We Google pretty much every combination of *'cycle'* and *'pregnant'* we can think of and we get a myriad of responses and information which ties our brains in knots.

From the Cycling UK site *'Both the NCT and NHS say pregnant women should not cycle because of the risk of falling.'*

From the Parents.com website *'As with most exercise, it's best to stick with what you were doing pre-pregnancy.'* (Erm, nothing?)

From the Total Women's Cycling website *'Although there's no concrete proof that high-intensity exercise harms your baby, cutting down the intensity of your training makes sense. Your body is already working extremely hard creating and growing your baby. Throwing a high-intensity work out on top of that is a shortcut to exhaustion but that doesn't mean you can't ride a bicycle while pregnant.'*

And then from the Guardian: *'Cycling while pregnant keeps you fit and prepares your body for the uphill struggle of childbirth.'*

Which should we listen to? It is pretty scary to read that even the NHS warns against cycling whilst pregnant. That warning isn't about the risk of exercising though but the risk of falling. Would I be likely to fall? Is this whole thing just too irresponsible? We can't do it next year though as our baby will be too small. Maybe 2020 but that is so far away.

A few days later, I am sitting in the office when my phone flashes up with a WhatsApp message from my husband, *'I'm not really sure we can do this cycle. I think it might be too risky for you and the baby.'*

For me, that was the moment. The frustration, annoyance and disappointment I feel when I receive this message answers the question quite clearly for me. I can do this cycle. I can at least try. We can keep the daily distances relatively short and take longer to complete it. We can stop and give up if I feel my body is too tired or under too much strain. I can easily get a train or bus for one of the legs and my husband and toddler complete it on their own. We could even have a support vehicle in case of emergency. We can try. It isn't too risky. We just have to be sensible. Which means we need to do it soon.

We settle on April, when I'll be about 14 weeks pregnant – I'll be out of the riskiest first trimester but I, hopefully, won't yet have much of a bump to physically hinder me actually reaching the handlebars. We start buying, begging and borrowing equipment including bikes, panniers, a child seat and a cycle computer. We put together a vague training schedule which we hope will help us to become, at least to some extent, fit enough for the 420 miles ahead. Unfortunately, the Beast from the East has some other ideas and we get out on the bikes three times before we set off for Paris. We are comforted by the fact that Sam actually likes sitting in the bike seat and has also managed a nap in there, but are pretty concerned about our fitness levels. However, I remember reading an article by Dave Cornthwaite, the founder of the YesTribe, in which he shared that he could hardly swim before embarking on 1001 miles down the Missouri River and this makes me feel at least partly reassured.

We're going to give this a go.

Back to the Cycle

We trudge slowly but steadily up the hill to Guise, singing as cheerfully as we can, praying that either the rain or hill, or ideally both, will come to an end soon. No luck with the rain but, after what seems like 3 hours, but is probably around 30 minutes, the traffic and puddle filled road finally becomes flat and we continue relatively easily for the final slightly quieter, house-lined stretch into the town of Guise. We arrive soaking and exhausted at 9pm, two hours after our toddler's usual bedtime and excited about a hot meal.

At this point we realise that the difficulty we had finding food at lunchtime (Rob had to take a taxi from our stopping point to McDonald's and back because not one shop, café or restaurant was open for miles around) is going to continue. Everything in the near vicinity is closed and boarded up. The streets are eerily quiet, devoid of both cars and people. None of the places we have found on TripAdvisor seem to be open or even exist and we're too late for what seems to be the only nearby supermarket.

Cue hysterics again, this time from us both. We're exhausted, soaking and hungry. It is only day three of ten. We are really not sure we can do this. At this point, I'm almost ashamed to say, we start to research trains.

Having Fun

Despite the next day being better, with sunshine and a disused railway path, the hills continue and the pregnancy and lack of training takes its toll. More than that, to be honest, is the fact that Northern France in April really does appear to be a ghost town. We continue to struggle to find shops and cafes open and have to load up massively whenever we see a shop. This weighs us down, but is essential when transporting a hungry toddler.

We feel similarly downcast at the end of day four and, looking at the route that we've planned, realise that the hills are going to continue for at least another two days. I burst into tears.

"I can't do this. The whole idea was silly. I'm not going to be able to do another two days of hills. This is too hard."

My husband realises that I'm having a meltdown and so humours me by reaching for the creased route guide, 'Namur-Tours a velo', and helped by our map obsessed toddler, we start researching trains yet again. I look at the map and the route we have marked in pencil taking us up towards the Northern border between France and Belgium. I'm not the most geographically intelligent person, so I stare and stare some more before tentatively asking my husband,

"Ummm, could we not just cross over into Belgium sooner?"

The border is close. It's just that we'd planned to cross it further up. We could surely cross it tomorrow instead.

My husband, not one for changes in carefully laid plans, takes some time to look carefully at what I'm proposing but soon starts to nod imperceptibly. I know this is a good sign but tap my fingertips on the table impatiently whilst he measures distances and gradients and looks at roads versus cycle paths. He's definitely the planner of the two of us and the combination works well as I'm liable to just launch into something without a moment's thought and everything turning to flames soon after.

I grin when he finally agrees and our giddiness, a combination of tiredness and excitement at the new plan, is evident when we burst into hysterics at the news that the new route will take us through the town of Willies the next day on our way to the Belgian border!

The rest of the trip is a perfect example of why I am such a fan of changing my mind and switching plans on a regular basis if things don't feel right. As we cross the border, the sun comes out, the cycle path improves dramatically going from bumpy gravel to smooth tarmac and, for half a day, is a glorious gradual downhill through a dense, sweetly scented, pine forest. We grin as we gently pedal past an old man walking his golden retriever; a family on bikes; a couple canoodling; and several people just sitting on benches enjoying the sunshine trickling in between the forest canopy.

We are also relieved to find a plethora of cafes and shops open which slow us down as we stop for delicious ice creams and Belgian chocolate treats along the route. Our toddler sings at the top of his lungs for most of the day, proudly holding out his Thomas the Tank Engine toy to show to everyone we pass and waving at birds, dogs, tractors and trains along the journey.

Day seven is a real highlight for us when we make a deviation from our original route plan that skirts us around the edge of Brussels and instead decide to make the most of an incredibly sunny Saturday and cycle right into the centre down the canal path dodging joggers, roller skaters and other cyclists as we point out the various barges and rowing boats to Sam as we leisurely pedal along. Arriving into the Grand Place on our laden down bikes definitely draws some attention, and we are the subject of a number of tourist photographs before we dismount and allow our toddler some time to charge around the pedestrianized square and burn off some energy.

As we leave Belgium and pass into Holland, the cycle paths and signposts continue to be amazing, although we are stupidly using a map from 2010 and are for some reason surprised when we kept getting lost! Google maps and random Dutch cycling apps come to our rescue. We are also somehow surprised by the wind, somehow not realising why Holland is so famous for windmills, which makes some easy, flat days actually quite a challenge and pretty exhausting – but the scenery and sunshine more than make up for it.

Before we know it, it is the final day and we arrive at the final stretch of our 420 mile cycle down the River Amstel into Amsterdam. We jump between cycle path and road as we speed along the banks of the wide, still river, past barges, houseboats, ducks and bridges on one side and multi-coloured terraced houses and cute café picnic tables and parasols on the other. I feel like I'm holding my breath in anticipation of the finish but, simultaneously, I keep asking my husband to pause for photographs and sips of water as I try to eke out the final minutes of our little adventure.

As we get closer to the city, hundreds of cyclists join our route as they commute, visit friends or go for their afternoon exercise. They hardly notice we exist but I feel like they're there for us, to accompany us to our finish line and cheer us on.

The Finish Line

As we reach our arbitrary finish line of a tiny canal bridge across a quiet, flower lined section of Amsterdam canal, we dismount for our victory photo. As we wished, there's no one there to greet us. It's just us. Our little family. We managed it together as a team, the three of us and the fourth little man yet to arrive. We squeeze on to the narrow pavement by the barrier and have a huge bear hug whilst I shed a tiny tear of pride, exhaustion, joy and relief.

We've done it. It isn't swimming the channel or climbing Everest, but it was our little challenge that got us back out of our comfort zone and showed us that parenthood did not have to change us completely.

And, whilst I'm proud of completing it, I'm mainly proud that we managed to have fun whilst doing so. Cycling solidly for ten days was a challenge but ensuring that our little man had the time of his life during the journey was even more so. The time with him on the back of our bike with no technology meant constant singing, guessing games and pointing to various vehicles and animals. Ensuring he was content, fed, watered and not too warm or cold was pretty tiring at times but the joy of spending such time with him without the daily distractions of life was unrivalled. I am brimming with pride and am completely in awe at how he took it all in his stride and the positivity he showed even when we were late, lost and caught in a rainstorm. Through it all, he had a smile on his face and a song in his lungs. Rather than feeling like we had an adventure that he joined us for, he was an integral part of the adventure and I think that he had the time of his life.

As we begin the journey back to the office and back to reality, I do so with a spring in my step that I haven't felt for a long time. We have broken out of our comfort zone and I now know that we aren't going to get completely lost in parenthood and routine. We still have to be more sensible than we once were but we really can still challenge ourselves, experience adventure and have fun as we journey through life. Having children does indeed make it all the more complex but, in many ways, it also makes it all the more fun.

So, as we settle into our orange EasyJet plane seats and watch the runway disappear into the distance, I turn to my exhausted husband, grin and say, "Right then, what shall we do next?"

Website: Littlefeetbigworld.com

Instagram: @littlefeetbigworlduk

Chapter 9

The Path to Everest

by Jo Bradshaw

I was perched on the summit of Everest at 6.45am on 19th May 2016 wondering, at the grand young age of 45, how on earth I had got there. Not physically, but in life. You see, I was never supposed to be a mountaineer, I was never supposed to tackle climbs like this, I had never even thought I would climb Snowdon, let alone be sat on top of the highest mountain on our wonderful planet.

Where it all started

Back in 2003 I had been a risk averse, no saying, height hating comfort lover. I had a steady job behind a desk, and although I would often say I was off to do various exciting things I would end up staying at home for holidays instead. My confidence had taken a major knock 10 years before when I had given up the career with horses that I thought would consume my life for ever.

Here I was, in August 2003, stood on the edge of the open doorway of a small plane at 12,000' with an ex-RAF PT strapped to my back, once again wondering how on earth I had got there.

I had been bored at work one day you see and, being in my early 30s, thought I had better do something to 'conquer' this fear of heights. 'I know, a parachute jump will do just that' I thought to myself, so my first 'Yes' was to sign up to do a charity jump not far from where I lived in Buckinghamshire. I raised around £400 just from sending out an email around the office. I think people were quite surprised to find that I was doing something like this as I was not known as a risk taker back then.

A good friend of mine, Caroline, offered to drive me up 'just in case you can't drive back' and I didn't stop talking the whole way to the jump site, simply jibbering and jabbering through fear. Just as my instructor and I fell out the aircraft (or jumped as he would have said) I remember opening my mouth to scream but all that came out was a stream of phlegm which of course went straight upwards and into his face, poor chap. The only other things I remember about the jump were 'when is this going to end' and 'god that hurt' as the parachute opened and the force of the harness stopping me from falling tightened against my groin. It was a tad painful to say the least.

Fortunately, I had a safe landing and as Caroline drove us back to Aylesbury, she said, "Brilliant… what's next?"

"Ohhh noooo! That's it for me, thank you. That was my adventure all in one hit." And we drove on.

A couple of weeks later a flyer dropped through my letter box, back in the day when e-marketing was still a bit of a new thing. I took the envelope with me to open at work and that was really when everything started to change. As Caroline walked into my office, she spotted the flyer on my desk which was from Asthma UK, the charity I had undertaken the parachute jump for. It detailed a charity bike ride in Peru, a cycle ride of around 450km from Lake Titicaca to Machu Picchu (or thereabouts!).

"Brilliant!" said Caroline. "That's what's next!!"

"Ohhh nooo!" I replied once again, my default answer to pretty much everything at the time. "I don't have a bike. I am not fit. I could never raise that amount of money. I'm not sure how I would deal with the altitude and the biggest problem is that I don't have the deposit so I'm out!" I exclaimed.

"Gosh," she said back. "Barriers dear, barriers! We can work everything else out but I can solve your biggest problem."

"Oh?" I replied with trepidation. I instantly knew my get-out-of-jail-free card had just been cashed in.

"I will pay your deposit so that you can sign up now, and you can pay me back in instalments. Easy!"

"Oh, ummmmm, thank you, I think," I said very quietly.

Time to train

The ride was to take place at the end of April 2004 so I had a good few months to sort out my long list of excuses to saying no and turn them into exciting reasons for saying YES. I had a lot of work to do!

First, I had to find a bike to train on. Another kind friend offered to lend me a mountain bike he had gathering dust in his shed. It was a lovely Kona bike and just the right size. I simply had to learn how to ride a bike again and properly this time.

Second on the list, which really should have come first, was to give up smoking. I didn't think that a smoker fundraising for an asthma charity and then heading to altitude was a marriage made in heaven. So I quit there and then, and it's been the best decision I have ever made. (Don't smoke kids, it's seriously bad for you!).

I was rather unfit too, so I decided to join a gym and spent the first couple of months gaining strength and fitness using a programme designed for me by one of the trainers there. When I went in for my induction, my body was a tad on the wobbly side with more insulation than muscle, but I most certainly did not expect what was said next.

"So, what are you training for?" asked the instructor. "Do you have an event you are planning on doing?"

"Yes," I replied nervously. "I'm cycling 450km in Peru in 6 months-time and I need to get fit."

"Oh, cycling 450km? In Peru? At altitude?" he asked in a rather more quizzical way than I expected. "You'll never do that," he said, straight-faced and with intent.

To say I was shocked was an understatement. I thought they were supposed to be there to help me, not to put me down. Despite his comments, we carried on around with the 'how to use the equipment' routine and I never saw him again. I went to the gym religiously and started to feel my fitness improving so I put my Brave Girl Pants on and started pedalling a proper bike in the great outdoors. Back then I didn't realise that you weren't supposed to be able to sit on a saddle and put your feet flat on the floor at the same time, or that you weren't supposed to wear pants under your cycle shorts, or that wearing walking boots wasn't ideal footwear, or that…..and so the list went on.

I struggled on through the winter, training on my bike during daylight hours and gradually increasing my distances with each ride, searching out for steeper, longer hills and finally enjoying the feeling of getting fitter.

Meeting the team

January came and down to Salisbury I drove for our challenge training weekend. The bike ride in Peru was being run by an adventure company called Discover Adventure who were based down there and with a few steep hills nearby it was a great training ground. I was a little late due to an inordinate amount of faffing because of nerves that morning at home so I skidded to a halt in the hotel car park and grabbed my bike out of the boot whilst everyone else was waiting patiently. Off we went for a much longer bike ride with much bigger hills than I had done before. I was definitely the slowest and least experienced of the group. I still didn't really understand how all of the gears worked, I was still riding too low, still wearing my walking boots, still wearing pants under my cycle shorts but I learnt a huge amount that weekend.

We bonded as a group of 22 thanks to a few beers on the Saturday night in a Salisbury city centre pub. I had my saddle height sorted, I was advised to buy some cycle shoes and maybe try some clip in pedals and Dear Lord, please get rid of your pants! "You don't want to chafe!" said many of the more experienced cyclists.

I felt much more confident as I drove back home on the Sunday afternoon. I had a little over 3 months until we met again at Heathrow and although I thought I was fit before the training weekend, I learnt that I still had a long way to go. I didn't want to have the sweeper bus right behind me and didn't want to get in it unless I was injured. Pride was kicking in and it was a great motivator!

Off to Peru!

Three months on and I remember standing at Heathrow, a mild panic raising through my body, being given a quick briefing by the company owner about how the adventure started here and that our cycle guides would meet us in Lima. Our trip doctor, Helen, was travelling with us, but I was too nervous really to chat. I hooked up with Jules who I had met on the training weekend and we found a quiet spot in the airport before we boarded. Jules had done a few bike rides before, so I felt like a bit of a limpet following her around,

I'm sure she didn't mind as it was everyone's first time once, just not hers then!

Arriving in Lima late at night meant that we went to a hotel before getting on an early morning flight up to Juliaca the following morning. We were met in arrivals by Dougie, our very tall Scottish leader and his co-pilot, Caroline. With 22 cyclists, our guides and doctor, our charity rep plus local crew all trying to put the bikes on the roof of a van in the dark, it was quite the baptism by fire. Dougie gave us a quick briefing before we headed off to bed that night. We were to get up early, head back to the airport and then take the short flight up to the Juliaca airport not far from Puno in the high Andes. Puno sits at 3,827m so we would have gone from sea level in Lima to 3,827m in a very short time. Our bodies may object so we had a day and a half to get used to the altitude before we headed off on the bikes.

'Yikes,' I thought. 'What happens if my body goes on strike? What happens if I can't do this? What happens if…'

"Oh be quiet, girl," I said to myself. "You said yes to being here. The rest will take care of itself."

Arriving at Juliaca was indeed a shock to the system. You go from nearly 100% oxygen to having almost half of it taken away. Straight away you can feel the chill in the drier air. The fact that it was harder to breath, even whilst walking on the flat, and being dehydrated from the flights was exacerbated by the dry air so the headache kicked in pretty quickly. Trying to take the stairs at the speed you would at home was out of the question and even getting out of bed to go to the many visits to the loo was a huge effort. This altitude lark was hard work!

After being a tourist for a couple of days, we were mostly coping well with the altitude and I was pleased to have acclimatised fairly quickly. Breathing was harder but my headaches had disappeared thanks to the extraordinary amount of water I had been drinking. "Water is the best medicine," said Helen, our doctor. Your body goes into rapid diuresis when it realises there is reduced air pressure and therefore less oxygen gets into your body. There are many changes that occur at micro levels within your body, but the main thing was to drink plenty of water which also meant that you'd be peeing like a pony and oh, how true that was!

Our first day of the bike ride saw us heading back to Juliaca and to our starting point, a petrol station on the edge of town. A salubrious start, I thought! Our bikes had been put together by Dougie, Caroline and our local crew of experts and a paper map was given to us. Not for navigating with but just as a reference. The first day had a straight line on the A4 piece of paper. 'It's straight all day' was written on the paper and it was!

The roads in Peru were a dream to ride on. Smooth with no pot holes and the drivers would beep at you, not in anger but simply to let you know that they were coming. The scenery was stunning with huge open vistas and mountains in the background, hundreds of kilometres away and as far as the eye could see. They looked untouchable and I had no inkling that I would be climbing any of them in the not so distant future.

Getting into the swing of things

Dougie's greatest announcement during our first day's ride was that it never rained in April, and about half an hour later with huge black clouds coming over the horizon, he quickly made an excuse that this was an unusual year as hail and rain pelted down on us. We were huddled behind the luggage truck whilst the worst of it swept through and I started to cry. Fortunately, no one could see the tears running down my cheeks as we were being soaked to the skin. I was really frightened, not because of the rain but from thinking what on earth had I let myself into. Once again, Negative Nelly popped up to tell me to get in the truck. Who was I to think that I could complete something like this? What a muppet!

The drenching finished as quickly as it had started and the sun soon came out, drying our soggy clothing just before we arrived in camp. I use the word camp in the loosest sense of the word. I thought, back then, that camps had proper toilets and showers and were situated well away from the side of the road. We were more on the wild side of camping. This was to be a real adventure!

We were still at a fairly high altitude so the temperature that night would drop dramatically. There are a few things that happen whilst sleeping at altitude.

1. it's really, really cold.
2. because you have to drink plenty of water during the day you pee a huge amount at night. If you need to pee, go pee. If you don't you'll start shivering which means your body is screaming at you – GO PEE!!!
3. it gets colder during the night and especially before dawn, it's really, really, really cold.
4. you can get something called Periodic Breathing where you or your tent buddy will stop breathing for a few seconds, but it sounds like they are never going to start again. You, or them, then takes a sudden and rather large intake of breath, scaring either yourself, or them, or both! You both fall back to sleep for it to then happen again, several times over. It's all part of the acclimatising to the rarefied air but it can terrify you in the process!

I remember vividly how bone chillingly cold it was that first night. My sleeping bag probably wasn't as warm as it needed to be, and I had all of my clothes on plus a blanket over the top. Another schoolgirl error on my part. What I was supposed to do was to go to bed with warm skin, strip off my clothes down to pants and a t-shirt along with socks and a beanie then quickly jump into my sleeping bag. My skin would warm up the sleeping bag which would then turn into a radiator. Ahhh, the benefit of actually taking the advice! By wearing all of the clothes that I had sat in in the mess tent, I did have warm skin under it all but slipped into my sleeping bag fully clothed, therefore not allowing my lovely warm skin to be the radiator. As my sleeping bag wasn't being heated up by my body, my body simply got cold and it was a miserable first night and a big lesson learned.

Our adventures continued on a daily basis. We were cycling for 6 days and our highest point was at 4,500m over a high pass. I seemed to be burping a lot during the cycling and hadn't realised that this was also part of being at altitude. It's in the medical books too, High Altitude Flatus Expulsion! Who'd have thought!! Because of the lower air pressure, gasses expand in your body and they need to come out somehow and oh, how they did, for everyone!

Guardian Angel Dog

One day I was riding on my own for a short period, just cycling down a long descent into one of our camps. Dougie had warned us about the dogs in Peru. Most were not pets and some not always friends, especially to cyclists who were simply there to be chased. Now, being a dog person, I hadn't quite believed this and once again, how naive I was. Merrily freewheeling down this descent on a super smooth road through a small village I spotted a dog eyeing me up in the distance. He was initially lying down but soon got up and started at a pace towards me. 'Oh crikey' I thought. 'What am I going to do?' I was on my own and the advice had been to get off our bikes and find some stones to lob near the dogs to put them off. It all happened quite quickly so I had no chance of stopping, getting off, finding some rocks or similar and frightening off this very determined dog. This dog was heading towards me a full pelt with great intent of doing some harm and I was frightened. Suddenly out of no-where another dog shot across the road, barking wildly, and chased off my intended killer (probably a tad dramatic but that's what it felt like!). I simply couldn't believe it and all I wanted to do was to stop and give my four-legged Guardian Angel a hug, but my brain kicked in to say, 'Get out of here and quick!!'

In for a bumpy ride

Then came the off-road mountain day. Gulp!

The night before, when Dougie did the briefing, he mentioned the various routes and options for us that following day. It was a huge climb with a bumpy descent, so they had to give some get-out-of-jail-free cards.

- Option 1 was to head around the mountain pass and ride 25km on the roads to the next camp – no thanks.
- Option 2 was to be trucked half way up the mountain and then carry on from there. Again – no thanks.
- Option 3 was to start at the bottom and do the whole lot – yes please! This was an unusual response from me as I was used to taking the easy option but as I was here, as I had become pretty fit, as I wasn't going to come back, I thought it best to at least give it a go. I know that there would be a mini bus following the cyclists at the back, which turned out to be me! I wasn't sure whether Dougie, Caroline and Helen would let me do the whole thing, but it was worth asking and, to their credit, they said yes!

Yes, I spent that night worrying if I was actually capable of cycling such a distance and to such a great height. We had already reached a 4300m col on road but, apart from the rarefied air, the tarmac had made for easy cycling. This col was at a height of 4335m but the whole way was rough tracks and fairly rocky. I was not a skilled mountain biker, I was a little bit scared, but I got on my bike and off we went.

It didn't take long before I was quite a way behind the other cyclists who had chosen to do the lot. They were not only fitter than me but also used to riding on this type of terrain. I was cycling at between 6 – 10km/h. I was riding pretty slowly but, given the altitude and the surface going under our wheels, not too badly and Dougie, who had the job of keeping me going, didn't seem too bothered until we hit a short downhill section. He shot off and expected me to do the same. I gradually bumped and slithered my way down to the next up with fear etched on my face, at which point he said, "We'll get you to the top but you're in the bus all the way down."

"Not a problem at all," I replied. "Quite happy with that!"

At the top of the col we all had a huge hug and I shed another tear or two. It was the biggest climb I had ever done, and I had survived! My bike was swiftly taken off me and secured to the roof of the bus, in I hopped with one or two other cyclists and down we bumped all the way to Pisac, where we were staying that night.

The final day of cycling came all too quickly and our destination, Ollyantaytambo, loomed into sight.

"Right. Well done, everyone. Today is going to be a toughie, not just because of the cobbles in the last 2km into the finish but also the headwind. Keep those legs going and you'll get there," said Caroline in our update briefing that morning.

She was spot on. As we were pedalling hard down a long and winding descent a local was freewheeling up it! We stopped just short of the hill up into Ollyantaytambo, the finish point to our 450km cycle for Asthma UK. There were 22 of us fundraising for the charity, all there for different reasons and we'd all put our hearts into this ride. We all got along well and it had been a blast of emotions for me and my fellow cyclists.

Cycling up the hill, we left the lovely smooth tarmac and were faced with round headed cobbles – yikes! This was a finish and a half! We rode in convoy into the main square of this ancient Incan city, dumping our bikes and offering each other a huge hug of congratulations.

All we had to do now was to pack up our steeds, have a shower and head to a bar to celebrate. As I walked to my hotel room I was in floods of tears. I simply couldn't believe that I had cycled 99% of the challenge and if anyone was going to take away the 1% of the off road downhill, more fool them.

A fellow cyclist walked past me and said, "What are you crying for? that's a bit wet." Nice. It had been his third or fourth cycle and to him it was now his normal. To me, it was my Everest.

Ready to fly?

With the first of our celebrations over, we boarded a train to Agua Calientes early the next morning where we then hopped on a bus up the zig zags to Machu Picchu. I hadn't appreciated just how exposed the bus ride would feel or simply how exposed Machu Picchu actually was. I had a big fear of heights back then, the type of vertigo where you felt like you wanted to throw yourself off and fly if you got too close to the edge. I put a lid on my fear for the first half an hour or so, long enough for our group photos to be taken, and then I broke down in tears, snot running down my nose and my wobbly chin, proper fight or flight fear. 'That was it,' I thought. 'I've blown my one and only chance to see this amazing ancient site.' I hot-footed it back to the café and then got the first bus down to town, back to terra firma and the comforting streets of habitation.

Life is a learning curve

After we arrived back in Blighty I tried to convey to family and friends just how amazing it was. They just didn't get it. I had been sucked into a great world of adventure. I had discovered that I was capable of surviving 6 nights in a freezing tent and 7 days in the saddle, at altitude, in the rain / sun / wind and snow. I had eaten guinea pig, had wild wee'd and drunk beer with 2 of my fellow cyclists in a local's house. I'd been to high altitude for the first time,

I'd learnt to ditch my pants and go commando and I'd learnt how to ride my bike properly. I learnt about drafting, about Guardian Angel dogs and that, at the time, I was pretty rubbish with heights.

Roll on to 2017 and now life is oh-so different. Little did I know then that I would head back to Machu Picchu another dozen times and relish in the marvels of that ancient city, the vastness of the mountains and enjoy all it has to offer, even the exposure of the walk in. Once back from Peru, I had the adventure bug and wondered, 'What's next?'

I didn't go straight from cycling in Peru to being on the summit of Everest. There were many incremental moves between the two. From cycling in New Zealand and Cuba to crewing adventure rides and international treks in my spare time. From changing my job and moving from Buckinghamshire to Wiltshire to becoming self-employed as a Mountain Leader.

Every step I had made to that point, standing on the world's tallest mountain, had been a tentative one. Every single time I knew I had nothing to lose. I knew that I was employable so if it didn't all pan out I could go back to full time work. But I also knew I had to give this a go.

I cast my mind back once again to that moment on top of the world, that feeling of 'how on earth did I get here?' and am grateful that I've been through all of the things that I have. Maybe not the earthquake the year before when we gave Everest our first shot. We lost 3 of our amazing team of Sherpas and other friends at Base Camp whilst we were at Camp 1 when the earthquake struck but going through that type of experience has an impact on you. I've recently learned about Post Traumatic Growth, which follows Post Traumatic Stress and I'm certainly in that period now. I'm probably a better person for going through something as life threatening as the earthquake. We thought we were going to die, but we didn't and I'm here to tell the tale.

I now work on the basis that if a job, or any offer of whatever kind, is not worth exchanging time of my life for, then I choose not to do it. Life for me now, is all about experiences and not things, and I'm hugely grateful for this wonderfully eclectic life that I lead.

And it's all happened because of that one moment when I said YES to jumping out of that darned plane!

As I sit writing this story, with torrential rain pouring down the windscreen of Bimble, my Adventure Van, and my DofE students safely tucked up in their tents in a soggy field in South Wales, would I have changed any of it?

Absolutely not. Each step has made this journey possible, even if I didn't really know what was to happen next. I had no idea when I said yes to that bike ride, or even the parachute jump, that it would lead to anything else. It's happened organically and with the support of my wonderful family and friends and those who I work with. In talks that I deliver these days, I speak about Champions. Not the 'Woohoo! I'm first!' kind of champion but the kind that is there to guide you along. The kind that has got your back, The kind who simply wants to see you succeed. They are in it for you and not them.

Look out for your Champions. They are closer than you think.

And say Yes to opportunities that come your way. You never know where they will lead you!

Jo Bradshaw is a former no saying sofa surfer turned mountaineer, who'd have thought! She has 2 amazing Springer Spaniels who help her to train and assess Duke of Edinburgh students from Bronze through to Gold and they also keep her wonderful Mum company when she is away leading expeditions to high places overseas. She is aiming to complete the 7 summits (2 to go!) by the end of 2019 in support of children's mental health charity Place2Be. Fingers crossed!

Website: www.jobradshaw.co.uk

Facebook: @jobradshawadventurer

LinkedIn   Jo Bradshaw

Instagram   @_jobradshaw

Twitter   @_jobradshaw

Chapter 10

SUP the Five Lands

by John McFadzean

The first time I visited the UNESCO World Heritage area of Cinque Terre, on the northwest coast of Italy, I had never heard of stand up paddle boarding (SUP). But that didn't stop me from falling in love with the place.

Cinque Terre, which translates as 'The Five Lands', is a series of towns, more like tiny villages really, strung along the Ligurian coast. They're penned in by mountains to one side and the Mediterranean Sea to the other.

So when I was planning a trip to Italy as part of my quest to SUP in every country in the world, a trip along the Cinque Terre coast, stopping at each of the five villages in turn, seemed like a wonderful idea.

For a number of reasons, I had decided to base myself in the small town of Levanto. Levanto lies to the north of, and on the other side of, a headland from Monterosso al Mare. Monterosso al Mare is the northernmost of the five lands. Access by car to Cinque Terre is very difficult, if not downright impossible, although there is a train line which runs through all of the villages. As I was travelling through Italy by car, it made sense to find a hotel which was connected to the road network. Not only that but there is very little accommodation available within Cinque Terre, with a consequential upward pressure on prices. But most of all I just wanted to begin my trip from outside the five lands and paddle into the area, rather than starting inside.

Levanto had the advantage of being relatively easily accessible by road, as well as having more cost effective accommodation. My plan was to paddle the twelve miles from Levanto to Riomaggiore (the southernmost town) over the course of one day, stopping at each of the towns in turn for morning coffee, lunch, afternoon tea and finally dinner. Then I would get the train back from Riomaggiore at the end of the day. Twelve miles isn't a particularly long distance to paddle in a day and the route I had mapped out in advance looked like a gentle, civilised day out. But would it turn out that way?

I had arrived in Levanto two days earlier, on the Tuesday, with plans to do some sightseeing on the Wednesday, ready for my SUP adventure on Thursday. There is nothing I enjoy more than visiting a warm place, especially if it's somewhere I've never been before, putting on my shorts and t-shirt, and going for a wander.

But it wasn't to be. The best-laid plans don't always work out as expected. During the course of 2018-2019 I was honoured to be the Division Director for the whole of the north of England for the public speaking organisation Toastmasters, and we had an upcoming Division heat of the International Speech Contest. A day that should have been spent walking around in the sunshine, without a care in the world, was actually spent in a gloomy hotel room, with the curtains closed, my eyes glued to a laptop computer and a mobile phone permanently attached to my left ear. It's safe to say I was very much looking forward to my SUP trip the following day.

Levanto

Wind is the enemy of stand up paddle boarding, especially if you have to paddle into it, so I was hoping for a calm day. I had the option of reversing my route if need be, starting from Riomaggiore and working my way north. But the weather forecast was for low wind, coming from the north-east. If I hugged the coastline, I would be completely sheltered by the mountains. Despite the calm waves I looked at the sea with trepidation. I had been warned that wind could be very unpredictable in this part of the world.

I arrived on the beach at Levanto just after 8 am, having already inflated my SUP board in the hotel car park. I got a couple of odd looks from some other guests who were in the process of checking out. I imagined they were thinking:

'What is that man up to?' or 'How strange.'

But I didn't care. I was looking forward to the day ahead of me. I was going to SUP the Five Lands!

The beach at Levanto forms a semi-circle of sand between the hotels and restaurants of the town and the Mediterranean Sea. There was no one about at all. Levanto is a holiday resort, but this was March so it was early in the season as well as early in the morning. The sun was just beginning to rise above the mountains behind me and I could feel the heat on my skin, gradually warming me up as I prepared to set off. Apart from the gentle lapping of some tiny waves onto the sand, there was absolute silence. I watched as a couple of birds flew over the open water in front of me.

Sitting on the sand next to my board, I took a moment to reflect on my good fortune to be here. I felt relaxed and grateful to escape the hustle and bustle of daily life, even for a short time. I was overcome with a sense of absolute peace and tranquillity. I felt at one with the world.

Although I was enjoying the moment, it was time to set off.

Paddling away from the beach in perfect conditions, flat water and virtually no wind, I was excited for the day ahead.

More or less immediately I was in trouble. As I made my way towards the headland on the left, I was suddenly plagued by a persistent, cramp-like pain running all the way down the back of my right leg. I sometimes experience cramp in one calf or the other but this extended all the way up my leg. Was that even cramp? I couldn't tell but I spent the first 30 minutes stopping every few moments to get down on my knees, stretching my leg out behind me in an effort to relieve the pain. I would describe it as an annoying pain rather than agonising so I didn't seriously contemplate turning back. It wasn't the most auspicious start to my day; on my knees, in pain and wondering whether I should continue. I hoped that this wouldn't be a harbinger of things to come.

Monterosso al Mare

At just under five miles, the leg from Levanto to Monterosso al Mare was the longest single section. Fortunately, the cramp had started to wear off by the time I pulled up onto the beach at Monterosso, the only proper sandy beach in Cinque Terre.

Apart from the pain, it had been a very enjoyable paddle. Some gentle swell on the sea, which I find highly therapeutic, and no wind. It was nearly 10 am by the time I arrived. The sun was higher in the sky behind the mountains and the temperature was rising rapidly.

'If it's this warm at 10 am,' I thought to myself, 'I'm going to be sweltering later on!'

I had some extra waterproof and windproof layers in the dry bag secured to the front of my board, but I didn't think they would be needed today.

There were a few people on the beach, even this early. Monterosso sits in a bay and has a typical arc-shaped beach, with a promenade behind and, further back, a thin line of multicoloured buildings, many of them hundreds of years old. Orange and yellow and pastel blue, the peeling paintwork merely served to accentuate the attractiveness of the village in my eyes. Like a fine wine, some things get better as they age. I would put Monterosso into that category. Behind the town lies a sheer cliff face, mostly rugged brown rock with some greenery in places. It's difficult to believe that this area has been cultivated for hundreds of years. The locals grew grapes, olives and other crops on tiny terraces cut into the hillside.

Leaving my SUP board on the beach, within sight yet far enough away from the edge of the water, I found a small beach-front cafe and treated myself to a cappuccino (well, when in Italy and all that!) and a small croissant as a reward for making it this far.

OK, I admit it, I had two cappuccinos and two croissants!

I deserved a reward for pushing through the pain barrier. I was in no rush to move on and so spent a very relaxing half-an-hour people watching. A young couple playfully pushing each other into the sea. A mother with two young children digging in the sand with their hands. An older man, his face glistening with sweat, out for a mid-morning run. Monterosso was starting to come alive. The beach was beginning to fill up and it was time for me to move on.

Vernazza

My next stop was Vernazza, a couple of miles to the south. By the time I got there, not only had the wind started to pick up, but it was blowing onshore (from the sea towards the land) rather than offshore as I had expected. There was a nasty side swell on the sea which is not something I enjoy paddling through. I know some stand up paddle boarders who love ocean paddling and will SUP through any conditions. I am not one of them. Although I was enjoying my SUP The Five Lands Tour 2019, I have a strong preference for flatter water. Give me a canal or a river or a small sheltered lake any time!

To say the least, I was delighted to enter a small harbour and reach Vernazza. And not only that, it was lunchtime.

As I paddled into the calm waters of the small harbour, I gazed up in wonder at the multicoloured buildings which appeared to be piled up on top of each other, packed into the tiny space between cliff and sea. If you wanted to recreate Vernazza from scratch, I think you would need to be an expert at three-dimensional jigsaw puzzles. If I had thought Monterosso was outstandingly beautiful, Vernazza was just incredible.

Parking on a small beach, I saw to my left, cut into the whitewashed wall, a small passageway leading to half a dozen concrete steps. Climbing these slowly, as my legs were wobbly and my back was stiff, I found myself in a tiny piazza enclosed by half a dozen small restaurants, each with a group of tables set outside. I chose a restaurant at random and spotted an empty table. It was still early in the day but almost all of the tables were already occupied. I can only imagine how cramped it must be here at the height of the tourist season.

Overcrowding is one of the issues faced by many popular tourist spots (think Venice) and Cinque Terre is no exception. If my small story encourages you to visit the area, whether to stand up paddle or otherwise, I guess I've made the problem worse. And that is the problem. It's so astoundingly beautiful here that anyone who visits will naturally want to tell the world how amazing it is. And then the world will come running.

Although I left my SUP board near the shoreline, I brought my paddle up with me to lunch. The tables were packed so tightly together that I almost knocked over someone's wine with my paddle as I swerved and squeezed my way through the gaps. And then, taking a sidestep to avoid his drink, I nearly beheaded an American tourist on a table behind me. I could see other customers giving me look that seemed to say:

'Oh no! I hope this fool doesn't come anywhere near me!'

I wisely left my paddle propped up against the wall of the restaurant before I could do any more damage and greedily tucked into a bowl of pasta, washed down with a glass of white wine.

OK, I admit it. I had two glasses of wine. If I had known what was to come I might have had the whole bottle!

My choice of restaurant turned out to be inspired. My waiter, Antonio, was a keen kayaker and he knew the waters around here very well. He asked me where I had come from and where I was headed. I shared my route with him and mentioned the side swell. I expressed to him my hope that conditions would improve as I travelled south, but sadly he had no words of comfort for me:

"The wind is going to pick up later on," he warned, a sorrowful look in his eye. "The sea will be much worse."

"In that case, I'd better have another glass of white!" I replied.

Corniglia

Leaving the pastel village of Vernazza behind me and paddling out of the small harbour to the waiting sea, I realised that Antonio's prediction was accurate. As soon as I left shelter, I found myself paddling into a strong wind, pushing me back towards the harbour. The gusts threatened to blow me off the board and the surface of the water was choppier than before. A succession of small bumpy waves crashed over the nose of my board. The wind was blowing onshore so I headed a hundred metres or so offshore to get away from the cliffs.

And just then the wind began to go absolutely crazy! It seemed to be blowing in two, or even more different directions at once. Wind onshore with offshore gusts. Or the other way round. I don't know if that is even possible but it's what was happening. The predominant wind direction was clearly onshore, and I was being blown ominously close to the rocky cliffs. The rocks looked dangerously jagged. The type of rock, I imagined, that was so sharp it could shred your skin without even being in contact with you.

I felt an explosion of adrenalin bursting through my body as fear replaced fun. My heart was racing. My mouth was dry. I could feel the back of my right leg begin to tighten again. But there was no time to stop and feel sorry for myself. I just had to get away from the rocks.

Messy waves were aggressively pouring over the front of my board. And the back. And the sides. Coming at me from every direction at once. Pushing me one way, then the other and then back again.

I got down onto my knees as it was difficult to stand and paddled furiously away from the shore. But it was impossible to maintain a straight line. The best I could hope for was an insane zig-zag vaguely in the required direction. It felt as though I was travelling three metres backward for every two metres I went forward.

Corniglia was only a mile and a half away.

'Surely I can make it to safety!' I thought.

And I began to feel cold. Really cold. The sun was still shining brightly, now sitting high in the midday sky, but my skin was wet and wind-chill was sapping the warmth from my body. I carefully removed my windproof jacket from my board bag and popped it on, which was a delicate operation in itself considering the gyrations my board was doing across the surface of the water at the time. My concerns from earlier in the day that I might be too hot were long gone.

The only option I had was to keep on going. And to keep on keeping going. But it was tiring, incredibly tiring dealing with the unwanted wind and waves. Without a shadow of a doubt, this was the worst paddling conditions I had ever found myself in.

I was alone on the sea, not another human being in sight in any direction, and feeling rather lonely and sorry for myself. Although it was a physical challenge, I know the biggest battle is always the mental one. The voice inside your head telling you it's time to stop. I know from previous exploits that the human body is capable of so much more than the human brain thinks it is. But knowing this and being able to use that knowledge to overcome adversity are two entirely different things. I tried to summon up a different voice from inside my head. A different voice that said:

'Keep going. You'll be fine!'

I kept reminding myself that I was only doing this because I enjoyed it, because it was my hobby and because it was fun! But there was only one problem. It wasn't fun. It wasn't fun at all.

"Why am I doing this?" I asked myself. "Why not stop?"

Why not indeed.

There is something called 'The Fun Scale' that tells us that there are three different kinds of fun:

Type One: Type one fun is an activity which is fun while it is happening. Also known as 'fun'!

Type Two: Type two fun is an activity which is not fun at the time, but is perceived as fun in retrospect.

Type Three: Type three fun is not fun at all, not even in retrospect.

I certainly wasn't enjoying type one fun right now. I could only hope that I would find the pleasure in retrospect. That way I could chalk it up to type two fun rather than type three.

A small yacht passed me by and I could see the crew on board having a good look at me. Perhaps they thought I needed help! So I gave them a wave and a friendly smile as they passed. Every bone in my body was telling me to quit. Perhaps the rational part of my brain was also chipping in with unwanted advice but I realised I had no desire to be unnecessarily rescued.

Corniglia is the only one of the five villages that doesn't lie at sea level. It actually sits 100 metres up, perched on top of a cliff, and as such I could see it from a long way out.

"Just keep going to Corniglia, John," the voices in my head told me. "Just keep going."

But Corniglia didn't seem to be getting any closer at all.

I began to count my paddle strokes.

"One, two, three, four…"

Anything to quieten my inner voice and to take my mind off the position I was in. And at long last, I found myself within striking distance of Corniglia.

I seriously contemplated finishing my journey here and returning to my hotel, or perhaps completing my journey by train rather than by SUP.

"Would that really be cheating?" I asked myself. "Would it?"

There is no shame in prematurely quitting an adventure if that is the right thing to do.

I'm not entirely sure where it came from, some small electrical impulse inside my brain I guess, but I made the decision to continue past Corniglia. Having decided that I was going to complete my journey I didn't even get off the water to explore the middle village of the five. Perhaps if I had decided to visit Corniglia, I would have found the temptation of the train station too much? Perhaps I just didn't fancy the 100 metre climb from sea level to the village? (Clue: I really didn't fancy the climb!).

Manarola

So I said 'No' to visiting Corniglia.

But, more importantly, by saying 'No' to Corniglia I said 'Yes' to continuing onto Manarola and ultimately to Riomaggiore, my final destination. I said 'Yes' to completing my small odyssey.

And then something unbelievable happened. A miracle almost!

Not long after I passed the Corniglia headland, the wind suddenly dropped. Not to zero, of course, I wasn't that lucky. But it was manageable and, more importantly, it was blowing in one single direction. Offshore. The wind was blowing from the land towards the sea. If only I could paddle towards the shore then eventually I would be sheltered beneath the self-same cliffs I had been trying to steer away from.

It was a tough paddle into the wind to reach shelter, but I dug in, kept my body low, and got there with a few minutes of exertion. The sea was still bumpy, an after effect of the previous wind, but nothing I couldn't handle. Hugging the shoreline on my left, I continued my journey glad that I had chosen to go on. Next stop Manarola.

And it was at Manarola that I received the first of my rewards for going on, but not before I had negotiated a tricky entrance to the village. Like Vernazza, Manarola has a cascade of pastel coloured buildings which appear to have been painted onto the cliff side. The penultimate village on my route also has a small harbour, with a breakwater providing protection from the sea, although by now the water was fairly calm and I had no need of the protection. But I was tired and had an overwhelming desire to exit the water and chill out for a bit. And I did need a few calories.

Paddling into the harbour, and along the tiny quayside, I spotted a perfect SUP board sized space between the small motor boats already moored alongside. I tied my boat to an available cleat, removed my dry bag and began to climb up to the village, stopping only to take a few photographs.

But my journey for gelato was to have one final twist. As I approached the top of the steps, I could see a group of men working, performing welding work on the iron railings. There was no way past! Fortunately, as my Italian language skills are vanishingly poor, one of the men spoke English. He explained to me that the pathway was closed, but that if I went back down to the water, I could get back onto my board and paddle across the harbour and exit on the other side. It was a minor inconvenience but I was feeling so exhausted by this point that he might as well have asked me to paddle to the moon and back.

I had no alternative. The gelato was calling for me!

Having climbed up from the water's edge for the second time in less than ten minutes, I was delighted to spot, in the far corner of the piazza, a tiny doorway leading down to a small shop. I could see people coming out of the shop holding gelato. What better way to replace a few of the calories I had burned off on my way past Corniglia?

'Heaven indeed,' I thought to myself as I ordered one scoop.

OK, you probably know me well enough by now. I did, of course, order two scoops.

I stopped at Manarola for much longer than planned, just relaxing in the sun and watching the world go by. A group of Italian youngsters apparently on a school trip. Teenage boys running around and climbing and generally acting up in an attempt to impress the girls. I guess the world is the same all over! A beautiful young woman posing for photographs at the water's edge. Judging by the pouting going on, the photographs were clearly destined for Instagram. A married couple, hand in hand, absorbing the romance and beauty of the setting, oblivious to anyone else. The village was busy without being overcrowded. A background buzz of people talking, laughing and sharing the day. I was feeling warmer again so I removed some layers and lay back allowing the sun to replenish my skin.

Riomaggiore

Gradually, I came to the realisation that it was time to move on. I had just one more leg of my journey to go, which was to be the shortest one, less than a mile to Riomaggiore, the southernmost town of the five.

Feeling much better now, I pushed on and was delighted to find no wind at all. Where had all the wind gone? How could it be so stormy a couple of hours ago and so calm now? I didn't really care, I was too busy enjoying the transformation.

And what a moment it was. What a reward. I reached Riomaggiore just after 6 pm. Not quite sunset, but the sun was low in the sky behind me as I paddled into the village. I'm not sure what colours the buildings of Riomaggiore actually are, as they were all bathed in an astounding orange hue from the sun behind me. And not just the buildings. Everything was orange. The cliffs orange, the harbour orange, the water in front of me orange. Even the people seemed to be orange.

There was a gentle swell rocking me into a sense of calm serenity and I was the welcome recipient of a hundred, or maybe more, waves, smiles, and hellos from the tourists who were lining the wall of the harbour to take in one of the most beautiful panoramas anywhere in the world, the setting of the sun over the Mediterranean Sea at Cinque Terre.

If you close your eyes and think of nothing else for a moment, maybe you can imagine the scene. I know I can.

A rocky headland sitting beneath brightly painted buildings, burgundy and yellow and grey. Beneath you, a small concrete jetty, being gently washed by the warm Mediterranean Sea. And straight ahead, that same turquoise-blue sea extending all the way to the horizon, where it meets, and seems to merge with, a brighter blue and cloudless sky. A sky becoming more and more tinged with pinks and reds as the striking orange sun gradually descends. And just there in the foreground:

A solitary stand up paddle boarder, silhouetted against the sinking sun.

This was paradise to me. My reward for completing my SUP the Five Lands Tour 2019. I really didn't want to get off the water, I could have remained there for all eternity. But of course, all good things must come to an end.

Time for dinner I decided.

It was a steep walk up from the harbour to the restaurant, but it was a walk I took with a massive smile on my face. Real ear to ear stuff. And I was delighted to dig into a well-deserved pepperoni pizza and an even more well-deserved glass of deep purple and very, very dry Chianti.

OK, as you've probably guessed, I had two glasses!

(Actually, I had three glasses - but I think I deserved it, don't you?)

And as I wined, dined and relaxed, I looked back on my day and on my quest to SUP the Five Lands.

I reflected on my decision to continue my journey. Had I made the right decision? Well, yes, with the benefit of hindsight, of course I did. If I had stopped halfway through I would have missed out on the best parts of the day: The thirst-quenching gelato at Manarola; approaching Riomaggiore on a gentle sea, with the sinking orange sun behind me; and of course the three delicious glasses of Chianti.

But nobody can predict the future. I had no way of knowing that conditions were going to improve so dramatically by the time I reached Manarola and, even more so, by Riomaggiore. In fact, based on the information from Antonio, I was prepared for the worst! The only reason I said 'Yes' to continuing my journey was a sense that I wanted to achieve my objective. To reach my destination. I don't like to quit. Most of the time, I am that type of person. But not always. On another day I might have made a different decision. In my opinion, there is no way to judge a decision until later on, when we have the benefit of hindsight. But as I looked back now, I knew I had been right to say 'Yes'. I hope I will have the courage and the wisdom to make the same decision next time I find myself in a similar situation.

Exiting the restaurant, all that remained was for me to make my way to the train station and the return journey to Levanto. Twenty minutes sitting on a warm comfortable train for what was essentially the same route that had taken me all day to SUP! I was satisfied that I had achieved my goal and that it had been yet another memorable day on my quest to SUP the World.

John McFadzean is a Say Yes More Ambassador for 2019. He is on a mission to stand up paddleboard in every country in the world. As of July 2019 he has paddled in 40 countries. John would love you to come with him, either in real life or by following his adventures online:

Website: www.suptheworld.com

Facebook: @SUPTHEWORLD

Instagram: @sup_the_world_

Twitter: @sup_the_world

Chapter 11

YesTribe Italia

by Laura Maisey

"I always thought I'd like to live in Italy one day."

"Why didn't you do it, Grandma?"

"Oh, you know. Life gets in the way."

"What do you mean?"

"Well, erm, I don't know. I don't know why I didn't. I just... didn't."

This scenario kept playing over and over in my head and was, eventually, the thing that pushed me out of the proverbial door and into a whole new world. My seven year relationship had just ended (amicably and by mutual agreement, might I add) and my good friend and manager had moved on and been replaced by a much worse model. The hooks that were keeping my life pinned to London, where I had lived for eleven years, were gently loosening.

At a YesTribe campout with Dave Cornthwaite, I asked him, "Why am I thinking about going to live in Italy? I don't understand it. It feels like an itch that needs scratching, but I have a great life here. All my friends are here. What will I do there alone?"

He just turned to me and smiled and said one thing, "You'll find people there too."

It was around this time that the Grandma Scenario entered my head. It was the conversation I imagined my 80-year-old self having with an imaginary grandchild while sitting in a rocking chair talking about the days of old. That was what finally did it - fear. The all-encompassing fear that life would pass me by and I wouldn't have done one of the things I most wanted to do in the world, for no valid reason other than *I just didn't*. I was so scared that I looked at my diary for the year, worked out when all my England-based commitments would be finished, then chose a date and booked a one-way flight. It was the weekend after Yestival 2017. I would give a talk at the festival about the time I ran from Rome to London (that's another story) then I would go back to my east London home, pack up my life and get on a plane to Italy.

Ah, Italy. The home of Caravaggio, gorgonzola, Andrea Bocelli and the Vespa. The birthplace of Dante, Petrarca and Machiavelli. The inventors of pesto, tiramisu and ravioli. Italy had utterly captured my heart after a trip to Rome years ago and since then I'd been dabbling in learning the language through apps to practise on the holidays I took there once or twice a year. On the earlier-mentioned run from Rome to London, I spent the first six weeks in Italy and relished every minute getting to know the land and its people the slow way, by foot. Travelling mile by mile, day in, day out, through the stunning Tuscan countryside in late September has to be one of the best ways to spend one's time.

Of course, planning to actually live in a country takes some organisation (not much, as I seem to just about survive by the seat of my pants). For starters, I had to choose where exactly in Italy I wanted to live. My list consisted of three top choices - Lucca, Torino

(Turin) and Genova (Genoa).

I had really liked Lucca when I'd visited it on my journey from Rome to London but realised that its beauty drew a lot of tourists and you could hear English being spoken everywhere so it wouldn't be great for practising Italian. Torino had good work opportunities, I had heard, and was beautiful but I had seen it only briefly so wasn't confident about how daily life there might be. One of my close friends in London grew up in Genova and had an empty apartment there so I went out for four days for a little holiday and loved it.

Everything in Genova is on a hill. When I say everything, I mean *everything* (which is a nightmare for anyone with mobility issues, as one of my friends found out when she broke her foot and was house-bound for weeks). If you go downhill, you find the most beautiful vibrant blue sea. If you go uphill, you find the wild unforgiving mountains. The city is a long thin dense band of teeming life, full of Vespas and people and dogs and focaccia shops and cafes and apartment blocks and medieval quarters. It was loud and busy and an assault on my senses - and it was exactly what I was looking for.

My lovely friend said I could move into one of the rooms in his apartment, which sealed the deal. His family all lived close by and had gone to great lengths to make me feel welcome on that short trip so I knew I'd have people around, if ever I was struggling.

I had found my Italian home.

Then, finally, after all this daydreaming, it was time to up my game and go and live there. Firstly, I wanted to experience life in Italy and see if it was as good as I thought it would be. Secondly, I wanted to improve my Italian. I had some lessons with a language teacher before leaving, to prepare myself, and then off I went!

For me, the concept of 'home' is always where I am right now. Where I sleep at night and where I drink cups of tea is home. I don't need to be in a place for a while and figure it out and 'get a feel' for it. No, when I put down my suitcase and unpack it, I am home. I remember walking through the door of the apartment with my stuff for the first time, saying 'hi' to my new Italian flatmate, heading to the room I knew would be mine for the foreseeable future, putting everything down, looking around and thinking, 'Okay, I live in Italy now. This is my new home.' I was completely comfortable with that thought. It didn't scare me. It felt completely ordinary, as though it was strange that it had never been true before. It felt like it had always been true. I guess my life experiences have taught me to take everything in my stride but this was extraordinary, the way it felt so natural.

I spent days wandering around, getting to know the streets, losing my way in the mountains, staring out to sea, watching the older Italian men drink coffee and argue, eating focaccia and generally marvelling at my wonderful good luck that I was able to make this choice to live here. So many people can't make such flippant life choices. I was able to say, "I want this thing. I will have it." I booked a flight for £20 and just did it. That choice isn't on the table for so many.

I moved to Italy with no idea what I would do for work My Italian left a lot to be desired. I had only a small suitcase and backpack worth of belongings to survive on. It is perhaps the least well-organised country move in history.

Yet, the very fact that I was able to choose to do that kept me mindful of how lucky I am. I always knew that, should I not find any work there, I could survive on my money until it ran out then move back to the UK.

Talking of money, I did spend some silly days early on, calculating amounts in my mind and worrying about whether I would be able to afford basic things like rent and food. Some days I would literally have thirty cents in my pocket and it would be all the money I owned in the world and I would be wondering how much a banana cost then something would always happen to keep me from starvation.

I had found work as an English language teacher after seeing a sign for conversational lessons and thinking, 'Well, it's conversational, and I can have conversations. What more could they want? (Hopefully not qualifications!)' It was perfect timing because the school had just hired a teacher who had bailed out at the last minute so when I wandered over, all naive and clueless, and asked if they needed someone to help with conversational lessons, they said yes and I taught my first lesson for them that evening!

The work took a couple of months to really pick up, so in the meantime, I would be tearing my hair out, with the aforementioned thirty cents and wondering how I would be able to pay rent the following week. Maybe I would cover a lesson for someone or do a bit of private work or the mum of a young student would ask me to do some paid babysitting, and then I'd get a little extra in my hand, which was exciting because then I could go and buy that banana.

It took quite a few times of being faced with pennilessness to realise that something would always happen to keep my head above water. One time it was the late payment of the remainder of my holiday pay from my old job in London. Another time it was a tax rebate from the UK government. Next it was my bank apologising for something I didn't even realise they'd done years ago, accompanied by a cheque for £500. You see what I mean about being lucky?

After those darker stress-filled, money-worry days, I learned to relax into it and trust the world. Yes, I sometimes eat plain pasta for breakfast because my cupboards are empty. No, I can't afford the bus today so will walk the one hour to work. Yes, I am living hand to mouth. No, I won't have anything to put into a pension scheme (just the concept makes me laugh). Yet, if we flip the coin we see what else I was saying yes and no to. Yes, I was living the life I want and no, I would not accept the Grandma Scenario.

Alongside being able to afford my new life, there were the language issues. It's fair to say that I didn't quite make the splash I had imagined when I arrived, mainly because I couldn't understand a blooming word anyone was saying! Apparently, a handful of one-hour lessons for a few months doesn't bring you the level of fluency you would imagine.

It was so frustrating. I could get *'buongiorno'* and *'ciao'*, of course, and some verbs here and there, but beyond that, I was just smiling and nodding and saying, *'sì'* (which landed me in some awkward situations but that's for yet another story). I felt so stupid.

I was invited to dinner after a couple of weeks and of course I went along. This would be my chance to find some friends. It's fair to say that I offered nothing of interest for a potential friendship so no surprises for correctly guessing that I made no new lifelong buddies.

How can you be friends with a silent nervous-looking face? That was all I offered to the evening's proceedings. Silence. Wide, nervous eyes. A small scared smile. I was unrecognisable as the Laura I had known in London.

It is startling what happens when the gift of language is taken away from you. You have nothing to offer, just a smile, and a frightened one, at that. This group was the warmest, friendliest bunch. They even spoke in English sometimes, to help me, but I was so busy trying to understand what they said in Italian yet not being able to, that when they spoke in English, my mangled brain had stopped functioning. I listened and listened and kicked myself because I just *didn't* know what they were talking about but so badly wanted to. I spent the whole evening wishing I was invisible and wanting to run away. I even convinced myself that if I went back to the UK, I could go back to my Italian teacher and I would probably learn faster that way.

After this, I figured that I just needed to study the language harder, so I did, for hours every day. I studied and studied and studied. I used textbooks, apps, read kids' books, everything. Yet every time I was faced with a real-life Italian talking to me, I was gripped by fear, unable to speak, and would start looking for ways to escape.

'Well then, Laura,' I thought to myself. 'You really are an idiot. You have moved your entire life to Italy, to learn Italian, and you are too nervous to talk to anyone.'

I still thought that more learning was the key so after six weeks of intense studying, when I visited the UK for Christmas, I took all of my textbooks with me. As it happened, I was so busy eating myself into oblivion and seeing as many friends and family as time would allow, I had no time to study.

I loved living in Italy. I enjoyed the way of life. I felt comfortable and at ease there. The food was obviously amazing. I could go to the opera or the ballet (Ten euro tickets! Amazing!). I could see stunning artwork by my favourite painters. Now, if only I could get my head around the language, things would become a lot easier.

When I got back to Italy after Christmas, I was determined to do better. The break from studying had helped my brain to relax. I became braver in my interactions and less worried about mistakes. I would ask people, "Is it this or this? Do I pronounce it this way?" Before, I felt I should already know everything so was afraid to let people see that I was struggling. I obviously still had a long way to go but I was finally, slowly, finding my voice.

One of the things that I had really appreciated when I first moved to Italy was having free time. London was my home for so long and I still love it dearly. However, the constant rounds of work, social events, group workouts and dinners with friends meant I was always slightly behind on sleep and always in a rush. I am not complaining at all about the life I had created. It was full because there were so many wonderful things to do and lovely people to see. It was full because I chose it to be that way. Despite this, I knew that when I arrived in Italy without a friendship group, I would enjoy that time of being almost entirely alone.

It took quite a while but, eventually, after about a month, my super-speed London brain learned how to live at a slower pace. I didn't need to walk at 200 miles-an-hour anymore. I didn't need to be frustrated at people going slowly. I allowed myself to sit under the fruit tree outside my front door and read a book for the whole afternoon. I didn't whip through art galleries just looking for my favourite painters and missing out on the rest. In fact, I remember gasping and being so mesmerised by an unknown painting that I had to stop and stare at it for about twenty minutes. It turned out to be by a painter called Orazio Gentileschi, a good friend of Caravaggio's, who I also love. I stood there grinning at this 400 year-old painting and imagining these two friends creating beauty that would live for so long that it could make an English girl in Genova smile centuries later.

In late January, however, while enjoying the solitary routine of work, reading, art galleries, museums, opera (I *almost* saw Andrea Bocelli!), studying Italian and eating too much focaccia, I decided that it was time to have some friends. Every Sunday, I would go walking, either up into the mountains behind my apartment or down to the sea. One Sunday, I had walked up to an old fort on a mountain top in my running clothes, the idea being that I would run the return journey. Whilst picking my way through the stony pathway downhill, it was as though the world had heard my earlier thought and decided to throw some people into my path who might just make a good fit.

The group of three people were walking uphill and as I passed, one of them said something incomprehensible.

I stopped. "*Scusa?*"

Again, the words that I didn't understand.

"*Scusa. Parlo italiano, ma un po'. Sono inglese.*" Excuse me. I speak Italian, but only a bit. I am English.

"Oh! Wow! I'm an English teacher. My friend is a translator. She speaks English too."

The two of them said, "Hi." their other friend saying he spoke only a little English. The guy who had originally spoken said something about me being brave for running back down the mountain. Then, again as though they could read my mind, they said, "There's an international event on at the end of this month, have you heard about it?"

By coincidence, I had joined the online international meet-up group before moving to Italy, with the hope of finding friends, so I had heard about the event and was already signed up. After saying our goodbyes and promising to look for each other at the event, I headed home with the little fuzzy glow that comes from human interaction. I was looking forward to having friends.

Sure enough, at the event, I saw the English teacher and sat with him and some others, turning my collection of three friends into eight. It was all very exciting. I mentioned that I liked walking and someone suggested a local trekking group that had a page on Facebook. When I got home, I looked for any events on the trekking page but there hadn't been any in months. I wasn't sure if anyone was even looking at the page anymore. With nothing to lose, I posted the message that would change my whole life in Italy.

'I am going on a walk to Forte Diamante on Sunday, if anyone fancies joining me? Let's meet at the Righi-Zecca funicolare station at 8am.'

At 7.55am on Sunday, I waited at the station, knowing that if no-one came, I would do the walk alone, like I had been doing for months and I would relish the time outside in nature. I think it is because I never had a problem doing things alone that it was such a pleasant surprise how things snowballed. On that first walk to Forte Diamante, three others came - three people who I would end up spending a lot of time with during the next year.

One of them, Jess, talked about how she had been living in a village in the mountains above Genova (more of this later) on and off for four years but had found it difficult to form friendships or find like-minded people. She wasn't the first person to say this to me. I had been told it would be hard to make friends in Genova (untrue, in my case), that the Genovese were closed, distant, didn't like outsiders. As evidence, many people told me of the months or years they had spent in the city with barely a friend to speak of. They still referred to the country or city where they were born as home and Genova simply as their current location.

Italy - and Genova - absolutely felt like home to me the minute I arrived. I was convinced that these people just weren't doing it right. Their preconceptions about unfriendliness made them, in turn, closed and distant, uninterested in the people around them. I figured that if I could just create a different channel for these people to experience the world around them, they might be able to find some people to connect with and maybe, just maybe, start to understand that friendships were possible anywhere, even in this 'most unfriendly' city.

My mind wandered back to London, to the places where I had found community. Two places came immediately to mind. The first was Project Awesome, an early morning free fitness workout that I had attended for three years before moving to Italy. A lot of my closest friends and the entire direction my life had taken came from this group. I wondered about setting up a 6.30am workout in Genova and realised I was too prone to oversleeping to be a reliable leader for such an operation. The second was The YesTribe which, as you know if you're reading this book, is all about community and connection and encouraging each other. It was also an as-and-when thing so I could plan events that would suit my schedule and if others could make it, then great. If not, I would make sure I organised things that I was happy to do alone, to allow for that possibility.

I explained my thoughts to Dave Cornthwaite, about how I hadn't been planning to start a YesTribe but it seemed that people were crying out for something that didn't exist here yet. More importantly, they seemed to want something that I was capable of providing. My involvement with The YesTribe in the UK (I often lead campouts and had spoken at various Yes events) gave me an understanding of how to go about it.

The plan was ready, then. I was going to make The YesTribe Italia! I got a Facebook page set up, translated the explanation into Italian (with help, of course! I still wasn't very good yet), got a logo and created the first event. It would be a walk from the centre of town, down to the sea then along the coast for a few hours before heading up into the mountains for a flower festival, the *Sagra Mimosa*, in the piazza of a small village called Pieve Ligure.

To my surprise, fourteen people arrived for the walk. The weather was fabulous for February. We all had sunglasses and walked in t-shirts, laughing, joking, making new friends, admiring the views and getting adorned with tons of yellow mimosa when we arrived at the festival after about six hours of walking. What a wonderful start! One of the women on the walk became my running partner for the next few months until she left Genova. Another was my regular coffee meet-up between lessons. Another needed help preparing for a job interview in English so we worked together for the next month on that. Another gave me information about a good Italian teacher (who I studied with for almost a year and can credit with any progress I made). Those fourteen faces became a regular feature in my life. I would sometimes see them around town or they would pop up at a social event or they would come on more walks. Suddenly, the city wasn't full of unknown strangers. It was a warm and welcoming place, it felt familiar, it had taken me into its arms.

Over the next year, we walked most Sundays (or occasional Saturdays). We did *Via Ferrata* in the mountains. We met for *aperitivo*. We went stand-up paddle boarding. We swam in the sea. We went for long bike rides on the coast. We ran 5ks. We slept on the walls of an old fort on top of a mountain (the very same one where I met my first friends).

More importantly, however, were the resulting friendships that came from these. We welcomed in newbies who had only just arrived in the city and gave them a ready-made friendship group so they didn't spend years despairing, like the aforementioned people. We had a sort of dinner club offshoot with a group who would take turns to make dinner for the others. We forged deep connections through the joy of introducing others to *Via Ferrata* and having to give each other a mental or physical helping hand to reach the top of the mountain. We realised a common inability to stay upright on a paddleboard in the sea that had us laughing for hours over hot chocolates afterwards. We pulled each other through the rather scary day when we were lost on a mountain in the snow and couldn't see a way down.

Strangers are just friends waiting to happen. Isn't that what they say? None of us knew each other before a tiny spark of an idea was planted by a woman I had never met. From that, we created a world.

My final big adventure before returning to England was another spontaneous move. I happened to teach a lesson at a small village near the one where Jess lived in the mountains. The utter peace and tranquillity grabbed me as soon as I arrived. After the hustle and bustle of the city for a year, I had been starting to feel that a break from the noise might be nice. The lesson came at exactly the right time. After commenting that the views and calmness were lovely, the mother of my student said, casually, "You should come and live up here. It's very nice. I know someone with an apartment you could rent."

Never one to miss an interesting opportunity, I said, (in Italian as I was good enough by this point), "How much would an apartment up here cost?"

"Around two hundred and fifty euro, more or less."

My apartment in Genova was four hundred euro a month. I gave it a minute or two (apparently that's all I need to make great sweeping life choices!) and asked her for the phone number of the landlady of the apartment. Over the next day or two, after a flurry of messages, I started packing up my life in Genova to prepare for yet another move.

This move was one of the best things I did in Italy. Linguistically, I knew I was capable of it now because this tiny village had no native English speakers. I repeat, NO-ONE could speak English! I was opening up the potential of friendlessness again, but this time, I felt sure I could offer more than just a scared smile.

It was utterly wonderful. When I first arrived and the electricity company took a week to turn my lights on, everyone in the village knew about it and helped me. When I walked into the only grocery shop, the lady at the cheese counter immediately asked if I was coping. I said I had candles and was fine yet a matter of hours later, my neighbour knocked on my door with an extension lead and rigged up some power from his place to mine so I could at least turn on the boiler for warm water. When I couldn't cook because I didn't have gas yet, I was invited to the local restaurant to eat and my meal was paid for. In fact, when I arrived and there were no free tables, the waiter (my other neighbour) asked if I didn't mind joining a table of three as they had a space. These three became close friends and every Saturday evening, I would meet them for dinner and I was never allowed to pay for what I had eaten. When I walked to lessons in my city-appropriate shoes, I was told they would never do for the mountains and bought some bigger, more substantial boots to help me deal with the cold. I was given coats when the villagers decided my thin jackets wouldn't cut it. I was taken for coffees if I had free time. I love walking but dreaded walking along the main roads as I would always see someone I knew (you know everyone after a few days) who would insist on giving me a lift.

After some months of living in my idyllic mountain hideaway, Brexit loomed large on the horizon, as did the possibility of another Yes. This Yes was to a rather delightful young man I had met in

England and with whom I wanted to explore the possibility of a life together.

Although I loved the mountains, I also knew that movement meant progress and I wanted to see what exciting things might be waiting in England. All of my students assured me that they would be waiting for me should I choose to go back to Italy. That made things feel less dramatic as I know I would be back for a few months of each year to teach.

A group of friends came out from England for a skiing holiday together in the Italian Alps and I joined them for that and also for the flight to the UK. Yet another new adventure awaited me and, so far, it's going amazingly well.

All in all, I am so delighted that 80-year-old Laura can now tell her imaginary grandchild that there was a time that she had a dream to do something big and bold and she went and did it. I can picture her in my mind's eye now. Her huge contented smile spreading across her face. Her eyes creased with laughter lines as she looks down on her grandchild with pride. Well done 80-year-old me!

For now, I can say that I no longer live in fear of the things I didn't do. Life is for living and that's what I'm doing.

Now it's over to you. Think of yourself as an 80-year-old in a rocking chair having a conversation with your imaginary grandchild. What will you say was the one thing in life you always wanted to do? What will your answer be when you are asked why you didn't do it? Think of all the adventures that could happen if you actually did it. Will you be able to say, instead, that you did do it?

Facebook: laura.maisey.54

Blog: lazylauramaisey.wordpress.com

Chapter 12

How One Yes Changed My Life Forever

by Laura Try

I'm bobbing around in the middle of the Atlantic on an ocean rowing boat with 3 people I barely know.

The boat isn't much bigger than a large family car.

When I look out, all I see for miles and miles, and miles and miles... and miles is the ocean.

Every now and again, a huge swell of water scoops up my oar and sends the handle crashing into my shin with all its might, confirming the fact I don't actually like rowing.

And then I sit there and think to myself, 'How on earth did I get here?'

I'm here in this wonderful book to tell you how I went from a shopaholic beauty salon owner to a minimalist ocean rower, but before I do that, I need to take you back a few years.

*

1989 - 7 years old

As a child I was a dancer.

I started out with a one-legged skip aged 3. That one-legged skip soon turned into me dancing 6 days per week after school and at the weekend. I'm not sure where this (mild) talent came from as my mum, who was a bookkeeper, and my dad, who did something on the gasworks (I'm still not sure what he does now!), didn't do anything creative.

Somehow I ended up competing in national dance competitions dressed as Mr Toad from Wind in the Willows. The rest of the competitors were dreamy princesses, delicate fairies and magical female characters. But not me. I was a toad! Saying that, he did get me quite a few medals despite my green face and funny little outfit.

I spent all my spare time in the dance studio, spinning around in ballet shoes and leotards and I wasn't interested in anything else.

I never went camping. My family wasn't into things like that. I didn't know how to climb trees and the most ocean experience I had was on a ferry to Legoland in Denmark.

*

1997

Aged 16, I realised my dream of becoming a professional dancer wasn't possible because my family didn't have enough money to send me to dance school. Instead I set my heart on being a beauty therapist and having my own salon. Being in the dance world introduced me to makeup and this option seemed ideal; I could play with makeup and cosmetics all day and get paid for it.

*

2006 - 24 years old

I was the owner of my very own beauty salon, a business I had for 9 years.

Looking back, I cannot believe I had that drive and strength to set up my own business from scratch. I had so much energy and determination at that age. I didn't have any financial or business support. I just went ahead and did it based on a business plan case study I'd done at college.

I got a £5,500 bank loan, went to Ikea, bought 4 trolleys of flat-pack shelves and proceeded to build most of my shop myself. Where did I get all that energy?!

I started the business solo, but within 2 years, I was able to move to bigger premises, hire staff and consider myself a real business owner.

The salon was really busy and the business was very successful, and by that I mean I earned loads of money. But the problem was no-one had ever taught me what to do with my money, so I spent it.

I spent it on things; gadgets, gizmos, the latest technology, furniture to fill my house and designer clothes to fill my bursting wardrobe. I celebrated my success with how many possessions I could own because that's what I thought I should do.

*

2010 - 28 years old

I was introduced to camping for the very first time! Can you believe I'd never stayed in a tent before then?

I only went because I fancied the guy who invited me.

I pretended to have a fabulous time but quite honestly I could not *believe* anyone would go camping for fun!

Why would someone voluntarily put themselves in the outdoors, sleep in the cold, inside a thin piece of polyester, wake up to condensation, try and make the best of a tiny camping stove and then pack it all away to take it home.

How about just sleeping in a house?!

*

2012 - 29 years old

As I approached 30, I began to panic. I had this weird feeling that time was passing me by. I stood in my house and looked around at all my things. I then looked inside of me and realised that all these things weren't actually making me happy.

The Apple Mac computer, the flat screen TV, scatter cushions, that piece of decorative furniture to fill that gap over there, the luscious silk dress and coordinating designer high heeled shoes. How about this designer bag? Yes please! This was all a mark of my success. To show people how well I was doing in life. Cringe, ah?

When would I want to stop wanting the bigger and better model? When would I stop wanting more? Probably never…

Even though 30 is still young, I felt as though it was a pivotal point in my life. In my younger years, I'd thought I'd have my act together by then. But as I stood there looking at all my stuff, I realised they were just things and they didn't mean a thing.

I began asking myself, "What is it that I really want in my life?"

What I'd dreamed about for years was being able to run through the countryside. I wanted to be able to run up mountains, take part in marathons and do all the cool adventures I'd seen on TV. The issue was I didn't have anyone to do it with or show me how to get started. The friends I was hanging around with only knew what shade of lipstick to wear with the latest nail polish colour.

So, with that, I decided to swap my things for experiences.

I started selling all of my belongings and thought to myself, 'I know what I'm going to do, I'm going to become a runner! That's the answer to all of this!'

One of the last things I bought as 'shopaholic, old Laura' was a pair of running trainers. A really expensive pair of running trainers because expensive trainers make us good runners, right?

I laced them up and decided my first run would be around the block.

At the end of my road was a bridge. It was 0.7 miles away. By the time I ran to the bridge I had to stop. The muscles in my legs were burning and my lungs were on fire! I turned around and walked back home, crying my eyes out because I was so frustrated. How could I not even run 1 mile?

Each day I ran to the bridge and walked back, and each day I got a little further home. Until one day I was able to run all the way to the bridge and back without stopping. I could run 1.4 miles! *does a celebratory dance*... Hurray! I was becoming a runner!

1.4 miles turned into 5km.

5km turned into 10km obstacle races.

And then within a few years I was able to run half marathons and marathons.

2014 - 32 years old

I was sat at the kitchen table scrolling through Facebook. I remember this so well. An event popped up, the kind of event I had always dreamt about doing but knew I wouldn't be able to do. It was a 24 hour adventure race.

I showed my then-boyfriend and he agreed with me, "Yeah, you won't be able to do something like that."

You'd think that his comment would have upset me but it didn't. Honestly, it didn't because I knew he was right. He confirmed what I already thought.

I gave the event a 'like', made a comment, something along the lines if, 'This looks really cool' and thought nothing more of it.

A few hours later I had a message in my inbox from a friend who knew the event organisers. He had a spare ticket and asked if I wanted it.

Crikey! My stomach did a little flip thingy. My heart pulsated at the thought of actually taking part in something like this. My palms began to sweat. My brain whizzing thoughts of doubt. But I felt excited.

I didn't have any of the right equipment. I didn't know anyone who was going. I'd never done anything like it before and I certainly hadn't done any of the correct training.

6 weeks later I was stood at the start line of the event with my team.

25.5 hours later we finished the event.

But not only had we finished it, we won it!

I never would have believed I could have done anything like that and thought to myself, 'If I can do that, what else can I do?'

I got straight on the internet and started looking for 'bigger and better' adventure races.

A few months later I took part in a 48 hour adventure race. It was an event navigating through the Peak District carrying everything we needed on our back; food, water and all our kit.

There was no sleep and I was awake for 56 hours in total.

It. Was. Brutal! But I completed it and became the second female to ever finish the event.

As the sun rose on the second morning of the event, about 34 hours in, I was shuffling along, soaked to the bone from the rain, chatting to my teammate Luke. I vowed never to do anything like this again because the sleep deprivation was agonising.

I'd be walking along between tasks and checkpoints, hallucinating because I was so exhausted. Have you ever been so tired you felt sick? That was us for the whole event. Fighting back the fatigue with everything we had. I'd pray for the gruelling PT sessions from the organisers just so I would get the adrenalin rush and wake up.

2015 - 33 years old

It was London Marathon Day 2015 and I was at a friend's house, lying on the living room floor stuffing chocolate into my face, watching all the incredible runners on TV.

It had been a few months since my last event and the pain and discomfort had disappeared and only feelings of achievement and elation remained. Watching the marathon was making me think I'd like to do something again soon.

As if on cue, my phone rings.

It was one of the organisers of the 48 hour event. I thought it was odd he was calling as we weren't chat-on-the-phone kind of friends.

I picked up with one of those curious, question-like hellos and he cut straight to the chase. He asked what I was doing the following Christmas and did I want to join him and his team to row across the Atlantic?

First of all, I asked if anyone had died doing it and he said he didn't think so.

Then….. wait for it….. embarrassingly, I ask where the Atlantic was! That was such a 'beauty therapy Laura' question. I didn't have a clue!

The phone call didn't last long and I told him I'd get back to him with an answer in a week or so.

30 minutes later, and a quick check where the Atlantic actually was (cringe!), I called him back and said, "Yes!"

Our team was called 3 Men and a Little Lady. 3 guys and I were set to become the first mixed team to take part in the Talisker Whisky Atlantic Challenge. It was going to be great!

But sadly, after several months, 2 of the team had to pull out because they had families and good jobs and couldn't commit the time to the fundraising and training.

But by this time, I had invested time, energy, training and money into the project and I couldn't let the idea of the Atlantic go…

*

During all of these escapades, I was in a weird limbo….

At the weekends I was crawling through dirt, running up mountains and not caring how I looked. I'd also started enjoying camping… even without the guy I fancied! Then, during the week, I wore my fancy dresses and high heels, and plucked people's eyebrows.

The 2 lives didn't seem to match.

As a result of downsizing my belongings, spending time in the fresh air and finding 'my tribe', I realised my beauty salon wasn't making me happy anymore. Sure, I earned loads of money but that wasn't fulfilling my soul and there was something missing.

My values had changed and that led me to fall out of love with my business. People often ask me, "If your business was so successful, why didn't you get someone else to run it?"

I tell those people that it's like being an a relationship with a man or woman who treats you really well, says and does all the right things, gives you all the love and affection you need, but you just don't love them. That was how I felt about my beauty salon. I'd fallen out of love with it and I wanted to split up with it.

I'd felt like something wasn't right with me and the business for about 4 years, but kept ploughing on. I rebranded the shop, experimented with different plans but the feeling and lack of passion always came back.

I used to be a very impulsive person so once I'd made my mind up once and for all, the locks were changed and I hung a sign on the door. The salon was no longer open for business!

gulp

*

I'd always been fortunate in life to turn my entrepreneurial hand to anything. Despite not growing up with a lot of money, I always had a little business idea up my sleeve.

Aged 16, I'd visit school fetes and offer face painting to the children. I'd come home with a bag of £1 coins and a feeling of accomplishment.

I sold nightclub tickets in the party town of Faliraki and vodka jelly shots in boozy Magaluf in my early twenties. Yes, this wasn't world domination stuff, but it taught me how to become a sales woman.

After closing my salon, I thought a business opportunity would just show up. I thought I'd have the head space to think of a new business idea and everything would be just as good as it was, if not better.

But as the months passed, I slowly realised I didn't know much more than the ingredients of skin creams and how to create the perfect eyebrow shape.

The more time went on, the less money I had. I'd lost my identity and the thing I was good at. There was no longer a reason to get up and be somewhere every day.

But still I hoped and believed something would just appear.

Then came the day when I didn't have enough money to pay my rent. This forced me to become homeless. But don't think shop front and cardboard box. It wasn't quite that bad.

I had a van and started sleeping in that. It was a small box van which wasn't fitted out. It all felt exciting and adventurous at first but it soon became miserable.

It was the middle of winter, I didn't have a stable job, I wasn't earning much money and my mental health was deteriorating as a result. What was my purpose? I was struggling to find the answer. I was on a steep downward spiral.

This world of adventure and closing my beauty salon was meant to open up new experiences and opportunities for me.

How could I have gone from a successful business owner to this?

I'd message friends saying I hadn't seen them for ages and that we should have a catch up. I'd hope they'd invite me over and that I might get a place to stay for a few nights and some hot food. I never told them I had nowhere to live. I was too embarrassed. Mortified in fact.

There was this one moment when I slept in my van in a supermarket carpark and all the money I had was a £1 coin. I bought a packet of cherry tomatoes that cost 98p and it left me with 2p. I sat in the back of my van, holding the 2p in the palm on my left hand and stared at it for ages. I had no idea how I was going to get out of that situation.

I sat there and thought to myself, 'How on earth did I get here?'

*

2016 - 34 years old

I lived in my van for about 5 months which felt like an eternity.

I was accepting any job that came along; cleaning houses, working at events, building obstacles races. The benefits of the latter was that accommodation was provided as part of the payment. It meant I was able to stay in hotels for a week at a time. Anything to get me out of living in that van.

Still no-one knew my situation. I painted a picture that everything was ok, even to my family. I had to pretend because if I actually admitted to them what was actually going on, I'd have to admit it to myself and I'm not sure I could have coped.

Through all of this, there was always this thought lurking in the back of my mind. A thought that kept me curious and somehow motivated. 'What would it be like to row across the Atlantic?'

Scrolling through Facebook again, (I promise I don't spend all my time on social media) I saw an event to row 1,800 miles around Great Britain. I thought to myself, 'This could be the perfect opportunity to get me out of this mess.'

It was a chance to try ocean rowing, something I'd wanted to do since being invited to row across the Atlantic a year earlier. I'd also get to see the beautiful country we live in from a completely different perspective.

My life wasn't going as I planned and figured I didn't have anything to lose and everything to gain. I was in the pits and needed something to focus on.

This challenge might get me out of this awful situation, PLUS, at least I would have a boat to live on for 2 months! (yes, I actually thought that). I called the company who was organising it and asked a few questions and at the end they asked me, "So, are you in?"

*

I spent the next 12 months selling my soul and raising the funds to do the challenge. By this time I had a kind-of stable job working in a gym and somewhere to live but was right at the bottom of the financial and stability hierarchy. Every day was a real struggle.

I'd sacrifice my tiny food budget for buying business cards, flyers and banners to help promote my round Britain row.

The next 12 months were filled with fundraising and were painful but at least I had a focus. I had something to wake up for and keep me motivated. And I felt excited.

2017 - 35 years old

In the summer of 2017, I stepped on an ocean rowing boat with 3 strangers to row around the whole country together. I'd had just 3 training trips in an ocean rowing boat and I was about to tackle to entire country!

Since my trip to Denmark on the ferry as a child, I'd worked as a beauty therapist on a Disney Cruise ship big enough for 2,500 people. It wasn't quite the ocean experience that would set me up for this enormous challenge.

I'd met the other 3 people just a handful of times. We were 4 completely different people from 4 different walks of life!

Above anything, this was going to be a social experiment as much as a physical challenge.

As we pushed ourselves off from the pontoon, I wondered what on earth I was doing. I didn't particularly like rowing and I was now on this tiny boat with 3 strangers. The fundraising for the row had completely rinsed my energy and I felt knackered. I hadn't been sleeping well and hadn't been eating enough for ages. How on earth was I going to row for 2 months?

Our boat was 8.5m long by 1.5m wide. It was a tiny space for 4 people.

With each 2 hour rowing shift, we began getting to know each other, relaxing into our routines and feeling at one in our new and unique environment.

We had the time of our life!

At no point did any of us feel claustrophobic. We'd sit on the deck of our small boat and have the whole world right at our fingertips.

The stresses of the modern world had now faded and I was doing what I enjoyed. I was outside in the fresh air, riding the waves Mother Nature threw at us, pushing my physical and mental boundaries and doing what I had worked towards for over a year. I was finally doing something I enjoyed.

I had kind of hoped that rowing around Great Britain would put me off rowing across the Atlantic, but it did quite the opposite.

The team and I spent 56 days at sea together and completing the challenge confirmed my mega dream. To row across the Atlantic.

When I got back from the GB row, the organisers and the same company that builds the ocean rowing boats asked if I wanted to join their team taking care of their social media. This was the biggest and best offer of work I'd had since closing the beauty salon 2.5 years earlier. I jumped at the chance!

A stable place to live and consistent income was still a little iffy, but I felt as though things were starting to go in the right direction. Finance was tight and each day was a struggle. I wondered if I'd ever make the kind of money I used to make when I had the salon. The instability of the last few years had worn me down and really knocked my confidence.

A few months into starting my job, I was flown out to the Canary Islands to work at the start of the Talisker Whisky Atlantic Challenge, the exact challenge I had almost entered 2.5 years previously with 3 Men & A Little Lady.

There I stood waving 25 teams off as they left to row 3,000 miles across the Atlantic ocean. The whole experience was incredible… but I was sick with envy. My stomach was in physical knots because I was so jealous of those setting off on a journey of a lifetime. I wanted that to be me!

So when I got back to the UK, I decided enough was enough. I couldn't hold on to this dream any longer and I had to make it a reality. So I did only what I knew how… I made a video telling the world I wanted to row across the Atlantic and posted it on social media. I had no idea how I was going to do it or if the video would work but I knew I needed to make it happen somehow.

A few months passed and the video faded into the background a bit. My social media career had picked up and I had found a rhythm and passion for work again. Maybe this new focus would take away the desire to want to row across the Atlantic?

Then an email landed in my inbox after a night of cider. It was from a team of 3 strong women who were signed up to the Talisker Whisky Atlantic Challenge and they were looking for a fourth member. They asked if I wanted to join them.

It almost didn't feel real! Maybe I'd drunk too many ciders and had read it wrong?

I re-read the email the next morning and indeed they had invited me to join them. Could this be the chance for me to fulfil my dream?

I'll give you 3 guess what my answers was.....

*

A few weekend training rows off the Exmouth coast and 8 months later, we stepped off land and on to our boat, the same model of boat I rowed round Great Britain. This time it felt smaller because it was jam-packed full of supplies for the entire journey.

We wouldn't see land or any other humans for 6 weeks or more. I was excited about how this would feel, but also there was a terror I had buried deep inside of me about spending all that time on a boat with 3 people I didn't know very well. It wasn't like rowing around Great Britain where we stopped once a week for supplies on land. On that trip we got a little respite from each other, despite adoring each other's company. This time we were restricted to a tiny boat with nowhere to hide until we got to the Caribbean, 3,000 miles away!

There was no point in thinking about that at that stage, so I buried the feeling again.

We took our first oar stroke and that was it. After 3.5 years I was finally doing it!

There was all of the emotions at the start; nerves, excitement, elation and fear but they disappeared within 30 minutes of leaving the Spanish island. I was on the sea again on a tiny ocean rowing boat. It was the place where I felt the happiest.

People ask me if the Atlantic challenge was hard. Of course it was. We rowed in 2 hour shifts, non-stop through the day and night. 2 hours on and 2 hours off. In our off shift, we would need to take care of ourselves, our nutrition, hydration, the boat and navigation, leaving on average 1 hour 20 minutes to sleep.

One day we rowed for 9 hours non-stop to fight the headwind, with 6 hours of that with our left oar only!

We pooed in a bucket and watched our teammates do the same.

We ate dehydrated rations packs every day for 6 weeks, which made our guts ache.

Our bums were chafed, our hands were blistered and our joints swollen. One day we counted our steps and we only took 25 in a day!

But no matter how hard it was, I always felt grateful for where I was, the place I'd chosen to be, surrounded by Mother Nature and the ocean.

Ocean rowing makes my body tired and yet the ocean makes my brain feel so full and healthy.

There's something incredibly special about being at sea. I have the whole world right there! Sitting on my rowing boat I feel connected to the Earth, like there's a physical connection between me and the centre of the world. And it fills me up and makes me feel human.

There's something inside me that comes alive when I'm out there. The exact same thing that was missing when I owned my beauty salon.

*

So then, there I am, bobbing around in the middle of the Atlantic, thinking about my journey.

I realise living in my van had taught me resilience. The resilience I needed to complete this challenge.

I think back to how I used to be; the makeup, designer dresses and owning so much stuff. I think back to the pair of trainers and the bridge, the boyfriend who told me I couldn't it and the way life had unravelled over the last few years. And then I realise... I can do anything I put my mind to.

After 43 days, 2 hour and 20 minutes, the team and I crossed the finish line in Antigua.

We had completed the challenge but also won the female race category!

I'd love to tell you how it felt rowing over the finish line and into Antigua, but I can't. Words cannot describe how incredible and overwhelming the experience was.

All I can tell you is that it makes my heart beat fast just thinking about it and typing these words now.

I know I want that feeing again!

*

I suppose, after telling you all that, you may be wondering what's next?

From a girl that was only introduced to adventure aged 30 and introduced to the ocean aged 35, as a result of rowing across the Atlantic, I have been invited to row across the Pacific ocean, 2,400 miles from San Francisco to Hawaii.

Despite the route being shorter than the Atlantic, the weather and sea states are renowned for being a little less unforgiving.

Even though I know it's going to be my toughest challenge to date, I'm sure I'm going to have the best time because being on the ocean is where I am the happiest. And who knows what might happen as a result of me saying yes.

Website: LauraTry.com

Instagram: @LauraTryUK

Facebook: @LauraTryUK

Twitter: @LauraTryUK

LinkedIn: Laura Try

Chapter 13

Camino Steps

by Liz Dickinson

It was the Summer of 1984. Frankie Goes to Hollywood's 'Two Tribes' dominated the UK music charts for the Summer, the Miners' Strikes had started in earnest a few months earlier and national unemployment levels were at a record high. Perhaps in a bid to escape those austere times, my mum bought a second-hand Commer campervan and announced that we would be driving across Europe during the school summer holidays. I was eleven and was wondering why we couldn't just nip up to Skegness for the week rather than disappear off to the continental mainland.

Our Commer: home for the Summer, was stuffed with bedding, clothing and my reading library. For some unfathomable reason, I thought being a passenger would allow me to indulge in a spot of reading. It turned out that I would soon become the unlikely heroine of this fated road trip.

We traversed Europe in a south-easterly direction, and slowly the landscape started to unfold: in Provence, my fingers traced the symmetrical rows of lavender fields, disappearing to the horizon. I had only ever seen those shades of purple with bluish hues in art classes whilst experimenting with paint mixing. The Swiss Alps revealed rolling greenery, huge mountains with snow still on the peak. I was struggling to understand why there was still snow in July. Europe was already proving to be a rolling flora, fauna and meteorological education.

Travelling through Yugoslavia was full of contradictions: a volatile inflation rate, where petrol prices would spiral overnight, with a backdrop of that Adriatic coastline: brimming with concealed beaches, tiny islands and medieval towns. One afternoon, a kind family opened up their home in the middle of a picturesque mountain-range and invited us in for refreshments. Perhaps we invoked curiosity or pity; this English ensemble huddled together in a second-rate campervan, roaming through this soon-to-be war-ravaged country.

Our destination was Turkey: Istanbul, city of exquisite Mosques. We stopped at a petrol station 10 miles from the Greek/Turkish border. Suddenly, black smoke unfurled out of the engine, then thicker smoke and eventually an inferno.

Our cosy Commer was on fire at a petrol station.

The local fire brigade just happened to be passing and put out the flames. Once the shock had sunk in, my mum was on the phone to our insurance company arranging to repatriate our beloved, now severely burnt-out, van back to the UK. We gathered our belongings into pillow cases and stood like grieving mourners, lamenting the loss of our deceased Commer.

"We'll just have to head back to the UK. We can get a bus," my mum whispered forlornly.

"But Istanbul?" I wailed incredulously. "We've come all this way. We can't go home now. I want to see Turkey."

In my head I envisaged Istanbul as an Aladdin-inspired city, full of Arabian delights, flying carpets, exotic spices in markets and belly dancers.

Miraculously my mum came round to my way of thinking and we boarded a bus to Turkey.

The city of Istanbul was beautiful; the blue Ottoman Mosque with its unique six minarets and breath-taking interior, carved blue marble and handmade ceramic tiles. Whilst tourists marvelled at the 260 windows inside, I was shocked by the scale of homelessness on the streets. Aged 11, my eyes opened to poverty, never before seen in my own country or the previous European villages and towns.

When it was time to return home, we boarded a bus to Germany with our belongings still in pillowcases. We were in good company though as the other Turkish passengers, possibly economic migrants, also embarked with pillowcases and a couple of chickens in tow.

The bus journey took us north-westwards to Germany, then homeward bound. We sat with our Turkish counterparts, blending in with our pillowcases; we were temporarily displaced but they were now becoming permanently displaced from their home country.

That European adventure always stayed with me and when in 2001, I found myself working as an ESOL (English for Speakers of Other Languages) teacher at a Midlands FE college in the UK, my wanderlust had resurfaced. I needed a new adventure.

My students were refugees and asylum seekers from Iran/Iraq, Afghanistan and Somalia. Perhaps they too had arrived in the UK with pillowcases, weary-eyed, frightened of their homeland and needing sanctuary. Predominately male, ranging from fifteen to thirty years old, they had hollow expressions, haunted by horrors too unspeakable to imagine: it was like teaching a room of ghosts.

With due diligence and dedication to my profession, I did the only thing I knew how to do: teach. The basic ESOL classes started with the English alphabet but that presumed a level of prior learning in their mother tongues. The majority of these men could not read or write in their native languages, Farsi or Somali, let alone decipher the alien letters I was presenting them with. They wanted to work; earning a living was the only language they understood.

Periodically one or two students would simply "disappear". They had been dispersed by the Home Office to other cities with immediate effect. This added to a climate of fear. It was difficult to put down roots when, at any given moment, you could be transplanted into a new city overnight.

In the summer of 2001, I decided I wanted to fundraise and we had a designated bursary fund at the college for these students. Circulating my sponsorship form, I asked staff, family and friends to sponsor me per mile for a 60-mile hike across a section of 'El Camino Santiago', a medieval pilgrimage route across the north of Spain.

Though I wouldn't describe myself as a veteran hiker, I had walked 'The West Highland Way' twice previously and, despite the inevitable blisters and midge bites, I had thoroughly enjoyed hiking. I dug out my faithful, battered backpack and treated myself to a new pair of boots.

The difference was that I was doing this alone and in the middle of July in Spain, not in a Scottish spring.

Day One: Pamplona to Puente la Reina

I arrived in Pamplona with a backpack, not a pillowcase on this occasion, and armed with my trusty map. I didn't immediately feel like a pilgrim, (in Spanish: 'peregrino/peregrina) and with hindsight, I was relieved that I had narrowly missed the 'Encierro', the annual running of the bulls. I had lived in Madrid for a year previously and politely declined any invitations to bull-fights. The literary work of Cervantes, flamenco dancing and the enduring legacy of General

Franco was the Spain I was fascinated with. And tapas, naturally.

Leaving the *refugio* (pilgrim refuge) early after breakfast, the temperature was cooler, conducive to some steady walking. I wanted to avoid the predicted heatwave later that day. I needed to walk 18.5 miles and was focused on my destination. With my trusty, slightly battered walking boots and ancient backpack, I started my maiden voyage of El Camino de Santiago.

Although the Camino was well populated with walkers dotted in the distance, there was a deafening silence. I had never hiked alone before. I felt vulnerable. There was an overwhelming fragility in my solitude.

The sun was beginning to heat up and my fears of walking in a heatwave returned. I needed to keep moving otherwise the midday sun might cause instant dehydration, my body would roll into the shadow of a pine tree and then griffon vultures would snack on me for lunch.

A new fear of hungry griffon vultures forced my temporary loneliness to subside. I focused on my map, the scallop signs pointing the way and prepared myself for the ascent of Alto del Perdón: a 734 metre- mount with a promising view.

The view of Navarra was jaw-droppingly panoramic. I had only shuffled 7 miles from Pamplona but I didn't care, this was *my* first Peregrina view. In the distance, the triangular summits of the Pyrenees looked like the jagged spine of a long-lost Moors-land dragon, now residing on the Spanish frontier.

At the summit was a steel sculpture depicting twelve pilgrims beginning in the middle ages and continuing up to the modern day. The steel silhouettes shimmered in the midday sun, offering a history of the Camino in the form of beautiful artwork. I studied each pilgrim in turn: the first symbolised the beginning of the Pilgrimage, the next group of three showed the rising popularity of the Camino, then came merchants and tradesmen forcing their wares onto pilgrims. Next, a solitary figure symbolised a slowing-down of the pilgrimage on the grounds of social and civil wars from the mid-fourteenth century until mid-twentieth century and then lastly, two modern-day figures, showed a revived interest in the Camino in the latter part of the twentieth-century.

The solitary figure resonated with me but I had social and political freedom and I was here initially to help those in my classroom who had lost theirs. My perspective sharpened again. There is something truly uplifting about a collective pilgrimage, sharing a walk with complete strangers from across the globe. These Roman roads and stone pebbly paths had felt the sheer weight of history. Pilgrims had been walking, marching, staggering along this path for centuries, in some cases following the journey from east to west by charting the Milky Way. There is an inscription on the sculpture, '*Donde se cruza el camino del viento con al de las estrellas,*' (Where the path of the wind crosses the stars.)

On this Mount of Forgiveness, the wind whistled and whirled and below eco-farms of wind turbines now capitalised on mother nature's gift. The Camino follows the Milky Way: our galaxy containing a couple of hundred billion stars, including the Sun. I love the idea of the sky reflecting the earth; all those stars, gas and dust, held together by gravity, running parallel to this medieval, earthly pilgrimage. It already made me feel closer to this vast galaxy.

Descending this majestic mount, the wild pines stood to attention like evergreen giants, their musky, cinnamon scent wafting earthward. It was captivating. When we had hurtled across Europe in our Commer campervan, I had seen the French lavender fields and Swiss Alps from my windows but standing here, inhaling the pine, gave me an immediate lesson in mindfulness. We need to make time to smell the pine trees, to stand still, enjoy the moment and not worry about where we're going or where we've come from.

I had until now felt like a fraudster: a tourist pilgrim, sampling the

Camino for four days, rather than five weeks. In medieval times, pilgrims would walk from all over Europe into Spain, over the Pyrenees and then follow the holy, 500-mile pilgrimage to the Cathedral of Santiago de Compostela. There is a Spanish expression in my guidebook, *"El Camino de Santiago se hace por etapas,"* (The Camino Santiago is done by stages.) This was my Camino and I was walking a small stage.

That night in Puente la Reina, as I crawled wearily into my *refugio* bed, I reflected on the first day of my maiden Camino voyage. Whenever travellers and adventurers mention their unique epiphanies - that moment when they were staring at a clear night on a mountain side or in a desert, and felt their true personal significance or insignificance in the universe - it can feel at best clichéd or worst self-indulgent.

I was proud that I had walked alone for 18.5 miles, despite my fears of the heatwave, an attack by griffon vultures and a brief interlude with loneliness. The Navarra wild pines had lifted my spirit and taught me to commune with nature, savouring the moment, not simply obsessively race ahead to my walking destination.

Day Two: Puente la Reina to Estella

The next morning, my right ankle was throbbing. A blister had crept in during yesterday's walk but I hadn't noticed due to the distracting view of a Moors-land dragon on top of Alto del Perdón and that lingering, musky, cinnamon scent from the wild pine trees. My right foot was my dominant foot so I would be walking at a slower pace than yesterday, in a left-footed manner. A hearty Spanish breakfast and excited, anticipatory chattering from other pilgrims soothed my soul.

I set off towards Estella, determined that my blister wouldn't dampen my spirit too much. The wild pine trees lined up to commiserate with me, bowing as I hobbled past. The Navarra flora brigade had also come out to greet me: nestled in amongst the wild pines were an array of colourful flowers, from the Bermuda Buttercup, a bright yellow flower with shamrock patterned leaves to Onion Weed, a delicate white star-shaped flower.

The advantage of having a blister and walking alone is that I didn't have to feel guilty about walking a faster pace: I could meander, saunter or zigzag as slowly as I wanted.

My tiny physical impairment lead to some further emotional self-rumination: pilgrimages are supposed to be spiritual, a furthering of one's spiritual plane, an elevation of consciousness, perhaps an act of penance but essentially to benefit your spiritual health. Though admirable to be raising money for such a good cause, maybe I should really be checking into my own spiritual awareness.

Though I was perhaps paying penance with my blister for a past wrongdoing, it was difficult to be celestial when I had brought so much earthly baggage on the Camino. My heart was broken; held together by string and double-sided Sellotape. When a recent relationship ended, I moved to Madrid, thinking the distance between us would help me move on. Everything reminded me of him: the lovers kissing in Puerta del Sol, the flirting in Salamanca bars and tenderness in El Retiro Park.

Now, desolate and alone on the path to Estella, I started to feel helpless and lost. The vast open Navarra space was forcing me to confront my deeply buried feelings, which I could no longer run away from. I missed him. I realised I was grieving for my lost relationship.

The continuing, searing July heat on my second day was a challenging variable, alongside my burgeoning blister and backpack weighed down by grief. My first instinct was to react like a child on a long car journey, "Are we there yet?" Exhausted and grumpy, I inspected every numbered signpost, sighing inwardly at the day's remaining kilometres. Plodding onwards, I cursed the sun, the pine trees and the wheat fields which faded to the horizon. My Camino felt like a huge self-induced penance. That plucky eleven-year old who had persuaded her family to travel to Turkey had momentarily disappeared.

Stumbling down the dusty track, avoiding eye contact with other pilgrims, I almost missed them. A voice called over, "You ok? You look tired. Come and rest a while." Three pilgrims lounged at the side of the path, picnicking in the shade of the trees. A woman with cropped hair, a man with a baseball cap and a younger man with a mass of curly hair were cosily serenading me. The man took off his baseball cap and patted the ground next to him. Obeying, silently I joined these three amigos for the rest of lunch.

Three became four and we walked together for the rest of the day; my brooding, grieving clouds lifting, as the conversations deepened and we became acquainted. Agnes was a German Steiner School teacher, here for the summer to complete the whole pilgrimage. Alessandro was Italian-American, also walking the whole Camino and seemingly, fugitively on the run from the IRS. Josh was an English university student and needed respite from his academic studies.

They applauded my altruistic fundraising, whilst perhaps sensing a quieter, more emotionally therapeutic reason for my Camino. My focus sharpened again; the pine trees and wheat fields offered calming background scenery. By the end of the day, we had become firm acquaintances and once we had checked in to the same Estella *refugio*, we agreed to meet for dinner that evening.

That night in another squeaky bunk bed, I counted my blessings. I thought about those migrants with their pillowcases on our bus from Turkey to Germany, looking for a better life. Crossing frontiers, they journeyed thousands of miles from home, from that exquisite Blue Mosque to the pristine streets of Munich for a better way of being: an education for their children and medicine for their sick relatives. I remembered the faces of my refugee students: haunted by PTSD, childhoods lost in village warfare, identities stolen by tyrants.

Walking two days though Navarra in a July heatwave, grieving with a broken heart and a single blister was bearable. It wasn't life-threatening. My students had fled persecution by brutish tyrants and had travelled half-way round the world to find sanctuary in a country that tried its best to welcome them.

Nestled into my pilgrim cotton sheets, I dreamt, perhaps not surprisingly of General Franco.

Day Three: Estella to Los Arcos

I was no stranger to General Franco; whilst teaching English in Madrid two years previously, I had seen first-hand his legacy; a continued cultural language embargo on foreign films. More than three-quarters of the foreign films in Madrid cinemas were dubbed into Spanish, harking back to Franco's ban on all languages apart from Castilian during his dictatorship.

During the Spanish Civil War (1936-1939,) he had called upon the Apostle James (Saint James the Greater,) for support during the Battle of Brunete (1937) against the opposing Republicans. After his victory in battle, the Ministry of Tourism promoted the Camino to Spaniards and General Franco made offerings to Saint James at his shrine at the Santiago de Compostela Cathedral.

Interestingly, Saint James is the patron saint of Spain, the military patron of Spain and the Saint of Pilgrims.

Over half of my Spanish students were indifferent to learning English, preferring to routinely skip my lessons in favour of watching Real Madrid play football. There would be regular mutinies in class with the ubiquitous, contemptuous remark, "*no quiero hablar ingles,*" (I don't want to speak English) which invariably led to, "*¿porque no hablas español?*" (why don't you speak

Spanish?)

There was one exception. A small class of highly educated, professional Spaniards who spoke advanced English. They were overly keen to tell me their own family involvement with General Franco, at any given opportunity. This class facilitated their own learning, invariably setting the tone for each lesson, often resulting in huge intellectual philosophical discussions. Spontaneously a few students wrote epic family biographies, detailing atrocities and bravery, both on the Republican (anti-Franco) and Nationalist (pro-Franco) sides. The writing project snowballed and soon every student had written about their family involvement in the Spanish Civil War.

These were no longer English lessons.

It was therapy: collective catharsis.

Though 'The Valley of the Fallen', the memorial site which holds 34,000 bodies including General Franco's was in Madrid almost 300 miles from Estella, the ghosts of the Spanish Civil War had also started accompanying my Camino.

Some bodies had never been recovered: left hidden in woods or deep ravines, victims of The Falange death squad, over all Spain. Federico Garcia Lorca, the Spanish playwright and poet wrote, "In Spain, the dead are more alive than the dead of any other country in the world." He was shot by Nationalists, loyal to Franco and allegedly buried beside an olive tree.

Walking through the quiet morning streets of Estella, I noticed a lone olive tree in a garden. I stopped for a moment next to it, bowed my head and said a prayer for Federico Garcia Lorca: Andalusian literary trailblazer.

It was becoming increasingly commonplace for me to oscillate between deep musings about my sad love life and the plight of my refugee students; between a new contemplation on the Spanish

Civil War and more everyday concerns like food, sweltering heat, shelter and the direction of travel.

My stream of consciousness literally had two gears – profound or pragmatic.

I realised, and certainly not for the first time, that I was lost.

Not a little bit lost but adrift and disorientated.

Estella is a remarkably beautiful town, bestowed with medieval architecture worthy of architectural heritage. This means, however, that the streets have no right angles or defined street corners. I was becoming dizzy from walking in circles.

The locals found it amusing; watching myself and other unsuspecting pilgrims struggling with this labyrinthine architecture, commenting helpfully, *"Vale la pena!"* (It's worthwhile).

It was certainly déjà-vu but felt more frustratingly unnecessary than worthwhile.

The most immediate challenge was finding and following the Camino symbol: the yellow scallop with a blue background, often haphazardly located on a wall, obscured by a lamppost or other stationary landmark. Sometimes the scallop just mysteriously disappeared completely, like this morning.

It was like some extended metaphor for life: it would be nice to have a roadmap from birth and, throughout our lives, have constant guidance and instructions but we don't. We often feel lost, wander off, retrace our steps, start again and sometimes take the plunge. Learning to live with uncertainty is one of the best things we can do. It builds resilience.

However, as I was unfamiliar with the landscape and towns of Navarra, I had no sense of direction and made an educated guess about my pilgrimage route out of Estella.

It was at this moment, when I'd lost my way for the tenth time, that something lovely happened. A pilgrim with a camcorder noticed I was lost and came over to talk to me. He was a Hungarian documentary film-maker and he was interested in why people travelled from all over the globe to walk El Camino. We started chatting and he walked with me for a while until silently, we both knew it was time to part.

He re-joined his group and I carried on alone. There is something about hiking in beautiful scenery that is conducive to increased social interaction, often with complete strangers. It is not just increased conversations that are interesting but the quality of these exchanges.

At a bus stop in a town or city, we might discuss the weather or the expected arrival of the next bus but we are unlikely to ask a complete stranger about their spirituality or thoughts on pilgrimages. The surrounding skyscrapers inhibit our innate curiosity and dampen our conversational bravery.

Something magical happened in these Camino paths; normal small talk is bypassed and we got down to the nitty gritty in a matter of minutes. Everyone was walking the Camino for different reasons and it was not taboo to ask why. The interesting bit was that most people would also freely share with you their motivations.

The terrain had changed to low scrub and olive trees: evergreen trees with long roots that could withstand high temperatures and droughts. The midday sun was oppressive: a relentless, searing, airless heat that slowed down the moving line of pilgrims. An aerial lens would show our plodding in unison, our backpacks and nationalities indistinguishable; only the scorched earth and green dots of olive trees visible through the torrid heatwaves.

There was a welcome respite at the Monastery of Irache, near the town of Ayegui, which has a fountain on the winery walls. Pilgrims were encouraged to help themselves to a free glass of red wine or water.

Though habitually a red wine drinker, my hydration levels were rapidly waning, so I opted for the water. The majority of the other pilgrims gleefully drank the wine.

Shaded under the olive trees, sat my three comrades from the previous day, triumphantly sipping the red wine. Incredulous at my choice of beverage, they nonetheless still greeted me like a long-lost friend. We compared blister horror stories and later, our love of olive trees and a respected culinary appreciation of Mediterranean dishes with signature olives.

Joining my pilgrim comrades under the olive trees, noticing the green, silver oblong leaves of the branches, I thought about their longevity. Olive trees are amongst the oldest, cultivated trees in the world, with an average lifespan of five hundred years. Originally farmed in the Roman Times along the Iberian Peninsula, these trees have been harvested for thousands of years.

Over several lifespans, these trees have witnessed the Moors invasion, the Reconquista, the Spanish Inquisition, the Spanish Armada, World War I, The Spanish Civil War, World War II, the death of General Franco and more recently the 2004 terrorist bombing.

These trees with their twenty-metre height have seen encroaching armies, with bombastic generals, militant cavalry and the taste of victory and defeat.

These trees, with their extensive roots, reaching six metres deep and twelve metres wide, have felt the blood shed over centuries staining the earth.

Through droughts and floods, these trees have endured, witnessing countless genocides, their canopies lamenting the dead.

Quietly contemplating the futility of war, realising that landscapes though serene with evergreens and wild flowers have witnessed barbaric savagery, I followed my trusted pilgrims to Los Arcos, weary from the weight of history.

Later that evening, the Hungarian film-maker was in our restaurant, greeting me like an old friend and everyone sat together. We enjoyed *La Comida* in an almost carnival atmosphere, our collective endorphins celebrating our small achievement: walking and surviving in that blistering heat!

That night in my ubiquitous squeaky bunk bed, I reflected on the day's walking and lessons learnt. Perspectives and priorities shift depending on our circumstances. Whether we need sanctuary - economic or political - we gravitate towards what we need to survive before we can thrive. The Camino was starting to humble me once more. That blinding sun during today would be bearable tomorrow. I had chosen to be here, on this pilgrimage. In a few days, I would go home to my country that wasn't at war with a roof over my head, a job and a family that loved me. I was one of the lucky ones.

Day Four: Los Arcos to Logroño

In the morning, I took my pilgrim passport out of my backpack and smoothed the creases. To escape the heat, I needed to start walking before sunrise by torchlight. I wasn't the only one. Other pilgrims led the procession, their torches dancing like fireflies and as the sun rose over this medieval hinterland. My backpack felt as light as a pillowcase.

Walking away from Navarra into La Rioja, the terrain was changing again, we were entering wine-growing territory. This is where the wet and cold Northern Atlanta climate meets the hot and arid Southern Mediterranean climate. It was like crossing a frontier.

During this Camino, I had crossed immeasurable physical and emotional frontiers and, poignantly today, I had stopped measuring the Camino in terms of kilometres walked but in new friendships gained and kindness offered.

I never saw my three new amigos again. These were the days before social media and global interconnectedness. But we had connected at that point in time for a reason and I will always be grateful to them. They had helped superglue my battered, broken heart back together again.

Epilogue:

Returning to teaching refugees, it no longer felt as if I was teaching ghosts.

I had returned from my maiden voyage of El Camino de Santiago: a journey of Camino steps. The entire Camino is five-hundred miles, ending at The Santiago de Compostela Cathedral but there is an extension pilgrimage to Finisterre, a rock-based peninsula, on the west coast of Galicia. The Romans believed it was the end of the known world.

Walking sixty miles in four days and crossing the frontier from Navarra to La Rioja, I had been walking in the direction of the end of the known world.

It felt like Holy ground. This medieval pilgrimage is indeed tantamount to a spiritual awakening. Though I had not returned from a war, my soul felt as if it had just time-travelled through centuries of Spanish invasion and civil war. I had felt the ancestral bloodlines lying in the roots of those ancient olive trees.

I looked in the eyes of my students: I could see their villages burning. The funerals of their loved ones. The extinguishing of their old life.

Though I could never fully understand their traumas, see their nightmares, I could offer them the start of a new life, in a new country.

To cross the frontier, they needed to learn a new language.

We opened the window, let the autumnal light in and revealed the twenty-six letters of the alphabet on the board. Each cursive stroke illustrated hope for a new language and life to accompany it.

That plucky eleven-year old with the pillowcase was back.

Email: hills_liz@hotmail.com

Blog: dandelionmusings942967929.blog

Blog: typewritermum.blog

Chapter 14

From Outdoor to Insights

by Maren Frank

Imagine you are lying in a small one-person tunnel tent. You can see the first light of day seep through the dark green material surrounding you. Wearing two layers of warm clothes you are lying inside your sleeping bag feeling cosy, warm and comfy. The wind is blowing over the land. The tent is swaying with the heavy gusts. You hear the wind. You hear the ocean close by. It sounds wild, powerful. You are all alone and you are at peace. This was my first experience with nature quests.

Nature quest? What is that, you might ask yourself. Trust me it sounds more dramatic than it is.

I first had heard of nature quests at Yestival 2016. On that fateful Sunday morning, in a sunny field in the south of England, surrounded by hundreds of Yes-sayers I had followed the small voice inside and said yes to an invitation to go to Iceland, to go on a nature quest. Three months later I found myself surrounded by a small group ready to embark on a new adventure.

In the days before our nature quest we learned the following about nature quests. They have been brought to us from indigenous culture, where they are referred to as vision quests. In these traditions people go alone into the wild for various reasons (for example rites of passage or finding answers). They immerse themselves deeply into nature by staying in one place for a set amount of time. The tribe supports them by helping them prepare, by listening to their stories once they return and by making sense of those stories.

In a way a nature quest is a solo-campout where you decide to spend a defined amount of time in nature. To really immerse yourself into nature you spend all that time in the spot you chose when setting up camp.

In our case we had chosen our spot the day before we went on the quest. Together as a group we had prepared our nature quest by setting intentions and sharing stories.

Coming back to the group afterwards I described my experience as that of being reborn. Lying in that tent felt like being in a womb of some kind. I felt warm, safe, and at peace. At the same time the world seemed to be chaotic and powerful around me. Another picture that came to mind was that of a drop of water in the deep ocean. No matter how much the waves rise and fall on the surface, down there it is all still. I remembered having had similar experiences as a child. But this was the first time I'd felt such tranquillity since the busyness of my everyday working life had taken hold.

I was hooked. I wanted more. And so, I announced to the group that I was going to go on one twenty-four-hour nature quest each month for the whole year. I believed it was possible. It would be doable with my fulltime job and all the other stuff that I called my life.

It was decided, I was going to spend twelve of my three hundred and sixty-five days that year on my own in nature.

I have travelled a fair bit in my lifetime. I've also moved places, jobs, and relationships more often than most people I know. Early on I realised that the thing that always stayed was *me*. No matter how far I travelled, no matter where I lived, what I did or who I dated, *I* was the constant factor that was always there. Having consequently spent a fair amount of time in the world of self-discovery, self-help, and personal development, I knew one thing for sure: you cannot outrun, outwit or outsmart yourself. Instead, I tried to come to terms with myself and was disheartened by the same stuff coming up over and over again. In a way my choosing to do nature quests meant doing the one thing that I hadn't done so far: stop, be silent and listen.

My next three nature quests made it very clear to me why I probably hadn't gone down this route before.

Have you ever tried to follow your own thoughts? Or have you ever tried to be aware of all the thoughts you think in one day? Even more interestingly have you ever questioned what you are thinking day-in and day-out?

I thought I was pretty self-aware. I believed I knew my thoughts well enough. As it turned out, I didn't.

Spending twenty-four hours surrounded by ankle deep snow at a frozen lake, I had plenty of time to realise that the flow of my thoughts never stopped, never shut up and wasn't all that helpful. Instead of enjoying the stunning beauty around me, being at peace or even just relaxing a bit, my mind was constantly occupied with solving problems. Problems of any kind, small and big, my own, friends', the world's.

And when there seemed to be no more problems to ponder, my mind either started anew or came up with new ones. For example, have you ever considered how much pressure your bodyweight would need to create to form a solid block of ice from the snow below your tent? No? I hadn't either, until this random day in February. My mind considered how fast ice was growing downwards into the lake, and how temperature and growth were correlated. I also pondered how much snow my tent canvas would be able to carry before ripping. (If you hadn't figured out by now, I once studied engineering. I hope this information will relieve you of the burden of figuring out who on this planet would spend their time unconsciously thinking up these random mathematical questions).

Of course, there were other questions as well. Questions about why I was feeling stuck in my job, the job that I had started only a few months earlier and that (as every other job so far) had at the beginning seemed like 'the' job, the one I could finally stick with. My thoughts went in circles around my relationship. It was fine. We had a great house, an amazing garden and we shared dinner and a bed. Who was I to ask for more than that? That's how it worked, right? And people around me seemed to be quite happy with it, so why couldn't I just be at least content as well?

In the end, I was kind of glad the time had passed. I packed my gear and walked back through the snow and ice. The relaxing and peaceful effect of the first nature quest hadn't come. Instead I had become very intimately acquainted with my own thought carrousel.

*

March brought rain, so instead of the icy stillness I had a constant droplet orchestra. It helped a little. In between the whirlwind of my thought carrousel I managed to drop into simply listening to the magic of the multitudes of sounds rain creates in the natural world. Drops hitting different kinds of leaves, branches, the ground, my tent, the surface of nearby puddles, all mixed in with the sounds of birds and the wind. It felt good to listen. To stop worrying.

My aunt, my mum's youngest sister, had just come out of a major brain tumour operation and had decided in favour of chemo. I was trying my best to hold space for my mum, as she was doing the same for her parents and siblings. We both had advised against the chemo at this point in time. We had been there before. Eighteen years before. My grief was coming of age. I smiled while drying away some tears. My dad had taken the chemo, he wanted life, and we hadn't known better. This time we knew better. We knew that even though she believed to be choosing life she had probably, inadvertently chosen death. I felt sick to my stomach.

I focused on my breathing. I listened to the rain and the wind. By now I knew that I would be back to pondering just moments later. Still, these little islands of stillness, helped me, gave me the strength I was looking for to deal with the next round of merry-go-round in my never-ending carrousel ride of thoughts.

*

The temperature had risen for April and was now in the low positives. As it was dry as well, I decided to take the hammock. My first hammock campout.

I longed for the night, for the cool air around me, the stillness. It seemed so appropriate. My aunt had died earlier in the month. Her body had been too weak to survive the chemo. After all the hustle and bustle of the burial and family affairs, this was exactly what I wanted: to be alone.

I had chosen the day of my dad's death for this particular nature quest. It happened to be a Saturday and it seemed fitting. I wondered what he would be like now eighteen years later. I wondered how my cousins would feel in eighteen years about the death of their parent.

Death had taught me so much. At the same time, it had cost me so much. I had learned about the power of gratitude. The one healing balm that helped me grow through grief, loss and change. And I was grateful that death had taught me that I only have this one life, happening right now, in this moment.

Life doesn't wait till the weekend for you to come around. It's not at all like a book or a movie that waits to be experienced whenever you think you have time. Life is now. It is a full contact sport. You'll get taken down, slammed in the guts and bruised a lot (at least when you have my disposition to bruising). At the same time life is like dancing. It's moving with the flow, twirling to your own melody, rocking your own theme tune.

For me the lesson had been clear: dive into life. Fully immerse yourself. That's what I did going forward. I was full on. Always searching, striving, moving. And still, below all of my achievements, below the glossy cover of my CV, I felt I was missing something, something that I had lost when gaining my lesson learned from death. As if I were a toddler who wasn't yet able to hold more than one thing in their hands. Putting down something that I held close to pick up something that had just caught my eye. I knew what I had put down at my dad's grave: my trust in life.

How could I trust it? It'd just taken one of the most important people out of my life for no good reason. There was no fairness, no second chances. Why should I trust life? As I couldn't find a good answer, I didn't.

By now I had plenty of experience of how exhausting this could be. If you are in charge all the time and have to figure out everything by yourself, solve all the problems and make the right choices for your life, it is completely draining. It's simply impossible. There is only so much you can do in this vast and chaotic universe in which your life unfolds. The rest is up to chance or fate or whatever force you might believe in.

The night was cold and starry. I stared up at the fading grey of the trees against the black sky as I lay suspended between two trees in my hammock. The hammock being the last gift I received from my uncle / great-great cousin / ancillary dad before he died. Another death. Another lesson learned. I felt lonely and at the same time like I was in good company; the company of people passed.

A lump was forming in my throat. I choked up and tears were flowing again. So many tears. There didn't seem to be an end to them, yet I knew that at some point they would get less. I had been here before, many times before.

*

The sun was sending its light and warmth through the trees overhead. I stretched, then cuddled back into my sleeping bag, listening to the birds, feeling the warmth of the sun on my face. I felt at peace. Could there be anything more beautiful than waking up to nature on a glorious May day?

The more I listened the more I heard: the little creak a few steps outside my nature quest circle, the bees and other flying insects that filled the air, the woodpecker, the scratching of squirrel paws going up and down the trees, the faint rustle of branches swaying in the wind. It all emanated peacefulness. It seemed to me like I was bathing in the peace of this place.

I just hung there and for the first time in months my thoughts stayed away or, more accurately, they just moved on, flowing in and out like the water in the creek.

I looked out into the forest stretching far in every direction, taking in its beauty. Breathing in the fresh air I closed my eyes and enjoyed the simple smell that always tells me that I am in a forest, tells me that I am home. Opening my eyes again I just stared out into the chaotic array of trees, rows and rows of trees stretching away from me.

That's when it hit me. The forest was always there beyond my little circle of five trees. Just like the peacefulness is always there beyond my merry-go-round thought carrousel. The border isn't just invisible, it's illusionary.

I was there in the middle of the forest playing a game that said I wasn't to go outside that circle of five trees for the next twenty-four hours. But I could. There was no barrier holding me back, no fence, no force, just me and my thoughts. I had come up with the thought that this was the boundary and that's what it was. I could decide differently.

I realised that I could stop playing my own mind games any time. All it took was looking beyond, taking myself / my thoughts less seriously and instead opening up to what was going on.

It felt like I had just fallen out of one world into another. I was looking around in wonder, as if I was seeing everything for the first time. How could I have not seen the beauty of the tall green fir trees surrounding me? How could I have ignored the vibrant shades of greens of the underbrush? How could I have missed the gurgling laughter of the creek, the faint smell of forest earth and blooming meadows or the static of insects all around me? Everything was still the same and at the same time so much more. More vibrant, full of clarity and colour... more alive.

That day I left the forest full of energy. Slipping in and out of thoughts and the world of wonder. I had had many moments of peacefulness of simply being. What a refreshing experience! All those long hours of the other nature quests felt so worth it on that day.

*

Why this weekend? Couldn't they have come any other time?

My period cycle had been everything but regular for the last two months and so it had taken me by surprise on that morning. I wanted to go on my nature quest, at the same time I was having cramps and knew that I was going to be bleeding a lot during the next two days. I grumbled. I weighed my options. I was raging against the unfairness of being born a woman. But I knew that this was it and I had to deal with it.

I started packing my gear. It seemed like I was moving in slow motion. My body wanted me to lie down, to take care of myself not go on a crazy outdoor adventure. Our battle went on for two hours, then I gave in. Instead of going out I hung my hammock in my room (thanking the universe that this was a possibility) and opened the windows wide. I spent twenty-four hours in my room with the occasional visit to the bathroom.

From the outside it might have looked similar and coming out of it I knew I had a choice: pretend that this was the same or acknowledge that this was a nice day of taking care of my body that had no resemblance to actually spending a day out in nature. I opted for the latter and found myself one week later packing up my gear again, this time to go out and experience the wonder of being in and with nature.

*

The summer months seemed to drag on forever. I was going through the motions, trying to be my upbeat self, pretending that the heaviness wasn't there. But it was undeniably there. Every morning it seemed like I had to peel away a slightly heavier blanket. I asked myself why I even bothered getting up. I seemed to be going nowhere.

It wasn't that I didn't like my job. Yes, I felt bored out of my mind most days, but I had amazing colleagues and I loved hanging out with them, chatting with them, supporting them in their projects. Still it didn't seem enough most days.

On top of this I was facing trouble in my relationship. It hadn't been going great for a long time and I had been successfully denying it for as long as I could remember. A good gripe once and again to my closest friend in town seemed to make it bearable for another few months.

Somehow now seemed different. It seemed to me like the weight of the world, my world was pressing down on me. Frantically I tried to keep it all together, the job, the relationship, the house, the money, the social network. The more I hustled, the more it seemed to be slipping away. I knew I was losing this game, but I didn't stop. This is what I knew. Whenever everything seemed to go down the drain, I was the one fighting, tooth and nail. I wasn't going to give up, not if there was the slightest chance of winning.

But what did winning actually mean? What was I fighting for? These were the questions that came up during those days out in nature. It felt good to have a whole day of rest, to not fight, to simply take a step back and gain perspective.

Nature surrounded me in its full summer glory. It was green, lush, full of life. The stark contrast to the lifelessness of what I was fighting for became painfully clear to me in this environment. I was riding a dead horse. Staying with the analogy, I realised that I had loved this horse, that I had wanted to go on adventures with it forever. I was denying its death, not wanting to move on without it. It's so easy to deny death in the height of summer. How can all of this life, all of this vibrant, lush vivacity be gone in just a few months? It seemed so unreal.

But the death wasn't even the daunting part to me. As you might remember, death was something I was good at. I could be there and look at the death of my previous life with gratitude. Gratitude for the experiences and learnings of my job, my relationship and the years spent in this town.

Death wasn't the challenge here. What kept me stuck was my not knowing what was coming next. I was trying to control, plan and create spring. Putting it like this might sound a little crazy, but when looking at our lives it seems to be something we quite like to indulge in as human beings. We are staying in our known relationship, job or surrounding because we don't know what else to do. We believe we first need to figure out what to do next before we can leave what is there right now. Or at least I did believe those things back then.

I therefore spent my summer campouts asking for insight into what to do in the future, not now and here.

To put this into context I usually love spending my time daydreaming about possibilities. I find it fun. My awakening came when I realised that this only holds true when I am either doing it only for fun or I actually act on my dreams. As it turned out, constantly spending my time in a hypothetical future was draining me.

The spinning thought carrousel was back. This time my merry-go-round turned itself around the same possible future scenarios: where I might live, what I might be doing and what I would need to do to be there. Instead of getting better I was getting worse. On top of feeling low about where I was, I piled up pressure to figure out where I needed to be.

Interestingly, it led to me spending more time outdoors, especially at night. I would be lying underneath the stars, waiting for the thoughts to stop spinning, for sleep to take over. Lying there I awed at the vastness of space, the insignificance of my problems and the gift to be allowed to experience this. I was lying still, snuggled from all sides by my sleeping bag, listening to the faint sounds of the night, breathing the cool air, and marvelling at the miracle of being alive. Lying in this space of awe and marvel usually helped to find peace for another night.

*

Autumn came. For me autumn is proof of the beauty in death. It seems to me that only nature can be so accomplished as to make mass mortality look and feel so beautiful. Surrounded by the colours of autumn, the glittering cobwebs in the morning sun, dew dangling from every leaf, lungs filling with the cool and clear air, I saw a celebration of life. A life that is made possible through the continuous cycle of birth and death. Death is beautiful and full of its very own aliveness, nature seemed to whisper. For days on end, I could watch death's dance of golden leaves falling, being whirled around by the wind all the while illuminated by the autumn sun.

And then the rain, the life-bringing force of water, tapering away on my canopy, making the colours all the more vibrant and glowing. I felt at home. Nature seemed to be mirroring what was going on inside of me. Everything was dying, at the same time the core parts were staying alive, preparing for winter and spring. I had opted for the hammock. I wanted to be in contact with this, feeling fully immersed.

We had survived our first family gathering without our aunt. We had made it through not celebrating her birthday. My family had taken to worrying about me. They expressed it differently but the overall concern was apparent. Some worried about my being more detached, others concentrated on finding fault with my new diet.

Over the summer months I had gotten migraine attacks more frequently and with increased severity. My doctors were at a point where they saw only one option: permanent medication. I had been desperate to find an alternative and so I had gone searching. Changing my diet to make it less stressful for my body seemed to be a good first step in my ongoing cycle of living through stress induced inflammatory problems.

I had given up the battle. I couldn't win. Even worse, I was losing every day. My wellbeing was all but gone, my body was sick more days than not and I had more and more days in which I couldn't even pretend to the outside world that things were okay.

I knew that I wanted it to end. I didn't want to die; at the same time I didn't want to go on living life as it was.

This was the time when I came back to Yestival. Spending five days on a field beaten by heavy rains and winds. Spending time at first with the other volunteers and then with hundreds of Yes-sayers and listening to the stories of other people going through dark times helped me immensely. On the festival days I was more myself than I had been in months. I made new friends and re-connected with ones from the year before. I was happy, genuinely happy.

Coming home from this the heavy blanket felt otherworldly. How could it be that just a few hours before I had felt fully alive and now, I felt like I was a walking dead? Something needed to change! Yes, I still had no clue where to go or what to do afterwards but it didn't matter. I had snapped back into the moment of where life actually happens and I knew it was *now* that something needed to change.

For me that was taking myself into the doctors. I owned up to the fact that yes, next to the migraine there had been other things going on and that I was ready, ready to get help. I had been there before, I had tried to solve it myself, leaving jobs and relationships, just to start new ones with the ever-same outcome. I was ready for something else. I was ready to face what was going on, to stop, be and listen instead of running away and starting over somewhere else. This was new and scary.

Sitting in the waiting room of the doctor's office I reminded myself that it was possible. I had been going on these quests for nine months. I had learned to take it one month, one day, one situation, one moment at a time. I could do this. It didn't make it less scary and if I had known the struggle of the months ahead, I might not have gone, but I didn't. I just trusted that this was my best way forward for the moment.

I don't know if you have ever heard a doctor sigh in relief. That day in October I felt like I was sitting in front of a stranger having to tell her about my struggle. But as it turned out she wasn't a stranger. She had been there seeing me every couple of weeks for another migraine attack, seeing me struggle along and being unable to help me beyond what I was giving her leave to do. To hear me say that I needed help caused her to sigh in relief. I had given her permission to finally help. I had given up the fight for control and was trusting that others would take care of me, help me along my way.

Leaving the doctor's office that day I felt free and exhausted at the same time. My body ached, felt hollow and empty. Bu there was also a buzzing inside of me, the feeling of a new adventure ahead, of a first step taken on a journey.

*

November brought some early snow and so I was back in my tent on a field surrounded by snow and a view onto to two frozen lakes. I spent most of this nature quest inside my tent, listening to the faint sound of falling snowflakes. It was that heavy, wet kind of snow and every once in a while, a whole batch slid down the side of my tent, making room for new snow to pile up.

I felt like I had on my first quest. Lying in my sleeping bag with two layers of warm clothes on. I felt cocooned, safe and at peace.

Nothing much had changed so far. Don't get me wrong. Being off work helped. It helped a lot. It took away one weight for the moment. Also, my boss and colleagues had been amazing. They were all standing by my side, supporting me and emphasizing the value of my wellbeing. As it turned out, they were happy to help as well.

After having spent months and months feeling utterly alone in my battle it seemed so strange that all this help had been available all along. Friends, colleagues, doctors, all of them seemed to have patiently (and sometimes not so patiently) waited for me to come around and finally accept their help and support on my journey. No matter how little they knew me, they were happy to reach out and support whenever I asked for it. So even though my situation hadn't changed all that much, my feeling around it had changed a lot. I felt supported and most importantly I didn't feel alone anymore. I didn't need to figure this out on my own or face it on my own. It was a choice and had been all along.

Lying there in the early darkness of a late autumn afternoon, I became very still. I realised that everything was alright, that it always had been and always would be alright. Yes, the waves of life would keep on moving and storming about, but at the core I would always be that drop in the depth of the ocean. There would always be peace and wellbeing right there at my disposal. All it needed was to know, to trust, that the peace was there and that I was alright.

I felt at peace and I felt free. It was a different kind of free from what I had envisioned and different to the feeling of freedom that came from running away and starting over. It was the feeling of freedom granted by trusting in life. The freedom that comes with trusting in being alright no matter what was happening on the surface of my life experience. It felt deeper and more profound.

For a moment I was afraid it might leave, then I giggled. And being aware of myself, lying in my sleeping bag in a lonely tent on a snow-covered field in the middle of nowhere, giggling, made me giggle even more. I knew then that even though I wouldn't always be aware of this freedom and trust, that it would always be there, just like the stars and the sun are always there. It was only my perspective and limited senses that let me see them only at certain times.

In that night I knew what to do, not in the future, not sometime later but now. I knew what I had known all along: that I wanted to move on from my current relationship, that it had died and that it was okay. What helped me to actually move on was the trust that I was okay whether in or out of this relationship or any relationship for that matter.

*

In a fairy tale this would probably be the end. Drop the curtain and they all went on to live happily ever after. In this story however there was one more month, one more nature quest to go.

Five days before Christmas I packed my backpack and walked out to one of my favourite spots. In the summer it isn't suitable for a nature quest as there will always be a few people around. In winter however and with ankle deep snow it is a lovely spot, hanging between trees and looking down on a frozen lake. Hanging? Yes, I had decided to do this in the hammock. It was perfect for it. The temperature was just a little below zero and it was going to be dry.

Walking through the woods I could hear the snow crunching underneath my boots, the little crystalline structures falling apart. As I was losing heat fast the moment I stopped moving, I got ready to snuggle up in my sleeping-bivy-bag combo as soon as I had set up camp. A little bit of pacing and jumping jacks to get myself warm and there I was hanging in between two snow covered fir trees. In the growing darkness I could see the moonlight reflecting from the snow of the surrounding landscape. Everything was still, as if it was holding its breath, waiting for spring. Watching the sparkling stars through the canopy I feel asleep.

Splish, splish, splish, splish, splosh. I awoke with a start. My face was wet. No, everything was wet. The formerly snow-covered trees showed blotches of green in the grey hours of morning. Maybe I should have checked the weather forecast, I thought. Or maybe just pack something for the possibility of it not being dry. Well, I hadn't done either and so I was left with what I had.

The next few hours I spent underneath my winter coat hanging above my face to keep the snow from dropping directly onto it, but then I couldn't hold onto my bodily needs any longer. I had tried to hold out as long as possible, knowing that once I left the safety of my sleeping bag there was no way back.

Once I had peeled out of my layers, they had started soaking up the surrounding water no matter how hard I tried to keep this from happening. Putting on all my dry layers I started moving to keep warm. The melting snow made it very clear that the temperature had climbed above zero but with all the wetness around me it felt so much colder.

I started to pace and soon had turned the white snow of my nature quest circle into a forest-floor-brown mud pit. The roots where slippery and I needed to be careful not to fall. Time seemed to crawl by. The colder I got, the more it seemed to draw to a halt. The beauty of the surrounding nature was all but lost to me. The only thing that seemed to exist was the ongoing mantra in my head: only six more hours, only five more hours, only four more hours...

Around the time I had three hours to go I stopped feeling my toes. I tried moving more, jumping more, but the slippery ground and the confined space of my circle only allowed for so much movement. I was glad I had packed my gear right after getting up, as my hands had gone numb and clumsy.

Two more hours to go and my head was filled with only two thoughts: 'Who is going to know?' and 'That would be cheating!' Yes, I was considering leaving early, to abandon my mission of going on twelve twenty-four-hour nature quests in one year.

When the last hour came closer, I started feeling giddy and then I stopped feeling my feet altogether. Walking became a whole lot harder. It seemed like I had lost touch with the ground. Where my feet should have been there was just numbness, a hole of nothingness.

With forty-five minutes to go I knew that this was it. I shouldered my gear and left thirty minutes before the finish line. Every step was hard, as I was sinking into the wet snow and couldn't adapt to the ground beyond, simply because I didn't feel it. Slowly I was wobbling my way back.

Suddenly I was in agonizing pain as the pins and needles hammered into my feet. Tears were flowing down my face, partly due to the pain and partly due to the sheer joy of relief that washed over me. Somehow it had needed this last solo campout to teach me one of the most important learnings of adventuring: sometimes you need to leave early to come back another time.

Maren Frank is an everyday adventurer, saying yes to exploring a new route, having a weekend mini adventure, or simply taking the time to enjoy nature and smelling the roses. The time in between her adventures she spends having meaningful and transformative conversations in her role as consultant and coach. Three things that make Maren happy are flying high on a swing, soap bubbles, and falling asleep under a starry night sky. When getting in contact with her let her know what makes you happy.

Email: maren@kamanakai.org

Twitter: @Maren_F_F

Chapter 15

Children and Cougars and Bears. Oh My!

by Mel Findlater

The backstory

There are two reasons I needed to go back to this specific trip. First, to relive a memory, and second to remember who I am and prove to myself that I can still adventure, even with a child.

Reason 1- Remembering a peaceful moment

When I first met my now husband, still in my university years, we took our first adventure together only a few months after meeting. Him, showing off his strength and wisdom as many men tend to do in the early days of a relationship. Me, trying to show that I am an outdoorsy, strong woman, different to any he had ever dated before. I had never been backpacking before and figured it would be a piece of cake.

I won't go into many details from this trip but what you do need to know is this one key memory...the one that brought me back.

Picture this - The Juan de Fuca Trail on Vancouver Island in west coast Canada. It is the lesser known sister trail of the extremely popular West Coast Trail, with arguably just as incredible scenery. Hugging the coastline, walking through tall, beautiful red cedar and douglas fir trees with a view out over the ocean almost the entire time, this trail is stunning. It is 47 kilometres of breath-taking scenery and challenging terrain through a magical rainforest.

Instead of trying to complete the entire trail, we focused our efforts on the first 9 kilometres, heading to the second beach, Bear Beach, to camp for 3 nights. I remember the walk in being tough, up then down, then up again as we walked by stream after stream flowing into the ocean. I remember making it to Bear Beach and on our first night watching a tent near us get soaked as the tide came in overnight. So on our second night we walked just a little bit further and found the most beautiful beach which we had completely to ourselves. We pegged our tent right on the beach but above the tideline near the trees.

It was in the early hours of the morning that the magic began. Before I had even opened my eyes, I heard a muffled blowing sort of sound. A bear? I sure hoped not. As my heart beat faster, I zipped open the tent door, looked out, and not more than 20 feet from the shore was a huge gray whale feeding on the seafloor. It was as if time had stopped. My breathing slowed as I unknowingly let out a sigh, relaxed all of the muscles in my body, and just sat down to watch. It was the most peaceful thing I had ever witnessed. I felt such gratitude for being in that specific place at that specific time.

As an ambitious woman keen to travel, explore and try new things, I often find it challenging to slow down. When I need to, this is the memory that I go back to. When I close my eyes and think back to that hike, that morning, I can still smell the salty ocean air, hear the soft waves and the wind in the trees blowing behind me, and see that gray whale peacefully in front of me, likely unaware of my very existence.

It is this feeling, this specific moment, that had me return in 2017 with my husband and two year old. While I knew that I was unlikely to see a whale again, surely I could get that same feeling of gratitude and of peacefulness, even with a two year old.

How could it go wrong?

Reason 2- Proving to myself that I could

"Be careful!" they'd said. "One slip and you'll be pregnant!"

This scare tactic is what rang in my ears as a teenager, making me believe that getting pregnant would be easy, most likely an accident. It was anything but. Four years, two rounds of IVF and a miscarriage later, I was finally pregnant and well into my second trimester. I was happy, hesitant but excited. I was one of those annoying pregnant women who was glowing and feeling the best thing in my life with that big belly growing. Apart from having a ridiculously heightened sense of smell, I felt well. I was taking life very carefully, worried that doing anything other than a simple short walk would risk the baby, but I was happy and willing to do it.

And then it hit me. I'm going to have a baby, who will turn into a child. I had spent so much time trying to get pregnant that I hadn't thought much about the next bit. Self-preservation I suppose.

I am going to have a baby. What does that mean for me? Who will I be? Who can't I be anymore? What if I lose myself? What if I can't be spontaneous anymore? I have so many dreams...I want to travel, I want to adventure...I want to....know that I can say yes! What if after all of this I resent my baby?!

The first 6 months were a blur. I was recovering both physically and emotionally from a traumatic birth while trying to connect with the bundle of Bean that I was presented with. Then she smiled for the first time. Finally that rush of love that so many describe happened to me. Not the moment I gave birth, but the moment that I had recovered enough to connect.

The next year or so I really got into my flow. I worked for myself so brought her along to work meetings and conferences and she fit right in. I was with her 24 hours a day, 7 days a week, for those first 2 years and most of the time I didn't mind. In fact, I enjoyed the majority of it. I felt like I had finally found the reason I was here on this earth. So how is it that I also felt extremely frustrated with it all? Eventually, it clicked. I had put so much of myself into raising Bean that I was actually using it as an excuse not to think about me at all. Who am I when I am not Mama?

For 2 years I had fully embraced the ups and downs of being a stay at home mother while completely ignoring my need to take the space to reflect on our new life - to take time for myself. It turns out, being a parent is hard. Really hard. It's amazing and incredible and fills my heart with more love than I could ever imagine could fit in it. It also constantly tests the limits of my patience, mindfulness, creativity and what is possible on very little sleep. It's exhausting!

When I became a parent I almost forgot me. I needed to figure out who this new me was.

So, when my daughter turned two and my husband was gifted with a 5 week sabbatical from work, I knew we needed an adventure that would help me remember who I was, or figure out who I am now. Something that would give me the time and opportunity to reflect on me. Something that was outdoors. Something that would help me prove to myself that I can still do seemingly crazy things, even now that I am a mother. I had the perfect thing - hike the Juan de Fuca trail again, this time with a two year old strapped to my back. Easy, right? Crazily enough, I kind of thought it would be...

The preparation

I could sense that everyone I talked to about hiking the Juan de Fuca trail with a 2 year old thought we were crazy. My way of compensating for this was to be confident, perhaps a little too confident. I felt so convinced that the trip would be fine, that I had completely forgotten to bring our carrier with us to Canada from the UK where we now live. Queue asking a very old friend that I hadn't seen in 8 years to borrow hers. A great start.

Luckily, I did learn some things on the first trip that made us slightly more prepared:

1- I am terrified of being attacked by a bear alone, without anyone noticing. I learned this when every single time I had to pee in the night I woke Eric up to tell him. My theory, if a bear came to eat me, at least he would notice (not do anything, just notice). We're talking 5, maybe 6 times a night. He thought it was hilarious.

The learning for this time? Buy bear spray and bear bells. Check.

2- Blisters suck. I bought a pair of brand new beautiful high topped hiking boots just for that first trip. 10 minutes in I got blisters and by the end they were unbearable.

Learning for this time - wear well used footwear. Check.

3- My knees don't like hills and carrying a lot of things. I damaged my knees beyond repair that first trip and was almost crawling by the end of it because we had carried so much stuff in. I did physio for months and they have never been the same.

Learning - carry only the 2 year old and a small bag with diapers and wipes. Get my husband to carry everything else. Bring a lot less (somehow, with 3 of us now).

So, I was prepared right? I remembered that these parts of the trip were tricky and yet I still looked back on them with admiration. I didn't remember ever wanting to stop or go home. I didn't remember any regret. I conveniently forgot the pain and frustration. Any challenging memories were washed over by this incredible feeling of peace that I got from memories of falling asleep to the sound of the ocean and seeing that whale.

Bears, and cougars, and mud, oh my!

We arrived at the beginning of the trail later in the day than we had hoped. It was lunch time, we were hungry, and it was just before our two year old would have usually had a nap. It's fine, we thought, she will sleep in the carrier. After devouring some food we strapped the toddler onto my back and the rest of the kit onto Eric's and walked to the trailhead sign. I was nervous approaching it, as this is where it will usually be posted if there have been any recent sightings of bears or cougars nearby. I was relieved to see nothing of the sort. However, just as my nerves started to subside I began to read the sign which detailed what to do if you see a bear or a cougar, just to remind myself.

'Cougars may view children as prey targets due to their small size, high-pitched voices and quick movements.' I read.

My heart began to pound faster in my chest. Any nerves I already had increased tenfold. I knew the potential for bears and cougars was there but I hadn't thought about the fact that they would especially target small children. Was I being an unfit mother putting my child at such risk unnecessarily? The sign advised that you carry a stick large enough to be used as a weapon to fend them off. I was officially scared of my small child being eaten by a cougar and this fear did not subside for the entire 3 days of this trip. Bears? No longer the top of my fear list. Cougars, now that is what kept my adrenaline pumping.

Somehow, we mustered up the courage and started the trek. It was muddy - really, really muddy. The first part of the trail was downhill through a forest of vibrant green trees. It had rained recently and was still a little bit misty, so the smell of the trees floated through the air. I love that smell. This was the only part of the trail where you couldn't see the ocean until you reached it at the bottom of the hill but I barely noticed as all of my attention was needed to navigate the roots sticking out in every direction. Instead of trying to avoid them, our best bet was to try to step on the bigger ones in order to avoid sliding through the very thick, oozy mud. As you can imagine, we sang a lot of the Going On a Bear Hunt song. We can't go over it. We can't go under it. We will have to go through it. And through it we went. My feet kept missing the roots and I would stumble forward, off balance from the 2 year old on my back. My mind was distracted with looking for a reasonably thick walking stick that I could use should a cougar appear. Eric must have been thinking the same thing and shortly after placed the perfect walking stick into my hand. Phew. Now we're safe, right?

Take a moment and think about this. A ridiculously strong, large, hungry cat decides to come for Bean. I have a stick and motherly protect-your-young strength. The cougar has crazy strength, impeccable speed, sharp teeth and large claws. Clearly I would win that fight...

It turns out that Eric had these same thoughts long before reading the sign and had planned for this. It turns out he had bought bear spray in order to tip things back in our favour in the unlikely event of seeing a cougar. Who knows if it would even have any such effect on a cougar, being designed for bears and all, but it did make us feel a little safer.

After a few more minutes of searching and tripping, Eric found another stick for himself. Two adults, two sticks and bear spray against one cougar. Things are starting to seem okay again. Turns out the stick also proved extremely valuable going through the muddy trail as well, acting as a sort of third leg to keep me balanced with my uneven distribution of baby.

We let the little one down to stretch her legs for about 10 minutes of very slow walking in this first section. We made it about 20 feet but with so much mud and tiny feet and legs there was no way she was going to be able to walk much of this trail at all. It just wasn't going to work for her. So back on my back she went and we trudged through the mud, over the wiggly bridge and down the many stairs to our first beach.

Mystic Beach was beautiful and worth the 2.5 km walk down. Sheltered by cliffs and caves, this sandy beach gave us an unbroken, open view of the inviting ocean, while keeping us sheltered from most winds. Staying and camping here was very tempting. However, as this is where many people stop on their day hikes it was busier and wouldn't fulfil my need to chase the memory from last time. The sun was quickly moving down the sky and determined to get to our camping spot before dark, we hastily continued on our way.

We had approximately 7 more kilometres before we would reach our stopping point - another beach access. There's no going half way, you either keep going, or you turn around. Stopping in the middle for a camp was not advised and I would not have felt comfortable right in the trees with all of the animals. It was getting dark and we needed to get going quickly. However, if you know anything about 2 year olds, doing anything quickly is right near impossible. So, we did what we could.

On we went - up, down, up, down. This section of the trail was rated moderate difficulty but I would say that much of it was certainly more than that. We walked along the coastline, often on cliff edges a few 100 feet from the beach below, trudging through mud that was so thick at points that, if our boots hadn't been tied up properly, we probably would have lost them. Squilch, squelch. Squilch, squelch. Within every kilometre there were between one and three sharp hills leading us down steps into a little valley where we'd cross a small bridge to get over a stream and then climb steeply back up the other side. I was painfully reminded of how my knees felt during that first hike many years ago. I had conveniently pushed that part of the hike out of my mind.

About one kilometre or so from Mystic Beach the whining began. Bean was getting tired and was not a fan of being in the carrier. We figured she would nap in there, just like she had done so many times before when she was younger. Oh how wrong we were. Bean was cranky. She was bored. She was fighting sleep. She wanted to walk but, not only would she struggle on much of the terrain, with some of it being frankly unsafe, it was also getting dark and we needed to get to our campsite. We did not want to try putting everything up in the dark while keeping a 2 year old close by.

So on we trekked, distracting her by counting the kilometre posts and arrows in between. Instead of peacefully taking in the beauty of the trees and ocean surrounding us, we were constantly thinking of distraction techniques, counting 'waterfalls' that we saw when the streams entered the ocean at the bottom of each valley and guessing how many there would be by the time we got there. We would stop when things got too much for a quick snack and a stretch and then move on. Just as I was reaching the end of my patience with a wriggling, grumpy child on me, we would find another waterfall and bridge to count and walk over, and all was right in our world for a few minutes longer. Until it would start all over again. During one break sitting on a log I questioned whether we should turn around. However, we had gone past the halfway point. The walk back would be no better than the walk forward. So, big deep breath and onwards we walked.

Eventually, I moved her from my back to my front and after a big old yell and a struggle, she finally fell asleep. Thank goodness for that. We had a couple kilometres of peaceful, quiet contemplation as we took in the beauty of the scenery around us.

Every person that we passed looked at us with complete surprise when they realised I had a 2 year old strapped to me. I like to think that they were in awe of our incredible feat, but in reality they were most likely thinking we were absolutely crazy bringing such a young one with us, out of season in April, on a misty, muddy day... and what about those bears and cougars?! There were definitely times, many of them in fact, that I agreed with this train of thought... and then we'd see another waterfall and the world slowed down as we enjoyed the next few minutes.

Finally, 6 hours later we made it to the beach entrance. Phew! We were almost done! - or so I thought. By now, my legs were like jello and my knees screamed in pain with every step I took. The beach is flat, sure, but it's also full of sand and rocks and very, very tiring to walk on. After that initial boost of energy, I was walking slower than I had the entire hike so far, depending greatly on my walking stick to lean on.

Eric pushed on, looking for the perfect camping spot. It is requested that you use the designated camping spots on the trail in order to help preserve the environment and limit our impact on this popular trail. Each spot was also chosen wisely near a stream to get water from and bathe in, had an outhouse to do your business, and a bear box to put your food in at night. Eric waited for me at the first area. It was full of a group of teenagers who had come with some teachers/leaders. I love the idea of the self growth that they must be gaining from this difficult experience but I did not want to camp with them. It was not the quiet, peaceful memory that brought me back. I was shattered but we pushed on.

In my memory, on that first hike we had camped on a long stretch of sandy beach, just before the treeline, where you'd be unlikely to see others. Either my memory was wrong or we didn't walk far enough because this beach was not sandy. It was full of small rocks. I took a deep breath, accepted that this was a new experience, not the same as the old one, and we chose a great camping spot, just inside the trees, sheltered from the winds and occasional misty rain, with a circle of large logs to sit on and cook between.

No time for rest though, the sun was setting and we needed to get the tent up and dinner cooked before we had a hangry (anger brought on by hunger) toddler. Bean and I worked on setting up the tent while Eric cooked us some beans and rice. Have you ever tried to put a tent up with sore tired muscles, in almost dark, a toddler attempting to help and all the while trying to keep her within arm's reach in case an animal comes along? It does not make for a quick or easy endeavour.

Somehow, I managed to keep my cool and we did it. Bean excitedly threw her boots off and jumped into the tent. I set up the sleeping bags and she got all cosy, squealing with delight. It was the happiest I had seen her all trip so far and while the sound melted my heart from cuteness, it also made it beat faster in fear that a cougar would hear the squeal! After sufficient time by toddler standards, we left the tent to join Eric by the logs on the beach to eat our nice warm dinner.

Exhausted, with Bean and Eric beside me, I breathed in the ocean air around us and listened to the waves gently crash against the shore. This was our little bit of heaven for the next 2 nights. Then, it started to rain. After gathering the food and walking it to the bear safe container for the night, we went to bed, shattered but content. It was 8pm. Oh, the life of a parent.

A New Day

It had been a relatively peaceful night. I, surprisingly, only had to pee once (unheard of when camping!) and I didn't even wake anyone to go. Look at me being all bold and brave! Bean woke with the sun and we unzipped the tent to a cloudy but dry morning. With the tent door open we could see the ocean through a little bush in front of us. We laid there for a while, watching the water and listening to the waves and birds up above.

Then, the ocean smell was overwhelmed with that of toddler poo, slightly out of the diaper and up the back. Poo back, our favourite, and with limited wipes and ways to clean it up. Not to mention that we had to carry that diaper out again - the reality of backpacking with a 2 year old. We attempted to empty as much of the contents into the nearby outhouse as possible (not easy on a high fibre, vegetarian diet...) and tucked the dirty diaper into a plastic bag a ways away from the tent.

Finally, that not so lovely smell was replaced again by not only the ocean and trees but the smell of cooking breakfast. While I dealt with poonami, Eric was cooking us some oats with dried fruit, seeds and nuts. We huddled on the log eating out of our mugs and then replacing it with warm tea for me and coffee for Eric. We looked out at the ocean and took a breath. This is why we came here.

Just then, out of the corner of my eye, high up in a tree less than 20 feet away, I spotted a bird perched at the end of the branch. The wind blew this small branch and the bird around as it searched for prey below. I attempted to take a picture but by the time I got my camera out the bird had already gone. It was a bald eagle, one of the most graceful flyers around. I felt thankful for getting to see it so close.

We had that one full day at the campsite, before we would head back the next day. We moved about the day slowly. When the sun peeked its head out for a few minutes we strung a rope between a rock and a log and hung our wet clothes on it in the hopes that they would dry. We took turns taking Bean to the nearby stream to fetch water and show her how to put it through the purifier.

There was a solo man sleeping in a hammock in the trees and I ogled at him as I walked by, both intrigued and envious of the freedom and lightness of his kit, while also wondering how he was not terrified that a bear would come along in the night and sniff him or bat him like a ball in the trees. Eric, who is pure logic, explained that the nylon of our tent is no more protection than that of a hammock and that if a bear wanted in, it would come in. Thanks for that image Eric! Even though I knew this to be true, I think it will be a while before I feel brave enough to try a hammock in the trees in bear country. (I was, however, inspired to buy a camping hammock at home in the UK shortly after, keen to try it where I only have badgers and hedgehogs to contend with!).

The Way Out

We learned from our first walk and planned much better for our return journey. We got up early, woken by the two year old alarm clock anyways. After breakfast, packing up etc., we started on our way. We let Bean walk this first section on the beach, where it was relatively safe terrain. It was slow moving but she enjoyed the freedom. Just after we passed that first camping area I saw something scoot under a piece of large driftwood ahead. As we got closer we confirmed that it was an otter, bounding in and out of the log, taking a break from the ocean and having a play on land. It was fascinating to watch and guess at what it might do next.

Eventually, as it ran back to the water, we continued to trek onwards. Before we had even made it to the end of the beach section and up onto the trail, Bean wanted to stop for a snack. We happily obliged. We found some driftwood to perch on, nibbled our dried fruit, and she got out her magnifying glass to explore her surroundings. There aren't many things cuter than a 2 year old very seriously investigating her surroundings with a magnifying glass. I grinned and tried to keep my chuckles inside. So far so good.

We decided that at every 1 kilometre sign post we would stop, let Bean out, have a snack and a drink, and then let her walk for a short way. Sometimes her walking consisted of only 10 feet as the terrain wasn't safe enough in those places, but at least she got to have a stretch. With these ongoing breaks, continuing to count 'waterfalls' in the streams, and counting every kilometre signpost, the walk back took longer but was much more peaceful.

We made it to about an hour away from Mystic Beach, where we planned to have a big stop and a play, when Bean started to get really tired and fight it again. So. Much. Screaming. There was no concern that a bear would approach us with all of that noise. I transferred her onto my front and bounced her up and down jiggling all about. I even sang to her. All to no avail.

Just as we saw the clearing to the path leading to the beach, she fell asleep. I sighed. Hair sticking out in every which direction from sweat and just being generally frazzled from negotiating an overtired 2 year old, I had had it. I was getting to the beach and taking her off. If she slept a while longer on the sand, great, if not, she could wake up and play. I was not carrying her anymore.

Turns out 10 minutes is all a 2 year old needs when she is presented with a sandy beach, 2 waterfalls and a selection of caves to explore. We smothered her with more sunscreen and let her run. After consciously keeping her in arms reach for the past 2.5 days the sense of freedom on this beach was liberating for all of us. It is surrounded by cliffs so if an animal did attack, which is very unlikely with so many people around, you could see it coming from further away. I felt myself relax. We took our boots off, dipped our feet in the ocean, running gleefully in and out of the incoming waves. Bean pulled me by the hand over to the biggest of two small waterfalls and we put our hands right underneath the running water. She looked up at me with the most gleeful smile and my warmth and gratitude returned. We were so lucky to be on this trail, in that moment. It almost felt like all the screams, tired muscles, and pure exhaustion was worth it. Almost.

We spent much longer on that beach than we had planned for. With the sun shining down and the ocean by our side, it almost felt like every incoming wave brought us more joy and outgoing wave washed away the challenging times. Either that, or we were just dreading the final 2.5km walk up hill through the woods and were procrastinating because of it.

Eventually, we went on our way. Bean was now rejuvenated and content after her beach play so we let her walk quite a bit of that final upwards trail. She amazed passers-by with her sheer determination to climb up the initial flights of stairs that had been carved into large logs. The mud was still thick in some places but had dried in others and the path was much safer than the rest of the trail had been. We forged ahead at toddler speed, very, very, slowly. Eventually, she tired and asked to be carried again just before we crossed the wobbly bridge once more. Up through the rest of the woods we went and finally made it to our car.

Relief washed through my body from toes to head. We did it. It wasn't what I had hoped for but we did it. I was proud.

Time for Reflection

It's a funny thing, going on challenging adventures. While I was doing the hike, and even just sitting on the beach, I wasn't sure that it was the right decision. It was hard, really hard and not an experience designed for a 2 year old. There were many moments that were definitely not fun. It definitely wasn't the safest decision we have ever made, though the risks did bring with them a certain element of excitement alongside the fear. When we first finished the hike, I wouldn't have decided to do it again.

But then we got home and for months afterwards, Bean's play consisted of building mountains out of Duplo for her 'GuyGuy's to climb, waterfalls for them to play in, and bridges for them to cross. It turns out, difficult isn't always bad, even for a two year old. The parts that stuck with her, and I believe have truly shaped who she is as a person, are the fun parts - the exploring, the climbing, the playing and the fact that we did it, even though it was hard.

This is also what sticks with me. Now, looking back on it, I remember it so fondly, even the hardest parts. Even writing it out as I am now I am thinking about how I'd like to go back and do the whole 47 miles one day. Perhaps when the kids are old enough to carry their own weight. Okay, that might be just a little bit too crazy.

Did I achieve what I set out to? I believe I did. I didn't get my moment of awe and gratitude while I was on the trail and I didn't see a whale, but I did get those feelings after I got back and reflected on it all. I feel proud of the three of us for pursuing through tough conditions and realities of life with a two year old. Did I recapture who I am? Figure out this new identity? Not completely, I'm still doing that, but this trip definitely helped me take a huge step forward in figuring it all out. I proved to myself that I can still be a bit crazy. I can still take on challenges. Life with kids is an adventure in itself and yes I can still go on bigger adventures too.

Would I recommend this exact route to another family with a 2 year old? Probably not. Instead, choose a path with flexible camping spots, places where your toddler can walk safely, and time things so that you can go at the pace of tiny legs.

Would I do it again in that same situation? Probably not.

Do I regret it? Most definitely not!

In that moment, I needed to choose the hard path. I needed to prove something to myself. Now, I feel less like I need that. I will probably go back one day soon and walk with Bean and my 1 year old down to the first beach and camp. It's the perfect toddler distance. Now, I am in a place where I can embrace the version of myself that slows down and really enjoys things at the pace of my kids. Now, I let them hold my hand and walk me through the mud, showing me the way to my new self. I don't think I would have gotten to this place if I hadn't gone on that seemingly crazy first family backpacking trip.

Oh, and it turns out we didn't see any cougars or bears on the trip - but maybe they saw us?

Facebook: facebook.com/wearehappyparents

Twitter: @melfindlater

Instagram: @melfindlater

Instagram: @ordinarysuperparents

Chapter 16

Let's Go For a Little Jog

by Michelle Ellison

An astounding 5821 human beings ended their life in the UK in 2017.

5821 lives in a year is 485 lives lost per month. That is 16 people every morning in the UK waking up, who will go to sleep forever by the end of the day. It's too shocking. I started to wonder what 485 lives translated into in kilometres.

I've always been in awe of those people who run really long distances, Forest Gump style. I'm drawn to the fact that it's not a race but a long journey. It has nothing to do with time or speed. I'm not a runner but I love testing what I don't think I'm capable of. I imagined running from St David's Head in Wales to Lowestoft in England. 630km.

I thought to myself, if I can run the width of the UK, maybe that could be a big enough journey to inspire people to sign the petition I'm drawn to supporting. A petition to ensure that every person feeling suicidal that arrives at an Accident and Emergency ward in the UK, is given the best care possible.

How can there be no consistency in treatment in our UK A&E departments? When someone walks into A&E and says, "I am feeling suicidal!", why are they not treated the same in Aberdeen as they are in Brighton? How is it that some hospitals have brilliant support and care available and others don't?

This was something that I could help change. Each kilometre ran would represent approximately nine lives lost to suicide in 2017. That's 630km and 5821 lives. Every person who connected with the petition and the run could lead to another signature. The aim was 10,000 signatures to ensure the government would respond to the petition, so every individual signature really mattered.

For you and me: Ask yourself, what are you curious in? Keep asking that question and keep exploring what it is. You never know what you will learn, who you will meet, where it will lead and what you will change.

Connecting the dots

Steve Jobs was quoted, "You can't connect the dots looking forward; you can only connect them looking backwards. So you have to trust that the dots will somehow connect in your future. You have to trust in something - your gut, destiny, life, karma, whatever." Ten years earlier at 29, I had let a lot of years roll by, as I sat in the passenger seat of my own life, with my own life-defining dots few and far between.

When I had the courage to end my broken 12-year relationship to my best friend in 2009, feeling the lowest I'd ever felt, being a shell of the person I am today, I could not have guessed who I would become ten years later. I was a person who was always quiet in a room full of people, a person who never put herself in the front of anything, a person who hated the idea of running, cycling, mountaineering and yes, even dating.

Here I was, so many life-dots later in 2019, boarding a train leaving Paddington Station with my good friend Johnny. You would barely recognise the old me.

I never contemplated anyone running with me. In my head, I imagined doing it alone. I was going to be a nightmare. I could envisage all the times ahead where I would be in a bad headspace and I didn't want anyone to have to witness that. Or worse, I didn't want to have to hide it. I was happy to be responsible for just myself and my own feelings without inflicting them on someone else.

Returning from Cairns in November, when the seasons were changing and the leaves were turning golden in Clissold Park, I excitedly shared my new adventure with Johnny like a kid at Christmas. We were just going for one of our regular walks together around the park when suddenly something shifted.

Johnny said, "Can I come?"

I worked for many years as a Childline counsellor, which is where Johnny and I met. On our counselling shifts he was a bright light in the room that was often full of some heavy hearts. He knew exactly what to say to the kids when they called and you just knew from listening to him that kids on the other end of the line felt safe in sharing their lives. In the same way that he was the perfect counsellor, he was perfect to be my teammate too… positive, capable mentally and physically. Most important of all, he was someone I could spend 17 days with and be comfortable with when I would be at my most vulnerable.

I looked into his green eyes and saw the same excitement for adventure that I felt in my heart. "Yes!" I said.

The 6th March came. All of a sudden, or so it felt, we were speeding on the train towards Haverfordwest in Wales where our journey began. Our train pulled into the station close to midnight. We looked at each other and grinned. We were really doing it! A quick selfie and we ran for the first time together leaving the station, heading down the hill towards our hotel.

For you and me: What are the big dots in your life that have led you to where you are now? When was the last time you created a new dot? What new dot do you want to take on? Who knows what it will connect you to?

Ready, Steady, Go

We woke at 7am in our hotel in Haverfordwest and carried out what would become our three morning T's – tummies, talcum powder and tracker. We filled our tummies with loads of porridge, talcum powdered our feet before we pulled on our socks and shoes and turned on the tracker. With our bags packed lightly, we jumped on the bus that would take us to the most westerly point in the UK, St David's Head.

I had butterflies in my stomach. Were they due to the excitement or nerves? I couldn't tell. Day one of my denial began. "I'm only running today," I told myself willfully ignoring the other 16 days ahead of us.

At 10am the bus pulled up at St David's Centre. We both quickly realised that we were still quite a distance from the coastline. Oops! That wasn't in the plan.

"Sorry, love. I don't know where the Head is," said the bus driver unhelpfully, his thick Welsh accent almost singing the words. "Here's where I always turn round."

We needed a toilet and water stop anyway and I laughed. We hadn't even started running yet. So, we headed for a local café, for liberation, hydration and information.

It was perfect as that's how we met Cal working in The Meadow café. He had those eyes that smiled and was a young enthusiastic runner himself having just completed the local half marathon only weeks before. He was willing to share the petition and after a quick Instagram photo (of course!), we had our directions to our destination and our start point 3 miles away.

We didn't move far. While we were double checking our map only metres down the road, we met Nicola who had returned home for a holiday. She offered us an impromptu tour of her town. Super bubbly and with such passion for her home, how could we say no? It was a beautiful day, we had plenty of daylight and it was great to engage in another conversation about the petition. Was this a sign of our journey to come?

Battling the headwinds for our 3 mile walk to St David's Head, we kept repeating how grateful we were that we'd be running with the wind behind us. We reached the carpark at Whitesands Bay and turned onto the Pembrokeshire Coastal Path. We weren't sure how far away the point was, so we just kept going. Unlike the most easterly point of the UK, the most westerly point is unmarked. Luckily, we were able to ask another rambler on the path. Two hours after getting off the bus we had finally made it to the real start. A few photos and hugs later, we were eager to start this running business.

It felt like a crisp spring day as we started our jog along the cliff tops of the rolling Pembrokeshire hills. The blue sky and sunshine hugged us from above and the wind howled from below as the ocean waves crashed on the beach. We ran up and down the trail barely wide enough for our feet, before we turned off the path and onto the road retracing our walk and bus ride from earlier in the day back to Haverfordwest.

"We have to remember this moment right now," I said to Johnny. "Our bodies will never feel as good as they do right now!" Our running legs felt fresh, we had no injuries and our bags were as light as feathers.

For you and me: Denial can become your friend if you need to get through a tough situation. Use it wisely. Your body and mind might thank you for it, when used in the right situations.

Strangers

The sole purpose of running the width of the UK was to engage with as many people as possible. We wanted to raise awareness about the petition and ask people to consider signing it. But to do that, it meant engaging with as many strangers as humanly as possible, while also trying to make the running distance every day. Initially, at times, I felt hesitant to share with some people what we were doing and why. Do you ever worry about how someone would react? Do you imagine they won't have time to listen?

On day two, I was having a conversation over breakfast with a lovely lady in The County Hotel in Haverfordwest. We parted ways and I realised that I hadn't really shared my story. I couldn't understand why I hadn't.

"Johnny, what's wrong with me?" I asked as we left the hotel and started jogging down the road.

"What do you mean?"

"I didn't share my story with our waitress this morning. I didn't tell her about the run or the petition or anything."

"Nerves, I suppose. I'm not sure why I didn't either," said Johnny.

"I'm not running the width of this country for fun, you know. We won't get signatures for the petition if I don't share."

"Then you're going to have to suck it up and start sharing then."

And he was right. I made the decision right in that moment to share where we were running and why with *every* stranger, regardless of how I thought they *might* react to those words 'mental health' and 'suicide'.

Stranger is quite an ugly word isn't it? How does it make you feel? For me words spring to mind like unknown, scary, judgement, not to be trusted, strange. It reminds me of being told as a kid about 'stranger danger'.

If you talk to anyone in the YesTribe, one of the most supportive, positive communities I know, you'll hear them say, "Strangers are friends just waiting to happen." In all my conversations with strangers from the moment I made the decision to share with *everyone*, I was only ever treated with kindness and love.

I was expecting to breakdown at some point during the run. What I wasn't expecting was what would cause those breakdowns. I thought it would come because of the pain in my body, sheer exhaustion or even because of Johnny. But the tears came because of those people we call strangers.

- strangers who welcomed us into their homes, providing us with delicious cooked meals and a warm bed for the night;
- strangers who became our support crew for a day or two, ferrying our bags so we didn't have to run with them on our back;
- strangers who'd driven parts of the route with us to give us encouragement;
- strangers who were open and warm when I stopped them on the street, asking if I could share something with them, and going on to talk to them about mental health, suicide and our A&E departments' resources;
- strangers who waved at us from their cars, giving us loads of room as we shared the road with them;
- strangers who opened their front doors and filled our water bottles when they were empty;

- strangers who read the signs on the backpacks we carried, talked to us, smiled and called us crazy, taking away our little sticker leaflet to sign the petition;
- strangers who said they'll share the petition details on their work intranets and social media;
- strangers who bought us dessert and mountains of chocolate to help us refuel;
- strangers who showed their care and support for us in what we were trying to achieve;
- and strangers who openly and warmly shared the impact of mental health on their lives and the lives of those they love.

For you and me: Let's remove barriers. Let's smile to all those strangers around us - the shop assistant, the barista, the person we walk past in the street. They will most likely be just as kind, warm and generous as you and I. And you'll receive something beautiful in return. Human connection.

Wyn - Part One

The day we met a kindhearted, generous and extraordinary man called Wyn will be etched in my mind forever. It was our third day and we were suffering badly. We'd already run 46 miles over the first two days and, when we woke up and waited for the rain to clear, we left St Clears knowing that we would be running our first full marathon. We were still learning how much to eat and we were still getting it wrong. Food was no longer food. It was fuel and our bodies felt like they were always running near empty.

The first 9 miles were a killer, not only because I learnt I wasn't fueled enough, but because my knee had started to be a problem. My knees and I have an 18-year history of sharing life with arthritis. The bad times have been bad and my head started to play through what badness was on the way. I saw myself unable to walk very well, let alone run. It would mean letting down Johnny, the petition team and everyone supporting us. It would mean stopping and going home. I would feel embarrassed, ashamed and stupid to think my body - my knees - were capable of such a journey. My head was definitely going off on one.

But sometimes miracles are just around the corner. Tesco Extra came into view after those first 9 miles and it created a miracle. Yup, who would have thought a Tesco Extra was capable of that? We walked through the front door and smiles appeared on our faces as we knew we were about to eat!

An elderly gentleman came over to us to chat in the Tesco Extra café, as we sat eating our second breakfast for the day. He was curious as he had spotted our laminated signs attached to the outside of our 20L bags, which carried everything we needed for 17 days. As we chatted, a mother and her 10-year-old son joined in from a nearby table. She shared that after her son's football game that very morning, they attended a memorial for a 27-year-old young man from her village who ended his life only the week before. Goosebumps formed on my arms. Standing back in line for our third breakfast, a grandmother started chatting to me and invited Johnny and I over to her table to meet her husband, her son and her grandson. We talked about how running and the outdoors is good for your bodies and more importantly your mental health.

And those conversations continued as we walked around the shop collecting more food supplies and much needed chafing cream, engaging in conversation with staff working in the store, who were happy to put the stickers we carried with details of the petition on their staffroom notice boards.

I felt like a different human being when we walked out two hours later. My knees were still unhappy and I was going to listen to them, but for the moment they were able to run. I still had no idea if I was physically capable of completing the journey, but I was so humbled by our experience that I wasn't going to let my negative head-chat stop me. It's possible that my knees would be ok and it's possible that my knees wouldn't be. But I sure as hell was going to find out.

I decided that every conversation I had with a human being counted, and more importantly every signature we gained for the petition counted. So, we ran.

Tesco Extra started to fade later in the day like a distant memory. The afternoon brought excruciating shoulder pain, from the weight of my bag. I kept checking if my shoulders were bleeding. I could feel the straps cutting into them. There was nothing I could do about it as they continued to bounce off my shoulders, as my feet pounded the pavement and I continued to run. I mentally started throwing things from my bag, but I knew in reality I couldn't as every item had a specific purpose which was essential on the trip. Well, apart from my hairbrush. This was my only luxury item and I was *not* throwing it away!

We were running along a fairly flat and smooth part of the road. Like most of the 630km we ran, there was no footpath so we had to constantly crisscross the road to ensure we weren't running into a blind corner. As we rounded a bend, I spotted a few men near a river who looked like they are about to go kayaking but with no kayaks. I was intrigued and saw an opportunity for a petition chat so I ran over to them.

There were five gentlemen in their 60s. Some of them were dressed in bright red toweling onesies, others were wearing full jumpsuits. We made our usual introduction and quickly learned what they were up to. They were cavers and on the other side of the road was a big steep hill which they were about to climb into to explore.

Within minutes these strangers, these men, these fathers and grandfathers, started sharing with us their struggles with mental health and the impact suicide had had on their lives. Stories of a wife and her 30-year-long struggle with mental health and attempted suicides, and another about his struggles with his teenage daughter's mental health illness. More goosebumps. Humbled, moved, touched and inspired, we all hugged wishing each other well as we said our goodbyes.

As we continued running, I was left wondering about the impact we'd all experienced in sharing those brief moments of our lives with each other. For me, I was transported out from the pain I was experiencing, back to the purpose of why we were running. Did they know those stories about each other? If they did, when was the last time they talked about them? What kind of conversation were they having with each other now as they walked up the hill to enter the cave and explore the underworld beneath?

More miles down. I could see Johnny's feet getting heavier as they pounded the road harder and harder. Each step seemed to be taking more and more effort for him. Our last meal was over four hours earlier and the gels and bars weren't enough substance to get us happily through the last 9 miles. I was willing and hoping the cafe on our route ahead was still open at this time of the day. I kept saying to Johnny, "Not long to go now!" but, about 10 minutes away from the cafe, I looked over my shoulder to see him grimacing in pain.

What would you do? We couldn't stop. We needed that cafe to be open. I needed to lift him somehow, so I did the only thing I knew I could (apart from calling an Uber of course). I stopped running forward and started running back toward him, smiling, dancing, acting like a crazy person and it worked. His eyes and mouth lit up with a big smile. We carried each other in those last few minutes to the cafe and saw our second miracle of the day. It was open! With a comfy seat inside, hot delicious food and cake, iced cold water and a flushing toilet – we were in pure luxury.

Chomping down on our fourth meal of the day, a waitress came over and I instantly spotted her rich dark brown, thick wavy long hair. The kind of clean glossy hair to be jealous of, especially after a few days on the road.

"Hi guys" she said. "If you can fit this in your bags, I'd love to give you this chocolate treat for later." I instantly got up and gave her an apologetically smelly and sweaty hug. I was completely overwhelmed by her kindness, as we hadn't even told her what we were doing. She must of read the sign on our bags.

As she walked away, I sat down and Johnny looked into my eyes from across the table. The pain and emotion that had been brewing inside for the whole day suddenly felt like a volcano erupting, and I burst into tears. Great heaving sobs racked my body and Johnny looked at me with worried eyes and then said clear-as-day, like it was a fact, "We've got this". I half smiled and nodded, holding his gaze and quietening my tears.

I'll never forgot his eyes and his words in that moment. I knew we had the mental strength and support in one another to tackle the challenges we'd face ahead over the coming days. As the tears passed, there was only one thing left to do. I inhaled the biggest piece of delicious cake in the world! Because life is always better with chocolate cake!

As we were caking down, in walked a family of three. They looked conspicuous because they walked straight up to our table, like they were expecting us to be there.

"You're those crazy runners, aren't you?" said Kerry introducing herself, her partner and their 6-week baby.

"Er, yeah," I said, wiping cake crumbs from around my mouth.

"Wow!" she said. "We heard about your run and the petition from Cal and it's awesome that we've bumped into you!" My tired brain ached for a moment as I tried to recollect who Cal was, and then it came to me. The guy with the smiley eyes who we met in the cafe on our first day! He'd shared our message on Instagram and, through another little miracle, the stars aligned that afternoon for our paths to cross.

"Come join us!" I cried pulling over a couple of chairs.

We chatted about our shared love of the outdoors and the importance of sleep. I decided that running across the country was definitely easier than taking care of a six-week old baby! Again, it was a beautiful chance meeting and we left the café with happy tummies and full hearts.

Ahead of us lay 7 miles of grueling pain. We didn't know it, but thankfully we were about to meet our fourth miracle for the day.

We were willing the miles away when a car slowed down next to me and slowly wound down its window. I was ready to receive a load of abuse, as I had felt the frustrations of some drivers sharing the road with us that day. No abuse came.

A friendly voice from the interior of the car called, "Hey! Michelle!" I quickly recalculated where we were - Wales. No one knew us here... or so I thought.

He went on to say that he knew Sally (a fellow YesTribe Ambassador who I had only meet weeks before) and that he'd pull in ahead of us where it was safe to park the car.

As we ran up to the car, kind eyes and a big smile beamed back at us. We shared the warmest of bear hugs and he introduced himself as Wyn.

Wyn offered to be our support crew for the last five miles of our incredibly long day, kindly relieving us from our weighty bags and stopping every mile or so ahead to cheer us on. Of course, we said, "YES please!"

As Wyn drove ahead of us with everything we owned and needed for the run in the boot of his car, we laughed out loud. "Can you imagine doing that in London?" I said to Johnny. "Handing over everything you own, including your money and phone to someone you only met for a matter of minutes."

"Not likely!" Johnny said, as we ran following Wyn's car down the road.

We were on the home straight. As we ran over the bridge in Llandeilo, the big green house in sight and our finish line, we ran the last 50 metres cheered on by the supportive smiling faces of our new best friend, Wyn, and Alice who was taking us in for the evening (another good friend of Wyn and Sally's). Johnny was in pieces and I was feeling relieved.

What a mental day! We'd made it! Within minutes we were in the warmth of Alice's homely kitchen, sharing the tales of our journey so far, while Johnny was sprawled out on the kitchen floor stretching his broken body.

That night I experienced the kindness from a stranger like I'd never received before. Alice gifted us, not only the space and warmth of her beautiful home, but the most delicious stew and homemade chocolate brownies. I even had the chance to hand wash the few clothes I was carrying with me. Clean socks felt like heaven on my feet.

While I showered, Johnny called his son. And while Johnny later soaked his sore muscles in the bath, I had a moment alone and cried again. I felt alone because I realised I wasn't really sharing what was going on in my head, about all that I had experienced that day. I messaged my sister. I messaged my mum. I messaged my friends. I reached out for their support. I told mum that my knees were fine. I didn't want her to worry. I told my sister I was broken. I wanted her sympathy. They both gave me words of love and encouragement and I realised it didn't matter that they were on the other side of the world, miles away from me in NZ. They were there for me when I really needed them.

Later that night, we popped Johnny's growing blisters, one we aptly named 'the shower cap', took our nightly painkillers for our aching muscle and swollen knees and drifted off to sleep. We didn't know it at the time, but our longest and hardest days were still to come.

However, this was the day I became fully connected to the lives we were running for. It was the day I started putting those lives before my own negative head-chat. And it was the day I allowed myself to start being truly vulnerable both in sharing how I was feeling and in accepting kindness and support from people we'd never met.

Wyn - Part Two

A few hours into our morning jog, we bumped into Wyn, his wife Marg and their friends as they were out on their regular Sunday cycle. We smiled and hugged and chatted. Wyn mentioned something about seeing us later and we both continued on our route. I didn't know it then but Wyn was about to blow us away with another little miracle.

We left Alice's house in the morning in Llandeilo with our tummies full and feeling overwhelmed by her generosity and kindness. And it didn't end there. Alice drove our bags to our lunch stop, so we could enjoy a morning with our shoulders free to recover. As she passed us later that morning, she stopped to top up our water bottles and treat us with jelly babies. Johnny was in love.

It had been a tough morning with rain, hail, sunshine and, for me, knee problems that wouldn't let up. Actually, every morning was always tough. So today was no different. We had 25 miles ahead of us to Sennybridge.

With lunch only 10 minutes away, we both started to perk up. Walking towards me was a middle-aged man and his dog. I made a snap decision. One of those decisions that you might only ever think about but not actually carry out. I stopped him in the middle of the footpath and asked this 'stranger' if I could quickly share something with him. He kindly said, "Yes," and I went on to share what we were doing and why.

He introduced himself as Kenny and went on to share that he'd suffered from depression after he and many others were made redundant from their jobs in a local manufacturing plant. He said it was a dark time and it was his dog who helped saved him. Whatever happened, his dog needed taking care of. Kenny would take him into the outdoors to go for a walk. His dog provided companionship and love.

What was truly awesome is that Kenny had turned his life around. He'd just finished retraining at university and been for an interview at his local police station. What inspired me was his genuine openness to share with me, a stranger who had just stopped him on the street. Again, those goosebumps. The power of sharing our lives with another human being felt extraordinary.

I caught up with Johnny who was standing on a street corner waiting for me and entertaining himself by stretching. We ran together into town, collected our bags and I settled down for a big portion of lasagne, my favourite lunchtime fuel, in the local café.

A call came through. It was Wyn. Wyn asked me if we had booked accommodation for that evening and as I said, "No, we've only reserved it." he went on to share what would happen later in the afternoon and I was astonished. Johnny was eager to know why my mouth had dropped to the floor while on the call!

Approximately 5 miles before the end of our day, Wyn and his wife Marg came to meet us to, again, be our support crew and cheerleaders for the last few miles. Running past them parked on the side of the road, Marg's hand would come out of the car window offering us a Mars bar and all the encouragement we needed.

Reaching our 25 mile mark at Sennybridge, Wyn was there cheering us on to our very last step, and after a few photos and a pee stop in the local cafe, we piled in the car back to Wyn's place. Back at Wyn's we had the pleasure of meeting his lovely children, grandchildren, great grandchildren, his seven dogs and three cats.

Wyn and Marg instantly made us feel at home. After our warm showers, clothes dumped in the washing machine and a hot cup of tea and chat with the family, we said our goodbyes and headed out for dinner with this wonderful twosome. Over dinner we shared our lives and what we hoped for in the future. It felt like we'd known each other for years and they left me feeling touched and inspired by the lives they have lived and continue to live.

The night didn't end there though. Wyn had arranged a warm bed at his friends', Sandra and Peter. They took us in at short notice, sharing their home, their stories and feeding us up on porridge the next morning. We shared our love for cycling and all vowed to meet each other on our bikes next time.

Wyn drove us back to our morning start point in a carpark in Sennybridge where, wrapped in our warm jackets feeling a little chilly, we shared the biggest warmest three-person bear hug, before saying our sad goodbyes.

Waiting for us on that cold morning was Will and Duncan, our film crew who were ready to share the next stage in our journey with us. It was great to see their happy faces, and I remember saying at that moment very seriously, with a cheeky tone of course, "If this relationship is going to work over the next four days, then you guys are taking these in your car." I handed them a big bag filled with our gear. My day bag was virtually empty. My shoulders felt relieved.

For you and for me: Plans are great. They can give you confidence and reassurance that you know what you are doing. But you can't ever plan for every eventuality. Be open to the journey you are on and little miracles will present themselves to you along the way. It'll be those little miracles that make life and your journeys more memorable, not the plan.

Pain

I was excited to have Will and Duncan, two young British film makers, on our team. I loved their vision for the film and knew they'd be great company on the road. A film would be a great way to share the story of the petition and to raise even greater awareness of such a serious and important issue that we face in our society.

Will and Duncan were hoping to capture the essence of the journey, our little miracles and mishaps, and I think more importantly the pain and the tears (or the money shot some might say). They filmed as they ran alongside us, as they drove past us with the camera hanging out the window and as they waited for our tired faces and bodies at the end of a long day.

But things didn't quite go to their plan. They hadn't really got to know Johnny and I just yet.

What would you do if you saw two young smiling faces with big cameras, sometimes right in front of your face, full of great banter? Will, dressed in his jeans, boots, puffer jacket and long blonde hair blowing in the wind, running or sometimes lunging backwards down the road, pointing the camera in your face as the cars speed past. There is only one thing I could do. Constantly giggle and smile and feel ridiculous. I am definitely not giving up my day job.

"Michelle you need to look like you are in pain," Duncan would say.

"Michelle you are making this look too easy. Be more serious," Will would shout over the noise of the car engine.

"You two have run over a marathon today, but you are chatting away like you've just been for a stroll," Duncan would comment shaking his head, with that indifferent look in his eyes.

"Correction Duncan, we've just been for a little jog," I'd say grinning.

I couldn't help the smiles when I saw their faces as we rounded a bend or watched Will try and set up the drone camera in gusting winds. They would take my mind off the pain and provide that light relief and distraction that I needed.

Externally I was laughing, smiling and having a great time. Internally it was another situation. I did feel pain and my body physically started to change, but it very rarely came out in front of the camera, which is kind of like real life too, I guess. When I am around other positive, fun loving, interesting human beings, I bounce off their liveliness and energy. It's when my thoughts are in my head, in the times when I'm not with others, that I can more obviously see the pain.

On day five after having run over 120 miles, we only had 10 more miles to go before reaching Hay-on-Wye. The guys had been filming us throughout the day and there had been a lot of laughs, but it got to the point that I could no longer meet Will and Duncan in the eye. My eyes were glued to the ground and I stopped seeing them as I ran past. It was getting late. It was getting dark and I was really struggling. They were now waiting for us to capture that moment on camera when we made it to the end of our day. I stopped caring. I could feel that life was changing with my foot. It was no longer about my knees or shoulders. Imagine your left foot is inflated three times its normal size and looks like it's a brick connected to your leg. That's what happened. Instead of running, I created this limp-run type motion forward, throwing this brick of a foot in front of me like I was swinging a bag of heavy groceries.

I kept saying to myself…

"Am I breathing? Yes!"

"Am I bleeding? No!"

"Are my bones poking out? No!"

"Can I put one foot in front of the other? Well, kind of!"

"Then I have no excuse! Keep moving forward!"

I zoned out in my mind pretending that I was at home in London calling my niece Brooke in NZ. I missed her. I pretended we were chatting and eating together like normal, me eating my salmon for dinner and her eating her Rice Krispies for breakfast. Brooke munching loudly as she was telling me about what she was up to at school and Brownies that week. It made me smile. I was doing everything not to think about my 'brick' and what it would look like after I peeled my shoe off at the end of the day.

The camera was there waiting for our arrival and I can't tell you now if I was chatty with Will and Duncan or if I showed the pain I was feeling. We crossed the road and walked into our lovely warm B&B. We were shown to our room and I felt rude for not being my normal chatty self with our host. But I felt happy to see a big bath which I knew I'd be soaking in later. I collapsed onto the floor and it was time to take off the shoe, to see what damage I'd caused myself during the day. A brick was an apt description, feeling really hot to touch and incredibly swollen.

There is only one thing to do when your feet get fat and you still have over 270 miles to go! I sought advice from a physio friend. I shared photos of my 'brick' and identified where I was feeling pain. He was able to determine it was fat because of its overuse. That's right 'overuse', which is I guess what 5 marathons in a row can do to you. A trip to the shops to stock up on frozen peas, Tubi-Grip, Nurofen gel and pain killers, meant I had all the supplies needed to get me back run-limping the next day. Death and long-term injury were not ok, but I calculated neither would eventuate from this 'brick'. So, a good night's sleep with my feet hoisted in the air by three pillows and covered with frozen peas, meant I was able to squish that fat foot back into my shoe the next morning and keep going.

Over the coming days, the swelling reduced and the pain killers became part of our daily consumption, as they took care of the new pains which came and went. Our days rolled over, made up of more human connection, the weight of the stories behind all those eyes we met and the heavy hearts from those sharing their stories of mental health and impact of suicide. More days of exhaustion and collapsing on our beds at the end of the night. More days where we couldn't consume enough food to fill our energy-sapped bodies. And more and more signatures collected for the petition as we ran miles and miles over the Welsh and English countryside making our way to the other side of the UK.

Johnny and I woke up on our last morning. My heart was full of joy. Overnight we'd reached over our 1,000-signature target.

We left Bungay that morning with our new friend and AirBnB host, Terry, to run through the countryside and along a beautiful river. The morning was clear and crisp for our last 19 miles of our journey.

As we approached Lowestoft I saw the windmill in the distance. Our finish line at Ness Point. We danced and jogged and laughed those last few miles away, feeling grateful for all that we'd experienced, the signatures we'd collected, recalling the goosebump conversations, the little miracles and the lives we'd had the privilege of meeting along the way.

Johnny and I

We took a stand.

We said yes to making a difference.

We plotted and planned.

We started.

We jogged together.

We jogged apart.

We talked.

We laughed.

We cried.

We danced.

We hugged.

We talked to the sheep.

We peed behind trees.

We tended to each other's tired feet that no longer wanted to run.

We listened.

We talked with others.

We gave space.

We carried each other.

We shared our stories.

We ate.

We slept.

We lived in pain.

We lived with blisters.

We lived with swollen joints.

We lived with tired bodies.

We took on cars and lorries.

We made decisions together.

We disagreed over each other's bags – twice.

We watched each other's eyes.

We watched for each other's pains.

We social media-ed.

We dried each other's clothes.

We dried each other's shoes.

We consumed all the water.

We sheltered from the rain, the hail and the snow.

We ran in the rain, the hail, the snow, the wind and the sun.

We become weather masters.

We danced and hugged and laughed and cried some more.

We became runners.

We ran.

Michelle's challenge is to take on the world of adventure and living outside of her comfort zone, while continuing to work full time. Over the last few years, it has led Michelle to climbing the highest point in every European country, stand up paddle boarding between England and France, the length of the River Thames, the longest fjord in the world and cycling the length of the UK. Michelle loves to combine adventure with purpose and has more recently started sharing the blueprints of her micro-adventures, to allow others to easily create a self-supported adventure in their lives too.

To read the outcome of the Government Petition she ran 630km for, check out Instagram @suicideguarantee.

Website: www.melandmichelle.com

Instagram: @shells_ellison

Twitter: @ShellsEllison

Chapter 17

Recovery, Rediscovery and the Peaks In-between

by Pete Barty

I am not an avid adventurer of the rugged, battle-hardened, inspirational type you see standing up at film and outdoor festivals, reliving their amazing tales of skill and endurance. I love these people. I vicariously live their excitement. But they're not me.

Ten years ago, I was simply a 38-year-old, relatively fit amateur league cricketer, happily married with an awesome wife and 18-month-old daughter. I had a reasonably successful career as a Chartered Engineer working for a local authority. Then things changed.

After six months of pain and return visits to my GP, ultra-sound scans, an MRI and a biopsy, I was sitting in the consultant's office, with my wife, Helen, and my Macmillan Support Nurse.

"It's primary bone cancer in your right shoulder. It's potentially fatal without limb-sparing, prosthetic surgery."

The room seemed to go dark and I put my head in my hands as the implications hit me like an avalanche. I stared into an abyss of fear and uncertainty.

Having grasped the devastating diagnosis, and with it the realisation I was due for surgery in just a few days, my Support Nurse sat down with my wife and I. Somehow, in this darkest of times, she knew exactly what to say and understood the worries that now plagued us. She was patient, understanding, knowledgeable and optimistic without giving false hope - exactly what we needed. I will never forget that moment in her office.

Just five days later, I was sitting in a ward at the Nuffield Orthopaedic Hospital in Oxford, with my wife at my side, waiting to go for surgery. Prepped and dosed with pre-med, I was anxious and afraid, holding her hand tightly, desperately needing contact and support.

My consultant came and discussed what was going to happen. Although I can't remember much of what he said, I do remember looking at him with frightened, pleading eyes, begging him to do his best to save me. My Support Nurse came and sat with us for a while too, ensuring we were as OK as we could be. Her familiar, reassuring face, giving comfort where there was fear.

After eight hours of surgery, I woke up in post-op, in a haze of medication and with my entire upper-right side immobilised. It was a very surreal experience. Everything felt slightly fuzzy and I had no idea how the surgery had gone. I was wheeled back to the ward, joined by my wife on the way. I could see the tension and anxiety written across her face. While I'd been unconscious and oblivious, she had clearly been waiting and worrying.

Wired and tubed up, both my consultant and nurse came to see me. The surgery had gone as well as they'd hoped it would and the removed bone had been sent to the lab for analysis. Step one done.

Ahead lay a long road to recovery, but right now, one box was ticked. Time to rest.

I stayed in hospital for about a week, immobilised and anchored to the bed with wires and tubes. Pain was interspersed with morphine relief. Sleep alternated with discomfort and anxiety. Sporadically wheeled out for scans and X-rays, the reality of what lay ahead was starting to sink in. Visitors provided welcome respite, an opportunity to be brave and to put on a smile.

One such visitor was Big Al. Not a remotely ironic moniker, Big Al is 6′ 8″ with size 15 feet. I'm reliably informed, during a late-night bedside chat, we sparked the somewhat naive idea of climbing Kilimanjaro when I got better. If I'm totally honest, while I remember with crystal clarity a lot of things about my time in hospital, there were some aspects that were more a fuzzy memory. Of this conversation I have absolutely no recollection. He was either pulling a fast one or I was morphine-d out!

This seemingly innocuous bedside agreement would have a profound impact on the rest of my life.

The weeks following my discharge from hospital brought Christmas and the fellowship of family that accompanies it. However, all too soon the smiles and connections faded as a new school term arrived and my wife went back to her teaching job.

I was alone with limited ability, faced with my thoughts and the darkness. I didn't realise I was becoming more and more isolated from those around me as the whirlwind impact of the previous two months took hold. I found myself reacting angrily to anything and everyone, being unfair and unkind to those who had supported me and who loved me.

Into this mix came the news we were expecting another baby and I simply didn't know what to do with this. My mind was a whirlpool of worry and everyone walked on eggshells around me.

Enough was enough. I needed to do something. No-one else could do this for me – I needed help but it was up to me to decide to make a change. This acknowledgement was my first big step towards recovery.

Talking one-on-one with Lucy, my therapist, I soon broke down. Words didn't really come but the tears streamed down my face for what seemed like an eternity.

Looking back, this was a huge turning point not only in my mental recovery from cancer, but in my life since then. Over the course of half a dozen sessions, we explored my fears, my mental processes and what I could do to protect those closest to me. I was normal. My fear and anxiety were all valid and expected. We just needed to explore them.

My physio and counselling started to help me back to recovery. The physical side was extremely painful as land and water-based exercises slowly increased my mobility. Despite a new perspective, it was still impossible to leave the shadow of cancer behind, frequent x-rays and scans made sure of that.

The challenge of Kilimanjaro began to loom large in my thoughts, and Big Al was not letting me off this. We'd both signed up by now and the date was set. I'd be away for my 40th birthday. What better way to celebrate than being stuck on the side of a huge dormant volcano in Tanzania trying to get to the highest point in Africa?

I'd been forced to do nothing for six months and had piled on weight as my fitness had fallen through the floor. I was going to meet that challenge head on but I needed to get my fitness back to give myself every chance of success on that hill.

When I eventually got the sign-off to start exercise, I gently started running. I needed to be outside. I'd had enough of life indoors watching box-sets. Yes, I could do this. Yes, this would help me get back to a sense of who I am and my new normal. And yes, I was going to do everything I could to climb that mountain!

The local Great South Run wasn't that long away, so I signed up to give myself a focal point. And followed that up with a place in the Great North Run. I trained as hard as my shoulder would allow. My running action looked weird with a strange arm position but I plugged away.

An equally big challenge lay ahead - fundraising for Kilimanjaro. I believed in my ability to get fit but raising thousands of pounds was something new...! Nonetheless, I also knew how much help my Macmillan Support Nurse had been when we reached out, and they deserved my persistence to do the best I could. After all, someone had done the fundraising for me and made sure there was support there when I needed it. Fundraising continued alongside training, visits to the hospital, work and family life. Blatant begging emails, interest from local press, magazine articles, letters to local companies, a big barn dance and generally pestering everyone I knew followed. This was my window of opportunity to do what I could to help others.

I scoured for kit and advice about climbing 'Kili' as the date drew closer. Before I knew it, I was at the airport, feeling emotional, vulnerable and anxious, with Big Al by my side. I have since met some amazing people who've summited Kilimanjaro dozens of times, but this was my first time doing anything quite so adventurous and my nerves were bubbling away under a brave façade.

It was the first time away from my family (which now included our second beautiful daughter) for any length of time, and this presented a huge opportunity to reflect on my cancer and recovery. It was a massive physical challenge, bigger than anything I'd ever attempted up to that point, and at altitude with the added challenge that brings. My motivation for climbing was never far from my thoughts; a drive to help others who had been dealt the same devastating blow as me, and to prove there is life after cancer. To prove that amazing things *are* still possible.

After four days of rain on the mountain, acclimatisation, questionable toilets and a birthday celebration with a singing crew that I'll never forget (and a cake!), summit night dawned. Following a pointless attempt at snatching a few hours' sleep, we were roused around midnight to eat and then start our bid for the top.

The team was quiet as apprehension and exhaustion took hold. Then hour upon hour of placing one foot in front of the other up a ridiculously steep series of zig zags. It was never ending. Some turned back as the altitude got the better of them, but I was fortunate to see the sunrise through the clouds as we reached the final summit ridge.

Twenty minutes later, we were standing by the famous summit sign, shattered and looking dreadful! And, unfortunately, totally engulfed in cloud with not even a glimpse of a view to wonder at.

Standing on the summit of Kili with Big Al was a massive deal for me. It was proof that I could still live my life to the full even after the cancer diagnosis. And I was able to raise over £10k for such a worthy cause.

The emotion poured out of me when I phoned home the next day, interrupting my wife's teaching of six-year-olds at school. And again, when I called my mum and explained I'd done it.

But what did this mean to me? Fairly soon after standing on that summit, it became clear this was a springboard to the next Yes. I just hadn't yet worked out what that was. I'd proved to myself I could be more than a disease. I could be better than I was before, not despite my misfortune but because of it. This was quite a difficult paradox for me to wrestle with. I was being thankful for having had this diagnosis, for getting through a pitch-black period, and was ascending from it with a direction and purpose that, on reflection, I'd previously lacked.

The "what's next?" question answered itself. Sometimes in life the answers present themselves, we just have to recognise them. I won a 2012 London Marathon place through my running club ballot. My first marathon, and a chance to wear Macmillan green again. With the love and support of my running club, Fareham Crusaders, and particularly my trusty training and race-day compadre Dave (everyone needs a buddy like Dave to see you through dark, cold, wet, long training runs), I rocked up in Greenwich for the start, in what was the year of the London Olympics. What a brilliant time to run around the capital city.

The last two or three miles were all about digging deep, finding every reserve of energy and mental resilience possible and quite frankly not throwing up. I knew the pain and disorientation I was feeling was nothing compared to the despair and anguish I felt when I was diagnosed. Despair and anguish that was being replicated every day, all around the world. My token effort of stumbling toward The Mall paled into triviality.

I'd caught the bug for this challenge lark and so started to think of what was next. Everest Base Camp seemed like an ideal challenge which didn't require me using my shoulder to climb anything! This was my first experience of the Himalaya and what I felt constituted a "proper" expedition; weeks away, discomfort, culture, altitude, dodgy weather and whole load of unknowns. We felt like we were living right on the edge!

I loved every day; getting up before anyone stirred to see the sunrise over Ama Dablam in sub-zero temperatures, leaning between pilot and co-pilot on the flight to Lukla to get the best view, snuggling deep inside my sleeping bag at night to stop my breath from freezing, jumping out the way of heavily-laden, stampeding yaks, laughing in tea houses with my fellow expeditioners, meeting an enchanting Nepalese toddler as we walked through a village and messing about with my camera with her, and of course standing by the famous rocks marking as close as you can get to Base Camp. I was hooked. Leaving Nepal, I was sad, but I knew I'd be back. I didn't know when, but this wasn't goodbye.

Another resounding success to build on, both in challenge and fundraising terms. Challenges dotted themselves through the next few years; a handful of marathons and a shift in focus onto ultra and trail marathons as I pushed myself, not necessarily on speed but with endurance. I would always run with a slightly odd-looking, upper-body style due to my prosthetic shoulder, but I barely cared what I looked like when running anymore. The 33 miles of the Imber Ultra and the 40-mile Compton Ultra led into the sapping 100km of London to Brighton, which, despite some serious post-race recuperation, came and went.

But the mountains were calling. I decided it was time to return to Nepal. Before any decisions were made, a fabulous, but quick, foray to Morocco for a winter ascent of Toubkal gave me the assurance I needed that I could use crampons and adapt an ice-axe technique if needs be. A chance discussion with Jo Bradshaw, seven summit aspirant, whilst working together, planted a seed of a thought around summiting the Khumbu 3 Peaks; Mera, Island and Lobouche East. This seed germinated silently until soon a seedling broke the surface. Could I?

Island Peak looked so scary. That summit ridge! And look at that ice wall to scale! I can't do that! But the seed sprouted, and grew, and branched. Imagined barriers dispersed. My boss was fine with me having a month off work. My wife reassured me we could make it work. And one last conversation with Rolfe Oostra, well known mountaineer and co-owner of the expedition company, about my abilities and worries, confirmed I'd be fine. That was it – I signed up.

The Khumbu 3 Peaks was truly an awesome experience. Four weeks at altitude, missing family, lack of sleep, freezing cold, exposure, exhaustion, group tensions at times, camaraderie, immense satisfaction, connection to the people and place, pushing beyond previously believed limits, fun and laughter. And to cap it all, the knowledge that of the five out of our group of twelve who summited all three peaks, I was one. This was my biggest feat to date and for once I wasn't thinking about what was next. At least, not straight away.

Without really meaning to, I was beginning to build a track record, and I'd become a familiar face for Macmillan with a good story to tell; sets a challenge, fundraises and achieves his goals. And so back home, once the dust had settled, I began to wonder and browse through websites.

Aconcagua, in the Argentinian Andes, emerged as the next contender. It would be another month away, one of the seven summits at 6,962m and based in Malbec country - I was sold on the wine alone. This was how, on New Year's Day 2018, I came to be standing at Heathrow Airport with Welsh Ray, who I'd bonded with and shared many man-hugs on the Khumbu 3 Peaks expedition and had convinced to join me. I still had no idea just how much saying Yes to the challenge of Aconcagua would come to mean.

My story of 'Aco' is a monumental piece of personal discovery for me, around which I've journaled many thousands of very personal words. So many, I ran out of pages in the A5 book I took away with me.

Aco is a beast, renowned for harsh conditions and not giving up her summit lightly. I trained harder than ever, knowing my body would be pushed to its limits, with my shoulder forced to carry loads to higher and higher camps. All was well as we reached the Plaza de Mulas base camp at 4,300m seven days into the trip. Acclimatisation was working and we'd summited the adjacent Pico de Bonette at around 5,000m.

Twelve tiring days later and our ascent of Aco was on track. Like most summit attempts at these altitudes, it began in the middle of the night. Dragged from our pits, we wolfed down some porridge, kitted up and pushed out into the deep darkness and freezing temperatures. As we plodded quietly through the tents, shining head torches marked the movement of other potential summiteers, their beams lighting up the slope ahead. And on the path above us, tiny lights flickered against the inky sky.

Plod, plod, plod. My head space was absorbed by simple thoughts of just breathing and moving my feet, glancing up every so often to see that the world still existed outside of my cocoon.

The same pin pricks of light in the sky as before. All was well. We continued. Plod, plod, plod. It was utterly lonely. No companionship at all. Just our own thoughts for company. Darkness and separation.

Eventually I looked up and saw a glimmer of daylight in the distance. I'd made it to daybreak.

I lifted my goggles to remind myself of the gracious inevitability of a new day. Yes, here it comes. The anticipation made for a welcome, warming distraction. Despite allowing myself fleeting glances up to see this beauty, I still needed to concentrate on the task at hand, the continuous plod, plod, plod.

We reached Influencia Camp at 6,300m with the sun now up. It had been a really tough two or three hours to reach this point, made harder by the snow that had fallen over the last few days. I was physically tired and needed a decent break here, I could sense my legs starting to hurt like they do after a marathon. I could only assume the others felt this way too.

In this new daylight, I could finally take a look around me and right on cue, as the sun slowly rose higher behind the summit, the dark pyramid of Aco's silhouette lay out in front and below us, a truly wonderful spectacle. We could see other climbers around us, also sitting in transition, recuperating, rehydrating, re-nourishing and generally taking stock of what was to come - Phase 2, Windy Gap and the traverse to The Caves. All of this would be in deep, dark shade, protected from the damaging sun but with a biting wind howling across the traverse making for temperatures far below zero.

Many of those resting were Argentinian so our leader listened in on conversations about the conditions ahead. We were protected by a little bank, roughly ten metres high, which marked the start of the ridge traverse into the exposed, frozen shade. Every inch of flesh was re-covered, goggles on and buff tucked in tight. Along this traverse, any uncovered flesh would blister and possibly succumb to frost bite.

As we lifted our packs to leave, around twenty members of the Argentinian Mountain Patrol, a part of the Army, who had just started out before us, turned around shaking their heads and headed back in our direction.

It was too cold for them. But it was their job! How were we supposed to fare?

We sidestepped past them and trudged up the small slope onto the ridge where we could see what lay ahead - the long cold traverse into the distance. I felt my breathing start to quicken and shorten, increasing my work rate.

The noise was jet-engine deafening and the ferocious wind destabilised us as we broke the ridge line. Onwards we plodded. It was bitter in this shade, with a stinging rawness you could taste, colder than I'd ever sensed before, tiny exposed pieces of my face immediately yelling to me that they were at risk and needed covering. My breathing was becoming troubled, short and fast. Way too fast to keep my body satiated and I couldn't regulate it despite us walking along a relatively gentle incline.

Just like in the darkness, it was lonely and insular with the restricted goggle vision. Just my thoughts and fears for company. Most of all, I was alone with the sound of my breathing. Short, quick, and moisture laden, which was starting to cause a new concern. I was breathing too much, which was creating way too much moisture being held in my buff.

"You're generating too much saliva and moisture. That's a sign of

AMS," our leader bluntly informed me. "You could start to become uncoordinated."

This hit me like an icy blast. What? Acute Mountain Sickness? Surely this wasn't happening to me? I'd never had AMS before and we were only at about 6,500m. I'd been at the same altitude before in Nepal and had no issues.

Eventually, we reached The Caves, signifying the next stage. Out of the blasting, cutting shade and back into the warmth of the sun. I drank some lukewarm tea from my flask, tried to get down about a quarter of a litre of water that was almost ice, then stuffed some nuts in my mouth, quite a challenge when wearing what, in effect, were oven gloves.

The sun warmed me through as we gazed up at the next stage – the Canaleta, a very steep, high wall of snow and ice. Most other times when I'd seen this in photos or read descriptions it was rock and scree. Not this time. We faced deep snow and ice. Rarely had I read of crampons being needed here.

The wind had abated, the sides of the Canaleta protected those attempting this steep high-sided gulley. I sat in my own silent retreat, as we started to sack up and move. "Come on, Pete. Be the person you can be!" I uttered to myself.

We turned toward the throat of Aco, 6,500m and rising. We were nearly there. My legs started to scream at me, as with energy-sapping side-steps we started up the face. But their cries were nothing compared to the immediate worry surrounding my breathing. It was so troubled it was clear all my efforts to get up this slope were going be severely hampered by the amount of oxygen I could get into my muscles. With the sun beating down on us, we inched slowly and steadily up the Canaleta.

Then I felt something happening with my legs. A feeling they weren't quite connected to the rest of me. I carried on, one, two more side-steps up a particularly steep section, but they were on their own. One cramponed-foot slipped. Then the other followed. Suddenly I was lying on my side against the slope.

I heard it immediately through the confusion of my unwieldly limbs. Our leader and guide shouting to each other in Spanish and, with that very utterance, I knew the meaning of what was about to happen right now. What that meant for this summit push, for my summit dreams and for my ongoing drive towards being better than that disease.

It was over.

In that pivotal moment, my hopes dashed by our leader's simple instruction from afar, I felt floored like a punch-drunk fighter. Like a bystander, cast aside, chewed up and spat out. At that moment, I just sat passively and observed as our guide roped me up. Full of a combination of shock, exhaustion, AMS and resignation. The realisation of what this meant gnawed at the edges of my awareness, yet to fully engage. It really wasn't far downhill to Camp 3, Camp Cholera. All I needed was to reach the tent and regroup, to start to process what had just happened and somehow work out what was going to happen next.

And as the altitude receded and my cognition improved, my enduring thought was, 'I've failed.'

How do I tell Helen and my girls that I'd failed?

Reaching the tent, I rehydrated, pushed off my boots and crawled in. Wrapped in my down sleeping bag, with the sun's warmth on the orange Gore-Tex of the tent creating a soothing cocoon, I closed my eyes and despite the mental anguish that enveloped me, I drifted off to sleep.

A short time later, I cradled a mug of warm tea in my hands and started to face what had happened. I deconstructed this wall piece by piece, feeling more exposed with each course of brickwork that came down.

I had failed.

Even though it was just a failed summit attempt, it hurt. Since having cancer, I had focused on setting myself a target, working out what I need to do to get there and going for it... *successfully*. In my mind, I didn't miss peaks, whether on mountains, in a race or in life. But there was no hiding from it. It wasn't down to the weather or unforeseen circumstances. It was just me.

What pained more deeply still was the belief that what I'd represented over the eight years since my diagnosis, what I'd worked so hard to create, was now irreparably tarnished. Eight years of being better than a disease, of not allowing the malignance to define me, of proving my self-worth beyond cancer and a disability. I'd traded privacy to be a face of cancer and of charity. I'd established a track record, a 'brand' that could be used for good to raise money to help others.

But, it wasn't simply 'helping' others that I'd sought to achieve – I had striven to *inspire* them. To provide that glimmer of hope, a moment of strength, whether they had been diagnosed with cancer or were just drifting goalless through this precious life. If I could spur on one person living with cancer to find a better place and believe they are greater and better than a disease, then all the pain and hurt of family separation was worth it. After all, eight years on, I'd been given the all clear and a new chance at life. I could take risks that others could not.

As all this tumbled from my exhausted mind onto the journal page in front of me, I realised my cheeks were wet. My swollen, tired eyes were crying. Wiping my sore, wind-burnt cheeks did little to stem the flow of tears. I flopped back onto my sleeping bag, in the hope that more warm restorative sleep would give me a clearer perspective on the day's events.

That clarity took many sleeps, much processing, reflection, soul searching and Malbec with Welsh Ray, to get anywhere near the sense of understanding and inner worth I sought. But get there I did.

Several other small moments came together to help me accept what had happened. On our last day in Argentina, Ray and I toured vineyards, ate amazing food and were joined by a friendly priest from Buenos Aires. Over lunch, we shared life stories. He was working in the city slums, providing hope to the hopeless and love to the unloved. I was humbled. It may simply have been by chance that I met this man, on that day; my recently-deceased mum's birthday, and just when I was questioning my worth, but that shared experience helped me see things differently.

A simple quote on a Facebook message from a friend, read while I was still struggling in Mendoza, gave me such another jolt and helped enormously.

"...the tragedy of life doesn't lie in not reaching your goal. The tragedy lies in having no goals to reach. It isn't a calamity to die with dreams unfilled, but it is a calamity not to dream. .... It is not a disgrace to reach the stars, but it is a disgrace to have no stars to reach for. Not failure, but low aim, is a sin." Benjamin E. Mays

I've come to believe this is the key. Reach for those goals, have the experiences and accept that sometimes it might not go to plan.

Failure is just one end of a polarity with success at the other end, and sometimes the tossed coin falls the other way up to our expectations. But not tossing that coin in the first place is where real failure lurks.

Avoiding taking that risk, that chance of not getting to my summit - what's the damage really? Knocked pride, or not understanding the wisdom and strength that result from trying. For me, that damage was the pain I felt but that too has eased. The catharsis I felt while writing in my journal helped immensely, as I sensed the logic of the argument rolling out like a red carpet before me. We must try. Win or lose, it's the experience and learning of the journey that shapes the person. Not trying or experiencing is to not fully live, to cocoon yourself in a bubble where familiarity breeds boredom, shrinking boundaries and experiences left unfelt. Just embrace the YES.

My first YES led me on a path towards physical and mental recovery. A one in a million cellular mutation left me feeling helpless, but it gave me a choice. Surrender or choose an active role in the process. That decision led me to the summit of Kilimanjaro, and subsequently so much more. The full ramifications of one simple decision are rarely known, but the implications of not making a decision often are. I focused on being active, staying fit and proving to my body that whilst it may have decided to try and kill me, I was going to fight it every step of the way.

The second YES was different. That was a clear shift in mind-set, to look at life not as successful ticks in boxes, but an ongoing process of experience, development and learning. If I had summited Aco, I know that on the way down I'd have been signing up for something else without ever considering what I'd learnt. The escapist in me would have focussed on the endgame believing success was everything. Instead I came to realise that understanding myself was the far greater achievement.

"It's not the mountain we conquer, but ourselves." Sir Edmund Hillary

Pete is an introverted reflector who is occasionally afflicted by sporadic calls to action. Since his diagnosis he has been on the adventures you have just read about (and some since then), trained as a Mountain Leader and qualified as a Counsellor; setting up in private practice (www.findyournorth.co.uk). When he is not trying to stave off middle age by staying fit, working or helping people understand themselves better to be the best version of themselves, he can usually be found on the touchlines watching his two girls play football, doing his best to keep his mouth shut about a sport he admittedly knows very little about.

Facebook: peter.barty.73

Email: peterbarty@hotmail.com

Chapter 18

Driving to Mongolia in a Mad Machine

by Richard Matthews

"Smithy, do you want to do something mad next summer? I am not going to tell you what it is and you have to answer, yes or no."

Somewhat reluctantly and blindly he said, "YES." Little did he know, Smithy had just made the best decision of his life

The Mongol Rally is a drive from the UK to Mongolia. The vehicle must cost no more than £500 and the engine size must be no more than 1.2L. The challenge would be difficult at best. Smithy's complete faith in my ability to not get him hurt would be tested.

We set out to look for a third member to join our band via the power of social media. A mutual friend, Mitchell, jumped at the chance. He had recently overcome cancer and the trip was partly a platform for him to raise money for the Teenage Cancer Trust.

The three main routes for the Mongol Rally are the northern, central and southern crossings of different areas of central Asia. The hardest and most adventurous route was the southern route. Of course we had to choose that one. Crossing Europe into Turkey, we would pass through Iran, Turkmenistan, Uzbekistan, Tajikistan following the Pamir Highway before heading north into Kyrgyzstan and Kazakhstan, entering Russia briefly before driving deep into the heart of Mongolia. Honestly, it seemed like a truly daunting task.

Speaking to people who had been before or who were planning on going this time, it was obvious that there was so much to learn. It was exciting.

As Hannibal from the A-team would say, "I love it when a plan comes together!" We had the plan, but pulling it together would be a miracle akin to creating to a bulletproof tank out of a few sheets of corrugated iron and an old oil barrel!

First thing was first. We had to find a car. Cue lots of scrolling through Auto Trader, flipping through car magazines and asking just about everyone we knew if we could buy their car. On Gumtree I stumbled across a 1996 Nissan Micra with a 1L engine. Perfect! There was one downside. It had no keys. Before you ask, no, we didn't steal it. The owner had blissfully lost them whilst staggering home from the pub one night.

Next up, we had to modify our noble Micra ready to take on the 'roads' of Central Asia, the mountains, deserts and potentially through rivers. But before we could get in to do any of that, we had to get it started first!

Off to Nissan we went. We were sure that they would help us. There'd be no problems at all. We were about to embark on an amazing cross continental trip in one of their cars - why wouldn't they help?

Well they didn't and they weren't that interested at all.

Feeling more deflated than a week old party balloon, we headed back to Mitch's house to reassess our plan. If we couldn't get any keys, our Mongolian adventure would be deader than a dormouse at a dodo disco.

On another front, sponsorship was mercifully easy to come by. Mitch and Smithy's companies both agreed to back our cause financially and I approached a range of outdoor companies looking for more sponsors.

One of the companies that came back was DD Hammocks. They set us a challenge. If we could build a frame to hang the hammocks off of, they would sponsor us all sorts of outdoor gear (including hammock, obviously). Not being one to turn down a challenge, we readily accepted and, in no time at all, Smithy (our resident engineer) was daydreaming about all sorts of interesting designs for a hammock hanging contraption.

He came up with, what we dubbed, 'The Spider System'. 4 poles extended out from the roof-rack with outriggers attached. The hammocks would be slung between the poles (one on each side, one on the rear) with straps holding the 4 poles in place... It was brilliant, fast and simple.

Next thing on our ever increasing to do list was a full service including gaining a bit extra height. We needed bigger springs to hold the extra weight that we would be carrying with all of our gear. To add some extra protection, we bolted a sump guard to the underside of the engine. Then we packed the car with all the things that are needed to cross a quarter of the world with three muppets at the wheel. Spare engine belts, oil, two spare tyres and more jerry cans than an army surplus store and all the other random bits and pieces including, three top hats, a bugle and a golf club (no joke!).

And finally, we got the Micra started like stallion ready at the gates. It wasn't easy getting this far though. In the end, we had to give in to the demands of Nissan and buy three car keys at an outrageous price. They were not our biggest fans at this point.

We were as ready as we would ever be!

It was the start day of the rally; a beautiful sunny Sunday morning.

All manner of exceptional adventure vehicles were lined up at the starting grid of the Goodwood race circuit for a lap, four abreast, bumper to bumper. It truly was a surreal moment. The atmosphere was electric; people gritting their teeth behind steering wheels, the sweet taste for adventure filling their heads, their buttocks clenched and raring to go.

The excitement got the best of some of us. A Swiss team drove straight into the back of the our Micra at the first roundabout. Morons!

A gut-wrenching feeling came over us. Was our rally over before it had even started?

We all jumped out to inspect the damage thinking the worst had happened. There was, in fact, no damage at all. Finding out the Micra was far tougher than we had realised gave us the confidence and absolute faith in our little white car. We were sure it would hold its own over the next few months.

We drove on towards Dover ready to catch the ferry to mainland Europe and began our international adventure properly.

Staying true to our nature, we missed the ferry! Someone kept sending us on the scenic route, not mentioning any names (Mitch!).

Staying positive, we rolled up to the check in desk with fixed nervous grins on our faces and joined a line of 5 other rally cars. We acted like nothing was wrong and that we were meant to be there. "Missed our ferry? Don't know what you're talking about, guv! We're in the Mongol Rally."

Our ruse worked. We boarded the next ferry and were on our way to France quicker than you can say, "Ou est la bibilotheque!"

Joining us on the ferry was a plethora of other rally teams. Some of the teams we knew from chats and meet ups in advance of the adventure. Others we would soon get to know. One thing was assured though…

Our arrival in France would be complete chaos!

We had agreed on the ferry that we would ride in convoy through the port of Calais, but in the confusion of endless roundabouts and identikit cash-and-carry stores, we somehow all lost each other. How it was even possible, God only knows.

Eventually, we all came together outside a closed garage on the outskirts of town, handed out the radios that we had been given and set off on the long night drive.

We carried on through Europe, crossing the continent at a hair-raising speed before entering Turkey - our first proper border. None of us in the car really knew what to do?

The three of us went up to passport control and declared that we had a vehicle. As the car owner, I was sent on a goose-chase going to several different windows to get insurance, then an inspection and then back to this window with the paperwork. It was bureaucratic nightmare and quite a daunting process being on my own. I knew that I would have to get used to this situation. We had plenty of border crossings to come.

A few hours later and we were finally clear of the border and into Turkey heading east and towards our destination of Mongolia.

We drove through the night for 2 days to reach a town close to the Iranian border for a rendezvous with 6 other ralliers. We were going to make our way across Iran in convoy. It made complete sense. We needed to have a guide to escort us through the country and at $1,000, it wasn't going to be cheap. Having 6 teams sharing the bill was just logical.

I had expected something similar to the red tape debacle at the

Turkish border only, maybe, slightly more difficult.

It wasn't.

It worse than I could have possibly imagined.

I was pulling my hair out as I tried to wrap my brain around the complexities of the forms I had to endure. With us being such a large group from many nations with a load of silly cars, they were reluctant to let us just walk in. Our guide was incredible to say the least. Even with his help, it took 13 painstaking hours in the scorching heat to secure our onward journey.

Eventually we were in. We set off quickly, partly in fear of being called back to the border to be reprimanded for not ticking a box on an obscure form and partly to start exploring the exciting landscape of northern Iran. We even had time to visit what is supposedly the first church EVER before heading down to Tabriz to stay the night.

This was when I had my first opportunity to really say, "Yes!"

Everyone else had gone in the pre-booked hotel and I was just grabbing my bag, when a car pulled up alongside me with only its side lights on. I was instantly on high alert as I made a mental note of where all of my valuables were stashed on my person.

Inside their car was a bloke wearing a white creased shirt and sporting a wiry mop of thin grey hair. He leant across and called out of the open passenger window.

His English was slightly broken. He asked if I was okay and what was I doing before getting out, going around to the boot of his car and producing a pack of biscuits.

"These for you," he said passing me the Rich Teas reverently. "Where you staying?"

"Er, here, I guess," I said, thumbing the hotel over my shoulder.

"No. You come back to my house, meet my family and we have food together, yes?"

"Um... Er..." I stuttered. What was I meant to do in this sort of social situation? I was slightly scared and caught completely off guard. "Thank you," I said. "But no."

Being so unsure of the repercussions, I opted to stay in the hotel. What a regret! Just goes to show that it's not the 'Yeses' you regret. It's the 'Nos'.

It transpired that this level of hospitality was going to continue and, everywhere we went, people wanted to give us gifts, have a chat and invite us back to their place.

Sometimes when we stopped, hordes of people would rush up, all really kind and wanting to help. It was truly surreal and it crossed my mind that this is what celebrities must get all the time. I had to turn down many kind offers from tours around cities to exploring new towns, food and accommodation. My main concern was around what would happen if I was found to be away from our guide. I didn't want to get on the wrong side of the Iranian legal system.

After Tabriz we headed east exploring Tehran's palaces, markets and incredible architecture before heading south to Isfahan, one of the largest bazaars in the world, with its incredible mosques and river flowing through it. We had such a limited time in each place, we could only scratch the surface of what each of these cities had to offer.

On the last night in Iran we managed to enter into one of the greatest places yet, the Shire of Imam Reza, a mosque in Mashhad. It was enormous, so big that during the holy days over 4 million people would come through its gates to pray. Just incredible!

Entering Turkmenistan, we were greeted by a stunning road and views of rolling arid mountains with a river running below us where lush vegetation grew.

Ashgabat, the capital city, is a truly surreal place. It is held under a dictatorship and cast over by the Karakum desert which occupies 70% of the country. It was stiflingly. Ornate marble buildings were scattered across the city like... well, like marbles and every road was tarmacked to perfection. The high-grade stainless steel in every lamppost and gold cladding on all the buildings made the city sparkle in the sunshine. The huge park with fountains and immaculate gardens seemed completely counter-intuitive when set against the backdrop of the desert. The whole city was like a bratty kids' playhouse dropped in a sandbox. We even stumbled upon the largest indoor ferris wheel in the world.

We left the city and headed north to the infamous Gates of Hell, otherwise known as the Darvaza Gas Craters, a flaming pit in the ground 43m across. In order to get there, we had to drive several hours across some very interesting roads. With the heat being so intense the tarmac had melted forming deep ruts and large mounds. Some of the ruts were nearly 10cm deep, like long solid ditches into which our wheels kept veering. Having our plastic sump guard protected us from the worst of the road, but we would still hear the occasional scrape and bang. The underside and suspension took a hammering but the Micra held up.

Travelling at night on roads as bad as this is never a good idea, but with only 5 days on our visa we didn't have a choice. We had to keep moving fast if we wanted to see Turkmenistan.

We stuck to a dual carriageway to ensure we were making good time. Further along the road, I noticed some head lights that seemed to be on our side of the road, although it was a long way off so I wasn't too worried. It kept getting closer and closer. Then I began thinking, 'Maybe it's just the way the road was turning.'

Suddenly, with horror filling every ounce of my body, I realised that the headlights were not in a lane next to me. And the road didn't bend around an unseen corner. The lights were heading straight at me. More importantly, behind the lights was the bulky mass of a 14-tonne bus. On a collision course!

I cranked the steering wheel hard to the left, steering us off the road and into the sand. Simultaneously, I slammed my foot down on the brake. I was only just able to keep control of the bucking Micra as we smashed into small shrubs and anything that lay in our way.

Poor Smithy, who had been fast asleep in the back, was thrown in the air, crashing heavily into the ceiling with an, "Oomph!"

Seconds later, having avoided death by bus and using rally skills that Tommi Makinen would have been proud of, I steered the Micra back onto the road and brought it to a gradual stop. Stepping out and panting hard, I sat down on the warm tarmac with my head between my hands trying to process what had just happened and what the outcome could have been...

We all took a breather, decided to slow the pace down and that someone else should drive.

Several hours later, at around 11pm, we reached the gas craters where there were a whole host of other rally teams. A 4x4 land cruiser was giving people lifts to the crater a few kilometres in the desert. Not wanting to risk the Micra, although we all reckoned it could have made it, we jumped in the 4x4 and went for a hell of a drive. The night sky, which had been void of all light, suddenly had an orange and red glow, spreading across the horizon like a wildfire. There in front of us was the flaming gas crater.

It was immensely hot, so hot that it was impossible to stand on the edge. The changing air currents brought the heat of the fire raging up the sides of the crater. The ground appeared to be on fire with rocks glowing red hot. Confusingly, it seemed like there was no fuel. The ground was literally alight.

We could have spent hours looking into the fiery crater, but we reluctantly left with the last group back in the land cruiser to our cars.

The rest of the country, was very similar to what we had already seen; run down, poor roads, people trying to live as best as they could in places of incredible history. Rubbish dumps surrounded ancient mud fortresses dating back to the times of Genghis Khan.

It was saddening to see history being neglected and the deep poverty in which some people were forced to live.

Nonetheless, we had to keep moving east towards Mongolia. We crossed into Uzbekistan at the border with Turkmenabat heading onwards to Bukhara and Samarkand before moving on to Dushanbe, the capital of Tajikistan and last city before the infamous Pamir Highway.

We had heard many stories about the Pamir Highway and Wakhan Valley. "You can't miss it," said one blog. "Your car will never make it out alive," said another. "The roads are hell," said a third before going into the kind of detail about weather forecasts, mudslides and detrimental road conditions that only a Mongol Rally veteran would bother writing about.

I was pretty cautious about the next stage of our journey. Apparently, there had been lots of sightings of Taliban in the area. We would be following the Afghanistan border for several hundred kilometres as well. Prime bandit territory.

We prepared the Micra as best we could, giving everything a once over and ditching some equipment to save weight before we started. This was sure to be the most difficult section of the journey.

With Dushanbe in our rear-view mirror, the tarmacked road twisted and turned as it steadily climbed into the foothills of the Pamir Mountains. It didn't last long and, without warning, the tarmac stopped, changing into a dusty track. The start of the aptly monikered Corrugated Road.

Every inch or so, a small aggressive little speed bump would shunt the car up and down like the angriest and most repetitive rumble strips in the world. With the constant vibration, we began to imagine bits were falling off of our poor little Micra.

That was until we took the lead of our small convoy and pushed the pedal to the metal, leaving the rest of the group in our dust cloud. The faster we travelled the smoother the ride. The wheels didn't have a chance to sit down into the dips instead sticking only to the tops of ridges. The consequence of this, was that we had to drive around 45-50mph. Along a remote road. In the middle of Tajikistan. What could go wrong?

The road and scenery undulated. Sometimes sections of tarmac resurfaced around the villages, while in other areas we were driving across sand dunes. Then the bridges came that we had to cross. The rickety old things looked like they would fall down if a portly gentleman decided to stroll home after a hefty meal, let alone a car full of three buffoons plus supplies.

The road followed a river up into the mountains. It cascaded excitedly through deep narrow canyons carving its own path through the rock and mellowed into 100m wide expanses as it ambled over plains.

After a couple of days in the wilderness, we had our first encounter with recent civilisation when Mitch spotted a sign in Russian. We didn't understand what the text under the symbol said, but that didn't matter. The symbol was clear enough.

It was a minefield.

It was a quick and mutual decision to not really hang around. Moving further up the mountain we discovered a bottomless canyon – with no barrier! Fortunately, the road was wide enough for cars and lorries to pass each other... just!

Every corner brought a new horizon, a different landscape and a new challenge. It was incredible but also exhilarating. It was a buzz of excitement, with "Oooo!", "Arrrghhh!" and "Oh hell!".

"Oh hell!" was soon at the forefront of all of our minds. We were getting close to the border town of Khroug and 3rd gear kept popping out. It had done this in Turkey once, but we hadn't thought anything of it. Now it was getting relentless. We all looked at each other with a sigh of 'What's happening?'

And then, it got worse. Every time we went in to 3rd, it would jump straight back into the neutral. Not good. We pushed on regardless switching between 2nd and 4th until we could find a mechanic to help us out.

The mechanic in Khroug test drove the car, sucked his breath in like all mechanics do before dropping a bombshell and said, "The gear linkage has snapped."

We all looked around dumbfounded. "What's the gear linkage?"

He explained that it was a piece of metal that kept the gear in place while the engine put power into the gear. With it snapped it would continuously pop out. That was the last time we used 3rd. Who needs 3rd gear anyway? Old granny's pootling down to the shops, that's who! Surely, we could survive without it. We were going to have to!

At Khroug, we discovered that the road we wanted to take was blocked due to some landslides which left us with the only other option - the Wakhan Valley Corridor. This meant several hundred more kilometres hugging the border. While this may have filled us with dread when we started this leg of the trip, we now felt completely at ease with it. We had already covered large areas of the border, being met exclusively by hospitable, kind, generous, amazing people. Where were all the bandits we'd been warned about?

Over the next several hundred kilometres, we encountered a few sparse villages and shepherds minding their flocks on high mountain passes. It was while gazing at a particularly stunning crag that Mitch leant a little too heavily on the accelerator and ploughed us straight into a ginormous lake. Water flew all over the place. It crashed across the bonnet and more worryingly sloshed into the air intake. Mitch kept the revs going and somehow we managed to reach the other side, the Micra coughing and spluttering like someone struggling to breathe.

Suddenly, it gasped its last breath and died.

We were like a well-oiled Micra paramedic team as we sprang to life, clambering out of the stricken vehicle to rectify the damage we (i.e. Mitch) had caused. Was it the end of the line for our little Micra or would he live to see the end of the race?

Then the cavalry arrived. Having seen what happened to our Micra, the other teams in our convoy opted for a different route around the lake to come to our aid

Joe, a qualified mechanic from another team, and Smithy, our resident engineer, immediately dived under the bonnet twisting whotsits and inspecting thingummys.

Alex from the Australian Team and I climbed a nearby mountain to pass the time while waiting for the engine to dry. From our vantage point we could overlook the entire valley. It looked like a huge hand with taloned fingers had scraped across the land gouging deep crevasses into the earth. Barren and foreboding. Further on we could see the sun creep closer toward the distant horizon. A bird of prey, maybe a vulture, circled high in the sky above us. I looked down to the bustle of activity by our tiny little matchbox Micra and hoped to God that they could fix it. How else were we going to get out of this disastrous situation?

Several hours passed until below us, thankfully, we heard the purr of the Micra's engine kicking back into life and a cheer from the gathered ralliers.

It wasn't over yet!

With the Micra back on the road, we scrambled down the mountainside and pushed deeper into the Pamir Mountains. We bumped and battered the cars through the lowlands before climbing and heading north to cross the mountains gaining altitude all of the time. Camping at nearly 3,500m, things were a little different compared to the valley bottom, that's for sure.

The next day the altitude got worse as we pushed on towards Kyrgyzstan, hitting the highest point and, up until now, the remotest point of the trip. With towering mountains surrounding us on all sides, we crossed the 4,655m Ak Baital Pass. Nearly everyone was struggling. The cars were in an even worse state, not really able to pull themselves past 20mph on occasion.

And to add to the fun it started snowing!

At the pass we all got out take a photo and then pushed on down the other side as quickly as we dared, rocking the cars across more dips, sand, rocks, rivers and dried river-beds. We were racing to get to a lower altitude.

We pushed on north through Kyrgyzstan, crossing the country in just over 48 hours, staying over in Osh and Bishkek to get some rest. Here we realised that the rear shock absorbers were shot. But we didn't want to hang around. We pushed on to Almaty where we had arranged some friends to meet up with us.

With the car still in a state, we left the urban bustle of Almaty behind to cross the wilds of Northern Kazakhstan to Semey. This meant a 1,100km non-stop drive passing through rolling countryside and arid deserts on dirt tracks. The scenery seemed somewhat bleak as the Micra twisted and groaned its way along the undulating road. At least we were able to move at a fair pace compared to the slow going in the Pamirs.

As the sun began to set to our west, in what seemed an age on this flat terrain, something started to dominate the horizon in the distance. A large structure close to main road. Getting nearer we could see it was an abandoned building of some description which had been left for nature to reclaim. We changed our course and headed off the main road to investigate. The building was huge, reaching nearly 50m into the sky. We headed inside to discover that it was an old food silo.

Nearby was a broken set of stairs graffitied with Soviet images. It was an eerie place, especially as the light began to drain from the sky. Even so, we began looking for the best vantage point to admire the sunset. We climbed the stairs attempting to get the roof. It was harder said than done, as many of the steps were completely missing and we were forced to climb the concrete and metal debris.

The reward was worth it. The sunset was breath-taking. Red ochre stretched across the barren flatlands turning to the deepest blue above our heads.

Carefully we made our way back down to the car and continued on to Semey.

The car had to be fixed. Our shopping list of things that needed to be done was quite extensive. Rear shocks, gearbox (if that was even possible) and the oil leak were the main priorities.

We stopped by a garage and soon discovered that we needed a bit more work than expected. Our exhaust had more or less split just before the rear of the back box. Luckily, we were in good hands as Micras are readily available in Central Asia. The garage took us under their wing.

In no time, Mitch and myself were being whizzed around Semey visiting all the shops to get the parts we needed. We were taken to a huge warehouse full of small market stalls. It was like an Aladdin's cave if Aladdin had been hunting for car parts instead of magic lamps. One stall had gearboxes and nothing else. Another had the rubber seals for gearboxes. Then the one that we need most of all:

the suspension stall and our much-needed rear shock absorbers. Unfortunately, we couldn't get a gearbox so we decided to push on without 3rd gear. We had got this far without it. We could get through Mongolia without it as well.

We got back to the workshop to find Smithy having had an incredible lunch with the rest of mechanics. On our return, they quickly got to work to changing the shocks as well as plugging the oil leak in the gearbox. When the Micra was reassembled, we had a fantastic meal with the garage staff. What awesome guys!

With the Micra powered up (minus that annoying 3rd gear) we got a good night's sleep before heading off to catch up with everyone else. We were a day and country behind the rest of our small group, who were now in Novosibirsk. We had agreed to meet them at the Mongolian border in Russia.

Leaving early, we crossed the Russian border without any issues and in under an hour, which was unheard of for us. We opted for the most direct route. Even though we avoided the main roads we were still blessed with excellent tarmac and, to everyone's surprise, we ended up ahead of our small convoy!

I was pretty excited to re-join everyone to camp out for the night under the stars before we entered Mongolia. Choosing a campsite was, for the first time, quite difficult as the land was flat around the road leading up the border yet also barren and harsh, covered in small rocks and short tufty grass. It was something that we would get very used to seeing over the next week.

Camping so close to the border had its issues. We could easily get into trouble with the Border Patrol who could have mistaken us for immigrants, vagrants or other words ending in -grants. We turned off the main road and drove around in the dark until we found a small divot in the land to set up out tents for the night.

In the morning we would be in Mongolia.

Finally, we crossed into Mongolia. This was our last push to finish line. 2 months of driving madness was now entering the grand finale. Crossing the Gobi Desert, plains, mountains and rivers with little or no infrastructure. The country is the same size as Western Europe, yet is populated by only 3 million people.

This is what we had all been dreaming of. We had made it to Mongolia despite everything that had been thrown at our cars. Time for the ultimate test of them and ourselves.

The tarmac only lasted for a couple of miles before it finished and we got to experience our first true Mongolian road.

Dirt tracks, several hundred metres wide, generally headed off in the same direction. Fortunately, they also pointed the way we were headed. Many of the tracks were only just visible through the desert conditions. Sometimes they were sand covered. Others were rivets with pothole trenches. It was always changing from one to another and then back again while endlessly twisting and turning.

I was in complete awe of the landscape, roads and the people. How did people live in such an environment like this? Our somewhat reasonable progress slowed to a few hundred kilometres a day, which was fine by us. Besides, none of us had any idea what the time was. From when we entered Mongolia everyone in our 10-person convoy had completely different times, working on different time zones. The sun became our clock. We woke up when it rose and went to sleep when it set.

It was after yet another sleepless night in the unremitting heat that we had the first real fight in our team. I didn't think we'd have a falling out but we did. Smithy came out the worst of it with a deep bloody wound gashed across the top of his head.

Just goes to show that you shouldn't have an argument with the boot of a Micra!

I grabbed the first aid kit and strapped up his head making him look like Tutankhamun's younger and less attractive brother. We told Smithy that he had to settle his differences with the car and go and have a sit down.

We finished packing everything and headed off as normal. 20 minutes into the drive Smithy informed us that he was feeling cold and had put his down jacket on. Mitch and I looked at each other. We were sweating in shorts and t-shirts.

Alarm bells began ringing.

Next Smithy told us that he needed to get out as he felt sick. We quickly pulled over. He leant out of the door and projectile vomited across the sand.

Alarm bells were *really* ringing now!

Cold. Vomiting. Disorientation. A recent head injury. To make matters worse the group was at least 100km away from any kind of civilization.

When we stopped the rest of the group gathered around and, after the well-meaning banter had passed, began to look seriously worried about Smithy's wellbeing.

"Gents," I told them. "We gotta get him to a doctor... fast."

Mitch nodded his agreement and we all climbed back into our vehicles and hit the road, hard!

The Micra led the group with a cloud of dust following in its wake as Mitch drove faster than the road would allow, hitting 60 mph. Smithy was in the passenger seat strapped in, seat cranked back with myself sat between the driver and the passenger seat talking, sometimes shouting, doing whatever I could to keep Smithy awake.

We covered the 100km in just over an hour arriving at a small village looking for any kind of doctor/hospital facility. Driving around the town frantically, I spotted a medical symbol above a small building.

Our next problem was communicating with the doctor about Smithy's exact symptoms. None of us spoke Mongolian. Thankfully, Smithy spoke the internationally recognised language of puke… all over the doctor's surgery floor.

The doctor started looking Smithy up and down, gave him a few blood tests and other inspections and then disappeared off, telling us something in Mongolian as he left. Smithy at this point was still out of it and talking rubbish.

A couple of minutes later the doctor came back and handed me what I guessed was a prescription of some kind. I looked at him blankly, trying to ask, "Well, what do I do with this then?" Luckily he got the message and led me outside to what looked like a vault and then went in. I followed him and found myself in a heavily fortified pharmacy of some kind only this one had all sorts of extra medical equipment and drugs.

Handing over the prescription, the doctor was in turn given back a complete IV system.

Back in the surgery, the doctor got to work immediately pumping fluids into Smithy's body. It didn't take long. After only a couple of minutes Smithy was back to his normal self again. It turned out that he had dehydration, a mild concussion and heat exhaustion.

Over the next few days, we kept on heading east to reach the capital, Ulaanbaatar, a bustling place full of life and the vast majority of Mongolia's population. This to us was the goal, but the real finish line was over the border back in Russia in the city of Ulan Ude. And, after a couple of days recuperation and experiencing the urban side of Mongolian life, this is where we headed to.

Relaxed and recharged we completed the short drive back into Russia to get to the photo finish on the podium, just like we'd dreamed of all those months before!

Of course, nothing runs smoothly. They had already dismantled the podium by the time we arrived so we had to settle for a haphazard selfie outside the hostel instead.

But WE DID IT!

We had reached the finish line of the Mongol Rally. The Micra was as battered and beaten as were we, but we had learnt a lot through the tears, the pain and the laughter.

…and the journey home is another adventure story in itself…

When Richard isn't driving his Micra to places it shouldn't really be or on long road trips, he can be found outdoors in Devon or up in the mountains of the UK and further afield.

Instagram: @thermadventures

Website: www.rmadventures.co.uk

Chapter 19

Pedalling the Yellow Brick Road

by Susie Pike

2:46pm. Friday, 11 March 2011.

Japan had been hit by the worst that Mother Nature could throw at it. Not only had it been struck by the most powerful earthquake in its history, but it had also suffered a hugely destructive tsunami which had wiped out lives and towns in seconds. As if Japan hadn't suffered enough, the effects of the tsunami and earthquake quickly developed into a nuclear disaster in Fukushima.

I had been living in the beautiful land of the rising sun for eight months, working as an Assistant Language Teacher (ALT) teaching English in the prefecture of Yamagata.

"Susie, we thought you were strong, but yesterday you showed signs of mental illness".

I had suffered with bouts of depression since I had arrived in Japan.

Me, the proverbial chatterbox, in a country where I couldn't communicate with most people. And yes, I had struggled.

THE FEAR

It was the Monday after the earthquake and I was back at school. The earthquake and tsunami were beyond horrific, but it was the nuclear meltdown in Fukushima that quite frankly terrified me to levels I had never before experienced. As I stood in the staffroom, tears ran down my panicked face which prompted the comment above.

I cried because I was told to get home as quickly as I could because a radiation cloud was coming our way. We had to be home by the time the rain came.

I didn't get home in time.

I was told under no circumstances should I allow any rain to touch my skin.

It did.

I ran home and stripped within 15 seconds of getting through the front door. I was so petrified that I never wore those clothes again. I nearly passed out during a panic attack when I phoned a friend in sheer terror. There I was, a 28-year-old girl, sobbing, shaking, naked and cradling myself on my bedroom floor. I don't think I could have looked more vulnerable if I had tried.

My levels of fear were out of control. Fukushima was massively unstable, changing by the minute, and no one knew what was happening or what was going to happen. Teachers who had previously beavered away at their desks were replaced by a huddle watching the news. This new behaviour in a country where I couldn't understand the language petrified me. I was petrified for my life - petrified by something I couldn't see and something I knew very little about - radiation.

Radiation isn't something I have ever had to consider before and suddenly, according to Western news sources, there was about to be a nuclear apocalypse and our lives were in danger.

THE AFTERMATH

Weeks of uncertainty and stress passed. The constant aftershocks were deeply unsettling. I had four options. Leave Japan for good - right then and there; leave Japan for a month on unpaid leave and return; stay in Japan and see out my contract until August or stay in Japan until August 2012, which I had just signed up to do. I chose to stay. Despite everything, I couldn't abandon a sinking ship.

I volunteered to help twice after March 11, both times in the areas that had been heavily hit by the tsunami. The town of Kamaishi used to be a bustling seaside town and now... nothing. It had been reduced to a flat mud plain of nothingness.

When we drove away from the sea, we passed through other towns that had been hit, but which had buildings that were still somehow standing. I will never forget the smell of death and destruction, the red X's on the doors of buildings that had survived and had been checked for bodies, the completely mangled cars that the tsunami had swept away and dumped in the most ridiculous of positions, and the eerie silence only punctuated by the sound of recovery trucks working away. Survivors of the tsunami slept in the local evacuation centre which was located right on the sea front. I was astounded by the strength the locals showed. It was incredibly inspiring.

It was raining while I was collecting equipment from a van outside the evacuation centre. A couple stood smoking in the doorway and they offered me their umbrella so I didn't get wet and cold. This couple had lost everything yet I was struck by how they were still concerned about me. Selflessness personified.

HOME, SAFE HOME

I said my goodbyes to Japan eighteen months after March 11 and felt an overwhelming relief after two years of massive highs and despairing lows.

When I got home my parents had arranged for me to see a counsellor. "How was Japan?" he innocently asked. Three simple words that prized open a little door in my brain. I never realised just how much of the anxiety, stress and panic of March 11 I had suppressed and kept to myself. Flood gates opened and I found that talking through it with a stranger was my way of releasing everything. I assumed I was jetlagged when I was sleeping 15 hours a day on my return home. I never realised it was my body's way of dealing with my pent-up emotional stress, which was now manifesting in a physical way. It suddenly all made sense.

Eighteen months after March 11, Post-Traumatic Stress Disorder (PTSD) smacked me in the face, right between the eyes and knocked me out, literally, for months. Luckily, I was home where my parents helped me and I had the countryside to escape to. I was so mentally exhausted that my body ached. I needed the time to process events, to get help and release the underlying stress that I had kept to myself for all that time. I needed to feel safe again and being home made me feel safe.

I had left Japan because I wanted to move to London and experience it in my twenties, and then move to Australia before I was too old for the working holiday visa. Back in 2007, whilst in

New Zealand, I promised my 24-year-old self that I would, one day, spend a year in Australia. I knew I had to fulfill my promise in order to avoid future regret. What I hadn't factored in was the time it would take to recover from my time in Japan.

Early on, I was surviving on half a bowl of porridge a day and hardly any sleep. This combination made me feel like I was losing my mind and it was terrifying. I was deep in a black hole of despair and unable to summon the energy to claw myself out. My self-confidence and belief had been smashed into a million pieces and my personality wiped clean.

Things changed in a positive way when, months later, I felt strong enough to head to London where I was offered a job. Colleagues, who were oblivious to my struggle at the start, became close friends and part of the recovery process. I was also lucky because it was here that I met Finse.

FINSE

I never understood the saying 'a dog is a man's best friend' until I met Finse. Finse was a beautiful, yellow Labrador puppy whose owner was the Vice President of the company I worked for. Months into my recovery, her owner asked for volunteers to walk her during lunch breaks. I leapt at the chance.

I never imagined that walking Finse that day would contribute to me seeing the light again. Finse and I went on daily walks to the common and it became my favourite part of the working day. I would talk to Finse as if she were a human. I would talk to her about my worries, about my day, about the most trivial of things and about the future. In return for her listening in a dog type of way, I would spend hours throwing the ball into the deepest, muddiest puddles. Her tail would wag uncontrollably as we ran alongside each other. The muddier we got the better. We'd return to the office covered in mud, stinking of wet dog but with massive smiles on our faces. I loved it.

Thankfully, a combination of support from my amazing parents, incredible family and friends, therapy, time and Finse gave me the strength I needed to continue in my recovery. I loved the two years I spent in London but I finally felt ready to move on to the next chapter. Going to Australia had seemed so incredibly unrealistic just three years previously and yet now it was actually happening.

PLANTING THE SEED

I knew that I didn't want the normal backpacking experience Down Under. I wanted to achieve something to make myself proud. My mental vulnerability had shocked me and so I wanted to test my mental strength, my physical ability, my determination and my will power. Luckily, Australia offered large-scale adventure and endless exploration.

My brother and sister-in-law, Neil and Harriet Pike, aka Pikesonbikes, have always inspired me with the things they do, the remote places they have been and what they have achieved with loaded up bikes, maps and sturdy hiking boots. They told me about an event at the Royal Geographical Society, so I hesitantly went along. I was lucky enough to meet Anna McNuff, who introduced me to others, including Dave Cornthwaite. After hearing them talk at an event, I skipped home over Waterloo Bridge with endorphins flowing and my imagination flooding with ideas.

Plan A was going to involve crossing Australia with Nordic roller blades strapped to my feet and a buggy strapped to my waist. As I turned to the internet for help, I discovered that roller blading on roads wasn't legal, so on to plan B. That involved cycling from Perth to Sydney. I was lucky that Neil and Harriet are seasoned cycle tourers and were writing the 'Adventure Cycle Touring

Handbook' at the time. Getting advice from two people I trust with my life was incredibly reassuring.

I'd never owned a bike before May 2015. I knew very little about cycle touring and nothing about bike maintenance. A trio of reasons that justified my determination to get to the start line.

When I first told friends about my cycle, they reacted either as 'nudgers' who said, "Why wouldn't you do that!?" or as doubters, who said, "Why would you do that?". I naturally gravitated towards those who believed I could achieve it.

The seed was planted. Only *I* could make this challenge happen. Only *I* could pedal, one revolution at a time across Australia. No one was going to do it for me. There was only one way to find out if I could achieve it, and that was getting to the start line and trying.

THE JOURNEY

I arrived into Sydney airport with my backpack strapped to my back, two weeks before my 31st birthday, the deadline for the working holiday visa. At that point, I high-fived my inner self that I had kept my own word. It had been a long journey, but I was here.

When I first arrived, I had planned to stay with the incredible Lewis family for two days but those two days quickly turned into four months. Suzie and Jamie were hugely supportive of my cycle and without them I wouldn't have been able to complete it.

In Sydney, I bought a Trek 520 and named him Doogle, the best name in the world. I went on a free bike maintenance course and a 'Cycle in the City' course run by the council. The instructor asked everyone why they were there and I nervously said, "In three weeks I'm attempting to cycle across Australia". I was the only one to fall off my bike on the course when attempting to brake. It was a beautifully ironic moment.

I had decided that crossing Australia wasn't about speed. I prefer to have time to absorb my surroundings and appreciate everything around me. For me, the journey was about creating memories and meeting as many people as possible, all whilst fundraising for the Samaritans, BeyondBlue and TreeAid.

I wanted to WWOOF (Willing Workers on Organic Farms), where you work 4-6 hours a day in return for your food and accommodation. I also wanted to use both Warmshowers, which is a network for cycle tourers where fellow cyclists accommodate you for the night, and Couchsurfing. I wanted to experience what Australia was really like by staying with locals along the way.

WAIT, IT'S ACTUALLY HAPPENING?

It was finally time to disassemble Doogle for the first time to fly to the start line. There in front of me was a bike box, shiny unused bike tools and my phone. I watched YouTube videos for instructions and eventually started meticulously dismantling my most valued possession. He, being Doogle, was bubble wrapped to within an inch of his life.

I was ridiculously nervous and riddled with self-doubt. I had ridden the wave of positivity from the nudgers in my life, but now this was it. It struck me that this stress was entirely self-inflicted. I was alone. On a plane. On the way to Perth. A challenge I had dreamt up a year before was actually happening. When it takes five hours to fly somewhere by plane, you know cycling the route back will take some time. My start date was set – Tuesday 18 August 2015.

I was met by my friend, Elise, whom I hadn't seen since New Zealand. She drove me to a bike shop where Doogle was carefully assembled. "You didn't want your bike damaged, did yer?" they said as they removed metres upon metres of bubble wrap from Doogle. Thirty-three metres to be exact.

Some of my kit arrived on the day I left, and that meant I didn't get a chance to practise packing or cycling with panniers. In total my kit weighed 25kg, Doogle weighed 16kg and my body weighed 60kg. 101kg to haul across Australia.

I decided to split Australia into stages, with thousands of kilometres separating each milestone in order to avoid being completely overwhelmed by the task ahead.

STAGE ONE: PERTH TO ESPERANCE

I dropped Doogle twice as I pushed him to the start line. Luckily some nerves seemed to dissipate when I pushed down on my pedals and finally set off. Or so I thought. 400 metres from the start line I phoned Elise to check I was going the right way; she laughed at me and told me to head east for Sydney. I knew I was being ridiculous, but self-doubt beat logic to the phone.

The whole of Australia lay to my left and turquoise waters lay to my right. The sky was dark and moody as if encouraging me to pedal faster. Monsoon-style rain soon started to fall, testing every single bit of waterproof kit I owned. I met up with my first Warmshowers host to cycle the final 20km to his home. We arrived chilled to the bone and drenched, yet within 30 seconds of arriving I had a towel in my hand and directions to the shower. When I re-emerged, my kit had been laid out by the open fire and dinner was being prepared. I felt so content.

Soon, the ocean was replaced by fields stretching to the horizon. The flat terrain allowed me to casually slip into my cycling mojo as I arrived at my next hosts. I felt instantly as though I'd been transported into a scene out of Babe. Jack and Jill, the dogs, met me at the gate, followed by my WWOOFing hosts and some runner ducks and geese. I spent the week picking mandarins from the orchard, weeding the garlic, feeding the chickens and mulching the asparagus. It was the simple life and I loved it.

I weaved my way back to the coast and stayed with Lyalya, who showed me to her 'little piece of heaven in the back garden'- an outdoor shower. So excited by this shower, she hadn't had one inside since she moved in years before. The next day she left to volunteer and laid out breakfast - a tea bag dangling in a mug, bread sitting patiently in the toaster, cereal waiting to be poured into a bowl and a little note of encouragement wishing me luck.

I then headed inland and entered national park country where the road meandered over undulating hills. Blue sky, green trees and orange sand met the grey tarmac as Doogle's tyres edged closer to Sydney. My brain soon stopped having to think about pedalling as my legs turned involuntarily. Just like breathing, they knew they had to pedal to keep me alive.

I arrived at my next WWOOFing hosts who ran a chalet business. They let me stay in my own chalet, nestled in the dense forest overlooking a beautiful lake. I had my own jetty, canoe and hot tub. There I was carrying a tent and my survival gear on Doogle and yet for three days I was living a life of luxury. I spent my days cleaning and gardening while torrential rain saturated the ground.

I headed deeper into the national park, where the same views greeted my tired eyes. The rain continued unrelentingly, lashing the tarmac road and rebounding with intent. I spent seven hours squinting through the 5mm gap between my helmet and sunglasses just to see the road. I was greeted by an incredible rainbow when I pulled up at my next WWOOFing hosts'. It felt like I had found the pot of gold, but the gold on this occasion was a warm shower. It was magical.

My hosts ran an olive farm and took me out into the bush where they taught me about the olive trees and how the farm was managed. We explored the local area, climbed a famous diamond tree, fed a wild kangaroo and saw emus casually roaming. I felt as though I was inside the perimeter fence of a zoo, yet this was Australia.

As I inched closer to the end of Stage One, I kept myself entertained by singing until my lungs hurt. Only passing vehicles interrupted the silence until I polluted the sound waves. I belted out One Direction and Adele, laughing at how ridiculously good I sounded. Or so I thought. There was indeed no audience to confirm this. As I belted out ballads, I kept being caught out by huge flies. I stopped for a moment to retch and looked over to a field of alpacas all staring at me, quietly judging my strange human antics.

As I headed into outback Australia, I met the feared Australian road train. Terrifyingly powerful, monstrous vehicles that stretch for over 50 metres suddenly greeted me on the road. Drivers label cyclists 'road bumps' because if they hit you, that is all you will be. The enormity of them was terrifying. If one was approaching from behind, and one was approaching from ahead, I had to get off the road. There simply wasn't room for the three of us.

The Nullarbor was soon approaching - the desert stretch. So vast, so isolated, so daunting that the thought of cycling through it overwhelmed me. My anxiety levels were creeping up.

My hosts in Jerramungup decided to meet me at the end of the day so we could camp together. The logs crackled away on the fire as we toasted sandwiches and spent the evening laughing. When I rode away the next day, my handlebar bag had been stuffed full of chocolate, making me smile as I set off east.

STAGE TWO: ESPERANCE TO ADELAIDE VIA THE NULLARBOR

I WWOOFed for a week in Esperance, building a tunnel for milking goats. Esperance was jaw-droppingly beautiful. The water was crystal turquoise as the white sand squeaked under my feet. As I walked across the beach at Cape Le Grand, I came face to face with a kangaroo. The surreality and beauty left me speechless.

I met a cycle tourer who told me a group of cyclists were in Esperance and on their way to Sydney. Knowing I had to double my water carrying ability, I headed to the sports shop in Esperance and was told Peter, the bike mechanic, wasn't working. With a stroke of luck, he popped into the store and spent time fixing a basket onto Doogle. We talked for hours and I told him my plans and how worried I was about the Nullarbor.

I left to buy water containers when suddenly Peter rang. He'd got my number from my WWOOFing hosts and told me to run to the shop as two cyclists from the Geriatric Playgroup – John and Durn - were there. Later on, I met the group of 10 cyclists, with three support drivers, from NSW, aged between 53 and 73 years, who were cycling from Perth to Newcastle.

I left Esperance at 7am yet the sun was already piercing my skin and sapping my energy. After 40km, I was waved down by the group and given a cup of tea and cake on the side of the road. Instead of camping that night, Helen, the organiser of the trip, invited me to sleep on the floor of their cabin. In an instant all my worries about the Nullarbor evaporated after I asked to join them and they agreed.

With the group, my whole routine changed: we left at 7am to avoid the heat, and my panniers went into the support vehicle so I could keep pace with them. Though I had twinges of guilt, I knew this was ultimately the right thing to do.

The Nullarbor was beautiful. Unexpectedly beautiful. The vibrant colours of the blue sky, green shrubs, red sand and grey tarmac greeted my eyes on a daily basis. The road continued as far as the eye could see.

The vastness felt incomprehensible. So large, so overwhelming whereas I was a tiny, pedalling dot on the landscape. Even the road signs listed distances my brain couldn't process. Numbers with four digits informed us every day of how far our legs had yet to pedal.

Most of the nights we stayed in isolated roadhouses, small settlements nestled in an expanse of nothingness. As I wasn't a planned addition to the group, I was crammed in wherever there was space, but I didn't care as long as I could lie horizontal. The early starts meant for early nights and 7pm bedtimes became routine. The toddler lifestyle was divine.

Images I had seen in books and online became my reality as we passed the famous landmarks, excitably posing under the '90 mile straight' sign, Australia's straightest road. The level of focus and concentration required to keep pedalling on a straight road for 90 miles amazed me.

Our longest day was clocked at 182.4km. I was the youngest in the group, but I was first to bed, gobbling down Ibuprofen as I was unable to bend my knee. We had cycled in a rotational peloton and in my tiredness, I kept losing concentration and nearly clipping the tyre in front of me. 'SUSIIIIIIIIIE!' they shouted as I zoned in and out. My tank was running on empty so I limped first to bed.

We had been incredibly lucky with the weather on the Nullarbor, but as the days passed, the temperature gradually crept up and finally hit 48C. Our alarms were brought forward to 4.30am, leaving for the day in the pitch black, with only the stars and bike lights to guide us on our way. As the temperatures rose, the dry heat instantly zapped your skin of any sweat and your lips felt as though you hadn't drunk liquid for days. We had to drink 10 litres a day just to stay hydrated.

Ceduna signaled the end of the Nullarbor and with that adrenaline seeped through my veins. The part of the trip I was especially afraid of was complete. Together, we had done it. I said an emotional goodbye to the Gerries at Port Augusta after cycling 1874km in 18 days with only 3 rest days.

The landscape proceeded to change from a sea of wheat fields to vineyard country as I weaved my way to Adelaide. My WWOOFing hosts in Adelaide paid for me to have a body massage. Stage two ended polar opposite to how it started - relaxed.

STAGE THREE: ADELAIDE TO MELBOURNE

I headed south of Adelaide, cycling 100km in a hellish headwind. I stopped in the town of Meningie when a lady pulled up alongside me. "Some people collect stamps, I collect cyclists off the side of the road," she boldly declared. I was taken to her Aladdin's cave of a house, where I was fed, watered and slept like a baby.

I hugged the coast as orange dirt was replaced by green grass and I ventured into Robe. As I set up my tent overlooking the sea, fellow campers approached me with cake and donations. I then met a lady who invited me to her house for Reiki, a three-course meal and a two-hour foot massage. The kindness of strangers astounded me.

After being spoilt by my Couchsurfing hosts for two days in Beachport, I left to cycle the 86km to Mt Gambier.

Yet, I woke up three hours later.

I didn't make it to Mt Gambier by bike. I made it by ambulance.

When my eyes opened I realised that my Couchsurfing host was stood at the end of my hospital bed. Not knowing why I was there, how I had got there and where 'there' was, my host reassured me. "Don't you worry. Doogle is with the Police. He's fine."

I was high on Morphine and felt relaxed. I was bruised and my helmet smashed yet I hadn't broken any bones. It would have been game over but it wasn't. It was a miracle.

My host's neighbour had seen the commotion at the side of the road, recognised my bike and called my host. He phoned the police who confirmed I was in hospital and drove 86km to find me. 12 hours of tests, CT scans and a diagnosis of bad concussion later, I went back home with my host.

My confidence and strength were wrecked. I didn't have the energy to worry but I wanted answers, though I found none. I slept for a whole week, with my host's dog by my side.

Most of all my short-term memory was affected. I felt as though I was floating, unable to snap back into reality. Luckily my stubbornness kicked in. I wasn't about to quit 1500km from Sydney. I just had to take it slow.

I set off again, warily weaving my way through the countryside and cycling past vast forests, eventually finding myself back at the ocean. I reached Warrnambool, the official start of the Great Ocean Road (GOR). With my hosts, I swam in the turquoise waters, marveled at the incredible views, picked cherries from an orchard and stuffed my face with fish and chips. My brain needed this down time.

The GOR was a great distraction. The road hugged the coast and every corner revealed another incredible view. I felt as though I was inside an Instagram filter yet this was real - the vibrant azure waters, ragged cliffs, lush green national parks and deep blue skies. Australia was showing off and deservedly so. It was beautiful.

The hills made my lungs burn and my muscles ache. Even though I was slow, I felt like I was riding a roller coaster. Creeping up to the top of a ride and squealing with excitement all the way down. I'd replaced singing with screaming. Every time I stopped to gawp at the view, strangers would approach me to donate to BeyondBlue. It was incredible.

On my favourite day, I took 8.5 hours to cycle 72km. For every hour I spent cycling, I spent an hour taking photos. People shouted encouragement as they drove past and I fundraised $120 from strangers I met en route. I couldn't stop smiling.

As the city traffic built up, I decided to hitch a ride with my host to Melbourne. My fears about the Nullarbor had consumed me, yet 'falling off Doogle' wasn't even on my top 5 worries list. A life lesson learnt about worrying. Stage three had been unexpectedly the hardest and I was grateful it was over.

STAGE FOUR: MELBOURNE TO SYDNEY

I knew this was the last leg and my head was racing. I felt as though I was nearly 'home' but I still had 1500km to go.

I headed inland from Melbourne, staying in little towns as I crept towards Sydney. I tried to avoid the busy roads so instead cycled on rail trails where Doogle's tyres felt insignificant against the challenge of the terrain. I spent some downtime riding a fat bike with my Warmshowers hosts on the beach and stayed with more incredible people.

I dragged myself up the aptly named Mount Agony road and arrived at Anna McNuff's awesome friend's home. If only every road could describe the journey ahead. Doogle's back wheel had buckled after my accident so they bundled him into their car and zoomed us to the nearest town to get him fixed.

The final stretch was about getting my head down, funneling every ounce of energy I had left to edge closer towards Sydney.

I made it to Nowra in time for Christmas and arrived at the home of a friend I'd met in Zanzibar in 2010. Oli was working on Christmas day but invited me to his work's Christmas dinner. There I sat, in my nicest cycling clothes, surrounded by on-duty surgeons and doctors in a hospital staff room. It was surreal, yet it more than provided the few hours of people time I needed. I returned back to his house and spent the rest of the day in delightful silence. I craved being alone. Throughout my trip, I'd spent every evening, bar one, in the company of awesome hosts, and I was socially exhausted for the first time in my life.

I had two days to go.

Two.

I cycled on to Wollongong where I met a friend, Nat, who came to cycle the final day with me. Crammed into a hostel, I spent the penultimate evening packing my panniers for one final time and checking I had enough Timtams to carry me one final day. It felt utterly surreal.

As we headed north, I dragged Doogle up two huge hills for one final time, sweating as the sun beat down on me. We then headed onto the motorway which was horrendous so we agreed to take a train through Sydney to the north, to then cycle back south for 20km to make up the distance.

There, I was met by Jamie and Big Al from the Gerries. It was too surreal to be emotional. Too overwhelming to be true. We cycled the distance into Wahroonga Park, my finish line.

After 5031km, 132 days on the road, of which 64 were spent cycling puncture free, I broke through the finishing line tape. I was greeted by friends, my Aussie family and Matt the photographer. I expected to burst into tears, but I was totally overwhelmed. Happy that I'd finished. Sad it was over. Proud that I'd completed it. Relieved that I had survived in one piece.

REFLECTION

I was going to miss my routine. The simplicity of life on two wheels. The simplicity of having a goal every day that had to be achieved. A destination that had to be reached. The guilt-free justification to eat an inordinate amount of Timtams. The simplicity of only having belongings that fit into two panniers. The simplicity of cycle touring. I would miss it all.

I stayed with an enormous number of incredible hosts during my journey. Though I have been unable to write about them all, they all represented kindness, selflessness and generosity. From Japan to Australia, humanity shone bright like a diamond, sparkling in every way.

From family and friends back home who rooted for me from afar, to the strangers who became friends I met on the way, every single person contributed to me achieving my dream.

I had done it.

In the words of an Aussie, "I'd bloody done it".

Susie lives in London with her other half and escapes the city at every opportunity. She loves travelling, taking photos, taking on a challenge, hunting for good coffee shops, hiking, cycling (mountain biking and touring), swimming and recently, because of her other half, has taken up surfing. She used to not like the sea and was terrified of waves but has decided that life as a beginner surfer is super fun. She's in training to swim 10k in an event in November after not being able to swim more than 50m without gasping for air three years ago. She prides herself on being a nudger in the YesTribe and Adventure Queens community. When she's excited about an adventure/challenge she's basically the female equivalent of Buddy from the film, Elf. Shout if you fancy meeting up with her!

Instagram: @thetravellingphotoaddict

Chapter 20

Island Triking

by Tanya Noble

I was stuck in a rut.

At 37, nearly 38 years old, I was doing a job because it paid well, I was *still* single and when people talked to me about their five year plan – I was lost. I didn't even have a 1 week plan.

It was April 2018 and I was heading abroad to do a job I had done for the past four years, not because I was passionate about it, but because I didn't know what else to do. I had taken 3 months off previously to 'decide' what my future looked like. I hadn't of course. The thought of it was too overwhelming and it was far easier to find a personal trainer, try to surf, spend time in Cornwall and just carry on as normal.

During the 'decision making ' months I spent a lot of time on social media just mindlessly scrolling through the seemingly perfect lives of everyone else. If you could get paid to procrastinate I would have earned mega-money!

There is an upside to social media though and it meant I had discovered a group of folk that were 'making life memorable' – The YesTribe of course. The positivity and kindness oozed from the posts – if only I had time to get involved. "Well, Tanners," I said to myself. "You have to make time."

In February I attended my first YesTribe event walking part of the capital ring walk in London – I felt immediately at ease with this bunch of strangers. On the train home I booked without hesitation my ticket to the following weeks YesStories. Self-powered journeys, the power of saying Yes, going on an adventure... why had I not discovered this before?!

Work continued as normal – but in the back of my mind was this whole different aspect to life – I wanted to have a break to try something completely different. I'd enjoyed keeping fit in recent years but had never before thought of powering myself on a multiple day adventure. A hike, a run or a surf here and there but always one offs.

There was one particular evening I was sat in my little apartment after work. It had been a particularly tough and stressful start to the job – I was taking time out with a G&T, and then another one. And when I joined the rest of my colleagues by the fire, it was another one for the road. You get the picture! I walked to bed with that warm glow that gin provides and did my standard get into bed and scroll through the social media. Up pops a post by Dave Cornthwaite offering out the Ice Trike recumbent bike for an adventure. The thing about alcohol for me is, there is absolutely none of that thinking twice. There's no 'emergency brake' thought or apprehension. You see something, you think it's the most amazing thing to do – and before you know it you've filled in the form and pushed send.

The fuzzy wuzzy head the next morning was a thing to behold. Berocca and strong coffee to the rescue! My life at work consisted mainly of trying to stop my boss having a meltdown, looking after our crew's wellbeing and budgets, budgets, budgets. By the time I got to work that morning there was already an email in my inbox (curse those early risers!)...

It was from Dave Cornthwaite.

Uh oh!

'I love this Tanya! The Trike is yours whenever you need it, on one condition. When you're back you talk about the experience at Yestival :)'

This just got real! I had just agreed to take a recumbent trike on the Hebridean Way and speak in public about it!

There was an initial terror but I'd pretty much managed to wing my way through all new experiences in life and this would be no different! People asked me what I would do for training – training? The problem was I had work booked right up the point I would want to start the trip! Right – don't panic – we can do this. I spoke to Dave Cornthwaite about his 1000 mile journeys and training and he said he didn't – the beginning of the journey *is* the training (of course I naively believed him!).

So that got me thinking. Maybe I needed to make the trip bigger in some way so that the beginning was the training! I looked at a map of the UK, and some elevations of routes circumnavigating different islands of the British Isles – and if by some geographical coincidence – the hills got steeper the more north you went. Rather than just the Hebridean Way the trip became 'Island Hopping Mad for Mind'. I would start at the Isles of Scilly and plan a route North ending in Shetland.

I needed to buy a lot of kit for this trip. The last time I had been camping, it had involved paying a company to put up a bell tent for you at your campsite, complete with a blow up bed and a feathered duvet. I had done 'proper' adventuring once – I was a Venture Scout and did my Queen's Scout Hike in Ireland... but my lasting memory of that was waking up with all our kit in water and still having a whole day's trek ahead!

Normally with previous interests I'd have all the gear and no idea but this time it was definitely a case of no gear and absolutely no idea. What clothes should I take? What cycling shoes? What about lack of washing facilities? What would I eat? Should I carry enough food on each leg? What about a tent? So many questions whirling around my head and actually, so little time to prepare!

Despite my reservations at having wasted my life working on a career I now didn't want – the years of Project Managing and Logistics came in very handy. Who knew that spreadsheets and adventures work in such harmony? Now this side of adventuring I could do!

I worked out where I could get ferries to and from and what islands I could visit in a group while always ensuring I could make it back to the same place on the mainland to collect the car. I planned a route that consisted of 7 legs – The Isles of Scilly, the Channel Islands, Isle of Anglesey, Isle of Man, Inner Hebrides, Outer Hebrides (inc. Skye and Mull), and Orkney/Shetland. I worked out a rough mileage around each island to roughly plan the dates. Detailed route planning and accommodation booking was left to the rest day between each leg. This very much allowed me to a) stop panicking about the amount of planning that was required and b) find out how many miles I could cover in reality! I had no idea!

While some adventuring folk like to free-ride their trips and camp wherever they end up of an evening, the whole idea of wild camping on my own actually scares the bejeezus out of me! I get anxious enough living in a house on my own (and yes still after 6 years of doing it). The thought of wild camping was something I felt was a step too far. While in reality I know the odds of being savaged by some beast or ransacked for my valuables in the countryside are very low, try telling my subconscious brain that of a night time! I even tried my new tent out in my mum's back garden and had to abort due to snuffling noises outside. Sleep for me is a necessity, and very much the more the merrier!

I decided booking into campsites ahead of time not only gave me piece of mind of having facilities and other folk around – it also meant I had an aim for each day. Each morning I would know the distance I had to go (thanks to the Komoot app), the elevation along the route and approximately how long it would take (always double its estimation!).

I'm not sure how I got all the prep done in time. I certainly was not concentrating as much as I should at work! In the weeks before the trip a few issues were thrown my way but, in true Tanner's style, there was first panic and then finding that solution!

Two of the most major hurdles I encountered before I even started were:

1) The Trike would not fit in my Fiat 500 Convertible! This may sound obvious to you – but when one fits in my Dad's neighbour's Aygo Toyota I can be forgiven for thinking all would be fine! This was quite a large problem – the trip needed the car to travel between legs. I had always wanted a van – but with my previous luck in buying 2nd hand cars, an impulse buy was not advised for this trip. Luckily for me I have probably the most amazing Mum in the world. I managed to convince her that car swapping her Ford Cmax for my Fiat 500 convertible during the summer months, was a total win for her!

2) The weekend I was meant to collect the Trike – I got a message on the Friday saying that it required a part that wasn't in stock – so collecting the Trike would need to be delayed. This was NOT an option. The ferries were booked for the Wednesday and I had to get down to Cornwall. I went through a major panic – the kind where you don't know whether to cry, take a nap in the hope someone else would sort it or get really, really angry. I messaged Ice Trikes explaining what was wrong

– I had no plan B. Being the awesome and supportive guys that they are, they said for me to collect the Trike as soon as I could without the part, get it to them first thing Monday and they would see what they could do. Totally amazing! Just the start of complete kindness I was shown throughout the trip especially at times I most needed it.

I opted to pack the car heavy with enough supplies for the whole trip and take just enough with me on each leg for the days I would be on the islands. I was being mindful that the less I carried the easier the 'Triking' but also knew there were some home comforts I could not do without, a jar of peanut butter being one of them! I was going to need those high calorie snacks!

In hindsight I really did not use half of the clothes that I had in the car. Once I'd found a good combination of outfits to take with me I stuck with that. Generally a rest day would involve laundry. I think the most memorable was laundry machines in a petrol station just outside Oban. Oh the glamour – at least I had been prepared with coffee in my thermal mug! Multi-tasking at its best with the washing time used to edit videos and plan the next legs!

The 15th August arrived – I was as set as I was going to be! The Trike was back on the road and fully functioning. Time to set sail on what was going to be the 1st of 29 ferries.

It was a glorious sunny day – the ferry to the Isle of Scilly was known for being a particularly rough crossing so this was a huge relief – or so I thought. It was still pretty rough on this calm day. So rough in fact that a child had to be helicoptered off for being so sick; new found respect for the coastguard team who hovered above the moving ferry while transferring medic and patient.

I arrived at St Mary's and decided to have a quick blast around. The island isn't actually that big so it was probably less than 8 miles. This was my test leg to build those 'Triking' legs up slowly and test out my kit – remembering this was very much a marathon not a sprint!

I was following the directions to the campsite but I had to stop and stare in horror at the huge hill I was forced to climb. At the bottom I contemplated it for a moment while snacking on a few vegan cola bottles – I needed that sugar boost! Two local elderly ladies walked past. "You'll never get up to the campsite on that, sweetie," croaked one of the old dears.

Going on past experiences, whenever anyone tells me I cannot do something it makes me more determined to prove them wrong. Challenge accepted!

I made my way slowly – very slowly – up the hill. It gradually got steeper and steeper as I wound my way up. There was a natural break stop by a castle with a viewpoint across the bay of St Marys. Woah! From the limestone houses that surrounded St Mary's, it gave way to a sandy beach. Boats bobbed up and down in the harbour – all looking so small from up here. In the distance you could clearly see the other islands surrounded by light golden sand, the bluest of skies and the clearest of water. The first of many amazing views!

The next day I discovered why sometimes detailed research was required (and this wouldn't be the first time on the trip) when I realised there was no way of getting me and the Trike to the other Isles of Scilly! Trikey had to be left at the harbour while I took a round trip to Bryher and Tresco and back to explore another 2 islands on foot.

As I climbed to the top of a hill on Bryher, I actually felt quite emotional. My eyes filled with tears and my heart skipped a beat. The hardest part of the adventure, I had been told, is starting it and this was the beginning. I was actually doing it! The view was breath-taking – the sun was shining, the sea as blue as the sky gradually fading to teal with crystal clear water. You could have mistaken it for some paradise island far away!

I always feel so alive by the sea – I dream of living by it one day. I knew the moment I reached the top of that hill that I had definitely made the right choice of trip. From then on, I promised that I would always try to circumnavigate the islands with the sea by my side. My happy place!

I was so lucky on the next leg of the Channel Islands that I had fellow YesTriber Emma Fairey join me. I had only met her a couple of times before but we hit it off straight away. There was no hesitation when she asked if she could tag along on 'Trikey 2' for the Guernsey, Jersey leg. We were both in a similar position that we hadn't been on a multi-day self-powered journey before, so we were both learning as we went along. It was great having an 'adventure buddy' for this early stage. Very convenient when I had probably the most catastrophic mechanical failure just off the Ferry in Jersey.

Trikey 1 failed to get into gear going up a hill. Rolling back down ensuring the pedals could turn as I went, there was a metal ping sound and several small parts scattered across the road. In the very pit of my stomach I knew this was not good. Having no real mechanical knowledge and being on an island there was always a risk that something like this could spell disaster. I managed to collect all the pieces. One of the pulleys in the system that takes up the slack in the chain on the boom had shattered.

Thankfully my 'survival mode' kicked in. It's this amazing innate ability I have to find solutions in ridiculous situations. It has served me well over the years.

First step was to compare Trikey 1 to Trikey 2 – 'Houston it is clear we have a problem'.

Next step, call Ice Trikes. They had said that I should call them at any time for 'technical support' – I think this definitely required 'technical support'! After a long discussion we were able to identify that the Trike could function without the pulley system – we just had to get to a bike shop. Emma being the most amazingly organised lady I have met happened to have some PVC tape with her – I managed to construct the pieces of the pulley and tape together in a fashion enough to hold it in place.

"Ok, Google…" time to bring out the big guns and find us a bike shop. Amazingly at the bottom of the very hill we were halfway up there was a bike repair shop. In another turn of fate they were a charity that employed folk who might otherwise struggle to get a job.

After liaising with Ice Trikes and a YouTube video later, Trikey 1 was back on the road. All for free – I had told the owner what I was doing and raising money for Mind. Having suffered from Mental Health issues in the past, he was only too happy to help.

I had heard from others about the kindness of strangers on adventures like this – maybe it's until you really need it that you find it. The experience of it though stays with you as a lasting memory.

Leaving the Channel Islands I was on a high, Emma and I had had an amazing time. Playing word games on the steep hill climbs to distract ourselves from the pain, working through mechanical issues together, the so called 'short cuts' the Komoot app sent us down that were not fit for Trikes and laughing at our silly mistakes along the way.

What I hadn't been prepared for on the next leg when I reached the Isle of Anglesey, was the huge low. The feeling of being completely alone and the mammoth amount of miles I still had to go.

Having been single for a number of years being on my own had never really daunted me – until then.

I was halfway up my first hill out of Bangor to cross the Menai Bridge. Trikey would not stay in the lowest gears. I felt tired. I felt emotional. Suddenly without warning the whole journey overwhelmed me. Looking back I realise that I had had an awful night's sleep.

I decided to post on Social Media about my struggle. After all I was raising money for the mental health charity Mind, and it felt important to raise awareness at how mentally tough this was for me. Halfway up that hill I really debated with myself whether I was doing the right thing. I blamed the Trike, I blamed my lack of training and most of all I blamed myself for thinking I could do something like this. I was a mess.

One of my oldest friends called me after seeing my post. As I had a little cry she reminded me of my journey over the past few years and that this was nothing. It *was* nothing. No one had made me go. I had wanted to.

In my early 30s I had struggled with depression after a long term relationship broke down but working through this I had become resilient and able to find the positives in most situations. It was time to do that again! My mind wanted to give up but no way! "Tanners, there is no giving up now!"

I think it's best to brush over the Isle of Anglesey – it was most definitely the Type 2 fun you hear talked about. The weather was absolutely awful, the roads so busy and, with that low moment, I wasn't sad for those miles to be over and the island to be behind me.

It was time for the Isle of Man. I had a determination to get through this. I only had one person to prove it to – myself!

The Isle of Man, however, became another classic example of where I perhaps should have done slightly more research than before I started. As soon as I got on the ferry the back of my left foot along my Achilles had really started to hurt. The ferry was so full with lots, and I mean lots of motorcyclists. Now you would have thought that would have given me a clue to what was happening on the Isle of Man but no, I was none the wiser.

"Are you going over for the racing?" a guy in full motorbike leathers asked.

"No?" I replied and explained what I was doing.

"You do know it's the Manx Grand Prix this weekend?" he said, a worried look crossing his features. It was one of those looks your mum gives you just before you do something really stupid.

'The Manx Grand Prix!' I thought to myself. 'Perfect timing, Tanners.'

I spent the rest of the ferry journey scouring the internet finding out how this would affect my journey. I found out that:

a) the whole of the TT course was closed at certain times.

And b) the famous mountain road which I really wanted to try was closed to cyclists.

This would have been really disappointing if I wasn't more worried about the fact that I could hardly walk by the time I got off the ferry at Douglas. Somehow I managed to limp my way to the Airbnb I was staying in (now I know why all the accommodation was booked up and really expensive).

I decided that it was probably worth a trip to hospital to get my left foot checked out – along the back of the Achilles looked bruised and very, very swollen. I was given the all clear and told if I carried on it would hurt but I wouldn't do any lasting damage.

Phew!

I kept Triking to a minimum and it became a forced few rest days. It wasn't wasted though and I did conquer the mountain but rather than by Trike I took the train and horse drawn tram. I was blown away at how beautiful the Isle of Man was. As I stood at the summit of Snaefell Pike, there was a 360 degree view of mountains. Despite the mizzly rain, the mountains interlaced and meandered down the valley in their browns and greens and the famous mountain road snaked through the middle. A view to rival the Lakes most definitely.

From now on each leg of the trip consisted of multiple islands. The next leg being Arran, Islay, Jura and Bute. While researching the trip I had come across the five ferry crossing cycling challenge which covered Arran and Bute – I adapted this to cover the isles of Islay and Jura too and this became the eight ferry crossing route!

This was where I totally fell in love with Scotland and I totally fell in love with Triking. The hill climbs were tough – so tough – but the views were unbelievable that it was always worth the climb. In fact, I cannot think of a time when the climb wasn't worth it. With every climb came a descent and these were epic! I would get the giggles at the bottom every time.

One particular moment that really stands out for me was while cycling across Islay. It was one road that went through the middle. I felt like I was the only person there. Eagles soared above. Deer grazed and crossed the road ahead. Butterflies in abundance fluttered past.

I stopped. I listened. Apart from the sounds of birds there was complete silence yet it made me feel so full of energy!

I had found my stride. My Triking legs had got stronger. Hill climbs were still tough but there had been a shift in my mental attitude. Instead of wanting to give up, I believed I could complete the challenge. From now on I knew I could get up those hills no matter the pain and no matter how long it took me.

It was time to tackle the original challenge – the Hebridean Way. I had wanted to do this for such a long time. I guess it felt too complicated, too far away and far too out of my comfort zone. Now I was in Oban I felt ready to tackle the longest leg of the trip – 12 days!

I had become tuned to checking the weather reports. The weather had most definitely turned as I made my way north. On this leg I had decided that I would not camp and booked into bunkhouses and hostels along the way instead.

Weather on islands changes so quickly. I had lost count of the times I had watched storms and heavy rain out at sea yet I was, thankfully, completely dry. Rainbows were a common sight, doubles and sometimes even triples! The weather could be extreme but, being on an island, it always passed quickly.

I arrived at my B&B on Barra. The start of the Hebridean Way was past this, onto Vartesay and back. I decided to tackle this before nightfall so the next day was more manageable. In that 11.5 miles I experienced every single form of weather that could be thrown at me. Glorious sunshine, extreme downpour where the rain drops were so large they hurt your face, hail and full on head winds. It was so windy, in fact, that the Ice Trike flag had to be put away before it blew away!

It's not often I'm confident in my decision making but the choice to stay in bunkhouses, hostels and this first night in a B&B was most definitely the right one. I listened in the night as the wind howled and it absolutely threw it down. I was worried for poor Trikey outside and hoped he would still have his rain coat on in the morning. (and yes I'm aware that he is a Trike and they are kept outside but when it's just you and them for company you get quite attached!).

The Hebridean Way was everything and more. The hills were a little relentless, especially on Harris, but the white sand beaches and crystal clear water and views for miles were just glorious. From the bikers I met in the Berneray Gatliff Hostel who I blame whole heartedly for my fuzzy wuzzy head the day after; my adventure buddy, Martin, who joined me for Harris and Lewis with his electrically assisted bicycle, Monsieur Argent; to the couple, Murray and Vicky, I met when Trikey had a tyre failure on Lewis, who were one of 150 people that weave the Harris Tweed cloth in a garage in their garden!

Talking of tyre failure – that was pretty epic. We were on for some hefty mileage that day – I was determined to reach the end of the Hebridean Way and then it was another 15 miles back to our accommodation. The butt of Lewis really is that... in the butt middle of nowhere! I had become brave on Trikey – the down hills I would just let him go. We even became such speed demons that I would drop him into the high gears to get that little bit extra. We were on a roll!

We had left the tough hills of Harris behind and, predominantly, just had the rolling plains of Lewis to go. We were about 15 miles from the lighthouse... the end was very much in sight. I felt good. I felt strong.

Then came the dreaded sound that every cyclist dreads – one of air escaping very, very quickly like an angry hissing snake.

'That's ok,' I thought. Trikey had had a puncture previously and it was easy to fix.

I looked down. Not only was the tyre flat, the tyre had split!

I had spare inner tubes but no spare tyre. In fact the guys at Ice Trikes had said that the likelihood of one going was slim. There was no way that this could be fixed!

I Googled to see if there was anything I could do. It was a Saturday afternoon. We were in the middle of nowhere in the Outer Hebrides. Surely no chance of finding a Trike tyre here?

"Ye of little faith," as my mum would say!

By some miracle I found a total superhero in Alistair at Bespoke Bicycles, who was willing to drive to where I'd broken down with a spare tyre... and he had the right size in stock! Not only that but when I went to pay him, he gave me back the money he charged for his time as a donation to Mind.

I was so choked up by this. Not only an amazing service but it meant I could complete my journey. Without Alistair this story would have a very, very different ending!

Storm Ali caused a change in itinerary after all ferries I required for the onward journey from Skye to Mull got cancelled. This meant having to take a 5hr detour by bus to collect the car to fetch the Trike from Skye. Even being on a bus in that storm was scary enough that I felt this was ok to change the plan!

The final leg of Orkney / Shetland went without any drama! Orkney had some headwinds to tackle but it was also where my mileage got up to over 50miles a day. I felt proud of us – me and Trikey. We'd smashed my greatest distance ever cycling in one day. And on a recumbent bike!

I had to dig deep in those headwinds – the sudden gusts definitely caused a sense of humour failure. But I always made sure at times like this we found a cake stop – even if it added miles. It was amazing what my body and mind would do for cake!

I was tired when I got off the ferry in Shetland after Orkney – no matter what, you never sleep well on a ferry.

Shetland is stunning. There was a steep climb out of Lerwick and on the first descent I felt truly alive. My mind and body had done more than I ever thought they could cope with – all the apprehension had gone!

On the final day the headwinds were tough on Shetland. The climbs were steep and long. The 40 miles became a battle – Trikey and I against the wind. I would repeat, "Don't stop, won't stop, don't stop, won't stop," over and over again. There was a determination that day to get those 40 miles done.

The final night on the Isle of Yell, off mainland Shetland, was one of facing fears. A night in a Böd. Think Bothy but more hostel like – you pre-book and turn up with the key usually being under the mat. It was described as the gatehouse to the most haunted ruin in the UK.

I knew we were going to be on our own here, me and Trikey. We were in the middle of nowhere. It was the sort of place you had to walk around to find a spot outside to get phone signal. Apart from the farmer up the track we were completely isolated.

This for me and my mind was huge. I was testing myself far out of my comfort zone. I would also have 50 miles to cover back to the ferry home the next day.

Part of the battle of doing anything challenging is convincing yourself you can. Ignoring that scare mongering part of your brain that feeds the other with fear. I told myself, "I can do this. I've just done 710 miles. Me, a non-cyclist. I can do anything now!"

In truth that's how the journey had made me feel – and when I read these words back from my travel notebook – it chokes me up.

I woke up early on my very final day. It was around 6.30am. I found I had signal on my phone and a message from a radio station local to me at home, asking if I'd go on their breakfast show to talk about my trip. What a way to end an adventure!

At 7am I stepped outside to the 'good phone signal' spot. The golden sun was just rising above the 'haunted' ruin. The dawn chorus was reaching its crescendo and a brook was bubbling nearby.

I knew I had 50 miles to cover that day yet I no longer felt daunted. I had slept well despite those anxieties of mine. Most of all, I felt strong.

After speaking to the radio station, I set off back towards Lerwick and the final ferry. I finally saw the appeal of being an early riser. I knew my legs could take those miles but despite knowing I could, on this day, I felt deflated. My heart just was not in it. Perhaps it was knowing that once those miles were done this trip was over and it would be a return to reality.

But what was reality? I couldn't go back to what I did before – could I? This was my chance to embrace the change – I'd learnt so much about me, about kindness and about simplicity. If I didn't change now, when would I? If you want something but maybe it means earning a lot less than you earn now, it can be done. Folk living on islands off our main one have been doing it for years!

I made the final ferry back home. I met an 80yr old couple who were interested in the Trike. I told them about my trip. He put his hand in his pocket and took out a note and handed it to me for my fundraising pot. He said to me, "Keep doing it for folk like me who can't anymore even though we would like to."

'Yes,' I thought and started beaming inside!

I had done it and this is what it was all about! The life decisions could wait. As cheesy as it sounds, I wasn't going to be sad it was over. I was going to smile because it happened. I knew then that, while this journey had come to an end, my personal journey would continue. But, well, that's a totally different story!

After all, it's about far more than just the physical adventure. It's about beginning the journey, the kindness of strangers, the moments you wanted to give up but kept pushing forward and the many, many life lessons along the way.

It's a journey that started with that simple word – Yes. And it's by far the most rewarding thing I have ever said yes to!

Tanya Noble is currently on an unexpected journey. Having been critically ill at the beginning of 2019 she felt it was time to follow her real dreams - stage one, get a dog complete! Stage two put the house on the market – done. Stage three… well, watch this space! She likes photography, being creative, camping and getting outside. She's known in her close circle for her culinary skills and there is always room at her table for dinner - you'll just have to fight Cara the dog for a place on the sofa!

Instagram: @tanyanoble

Chapter 21

Losing My Mind in the Atacama Desert

by Tim Millikin

Saying 'Yes' is not only a mind-set which you need at the beginning of the big adventure but one in which you need to keep with you. It's a card in your pocket which you will need to play when the times are at their toughest and when you need to be reminded of why you started your adventure in the first place.

For me, cycling around the world was never meant to be easy. In fact, I pushed head first into a three-year, around the world expedition to test my resolve and my ambition. In reality, it was the times which were hardest which create the most memories for me.

I had been cycling around the world for two years when I had got to the Atacama Desert in northern Chile and had crossed the mountain ranges of the Caucasus and Pamirs. I had already cycled solo across the Australian Outback and had cycled on northwards through Patagonia when the winds were pushing me back with such strength that the metal braze-ons on my bicycle broke apart. So it's fair to say that I was used to being both uncomfortable and in difficult environments.

But that Atacama was different. I was beginning to snap mentally as I was pushing north across the desert and, here more than ever, I needed to play my best hand. I needed to remind myself why I was there and what I wanted to achieve.

The Atacama Desert is the driest non-polar desert in the world, receiving an average rainfall of just a few millimetres per year. Some weather stations had never even recorded any rain in over 400 years! This creates a flat, arid and inhospitable landscape and looks more like Mars than anywhere in which you would wish to ride your bike. There is just one road which runs north and this is shared by onrushing trucks and cars, which forced me to shout and raise my fist in anger as they rushed past leaving just inches between themselves and my handlebars. There is also a distinct lack of any real civilisation. Due to the lack of rainfall, towns and cities never thrived along the road. This created large distances between settlements. Large distances that I needed to cycle carrying everything I would need for about 7 days at a time. This meant that my heavy bike had to become even heavier. To make matters even more difficult the road elevation gains as your head north. So not only is it dry, arid, and desolate but I was constantly cycling uphill. Gradually the road turned east towards the Andes mountains and warm Chilean beach roads were replaced by cold long mountain ones.

Not only was the environment and the road difficult but my desire to continue cycling was waning. A few weeks before I'd had the tragic news that my grandad had died. It was sad and unexpected and really shook me. For some time I was in a slump, I had no desire to continue, my head looked down at the bleak unmoving tarmac rather than the beautiful scenery, each pedal stroke felt repetitive as my mind tossed and turned over what to do either carry on or return home to see my family and attend the funeral. It was only in a conversation with my mum that I decided I should stay on the adventure. She told me that he said that if anyone was to happen to him that I was not to return home but continue, and that he was incredibly proud of me and what I had achieved so far.

This gave me the resolve to continue, to carry on heading north in his honour. It was a difficult thing to do and, when things started to get hard, all I was able to think about was being at home with my family and sharing his memory at the funeral or in stories around the dinner table. As I was travelling alone it meant that I had no one to speak with. Even if I did meet someone I could speak with, my language skills were only sufficient to purchase bread, not to convey deep feelings of loss.

It was fair to say that I left the coastal town of Taltal with plenty of reasons to feel concerned about the road ahead. All I wanted to do was cycle back to the nearest airport and fly home and end my adventure.

When I began, I'd wanted to cycle from Reading, UK to Reading, USA. I'd been on the road for two years when I reached the central coastal road of Chile. I was a year away from completing my adventure and there was still so much I wanted to see.

But then there was this little voice inside my head that constantly asked why I was doing this? Why am I seeing these places all alone? Should I not be home with my family? Who am I to attempt to cycle across the desert?

Self-doubt and fear starting to creep in but the words from my mother rang true. My Grandad was proud of me and wanted me to continue. With the ringing endorsement from my dearly departed Grandad Ted, I decided I would see if I could make it through the first stage of the desert towards the town of Antofagasta.

As I left Taltal the weather decided to match my mood. The heavens opened and rain started falling heavily on the road, like big wet tears. I was feeling miserable and hungover. My head was pounding, my tongue dry and my eyes were painful to open. My whole body just called out to go back to bed. This all meant my mood was downbeat and uninspired. It made it even more difficult to turn the pedals as the road started its steep climb up from the coastal town towards the heights of the Andes mountains.

The road was the Pan-Americana, the famous road which stretches between South and North America. It's a network of over 30,000km with only a short gap where the Darien rainforest lies between Columbia and Panama. The first day I had no destination in mind. I just wanted to cycle, to get north, to put some miles between me and Taltal and to be able to forget and remember all at the same time. It was working, as, although my mood was low, I was making steady progress and would often stop to look out in wonder at the amazing lunar landscapes all around me.

I managed to cycle around 60km that day, mostly with a steady but comfortable incline. As the sun crept towards the horizon I decided to call it a day and look for somewhere to camp.

The wind was howling so I knew that to ensure I had a comfortable night's sleep, and therefore have the ability to be stronger both physically and mentally the next day, I would have to find some shelter. I soon spotted what looked like an abandoned building some 500m off the main road and I pushed the bike into the desert to see what was there.

I was pushing into the wind which howled with such ferocity over the empty plain. The wheels of the bike slowly sank into the soft sand. It was like pushing the bike through jelly.

As I got close to the structure I realised it was a train line and what looked like an abandoned station building. 'This must have been how they built the road,' I mused before setting up my bed for the night. I made a small fire and some dinner and looked up at the millions and millions of stars overhead. With nothing around me, there was no light pollution and I could see the milky way above me shining with all its beautiful might.

There was something in the air that night. Even though I was totally alone that first night in the desert I felt a presence with me. I felt as if my Grandad was checking on me. I felt like he was making sure I was OK and, in his happy, go-lucky way, telling me that I was on the right track and everything was going to be alright.

Everything went fine and I was sleeping soundly until 3am. The blow of a huge horn shattered the desert silence. The growl of a diesel engine approaching tore the last vestiges of sleep from me. I was startled and scared as I watched two bright beams of light coming towards me. The light was the brightest light I had ever seen juxtaposed with the backdrop of the desert darkness. My heartbeat was beating rapidly and loudly against my chest as I felt the fear of being caught. The secret sleeper had been rumbled and I stood up alert and ready to protest my innocence. "I'm just a wary bicycle traveller needing shelter in the building. Honest, officer!"

It was only when I started to gain control of what was happening that I realised the lights and sounds were from a passing train. A heavy goods train was rumbling down the track. It wasn't abandoned at all. In fact it was being used by the mines in the Atacama to transport their goods back and forth from the port town of Antofagasta.

The train did not stop but continued to blow its horn as it went. I guess its intention was to warn animals away from the tracks rather than in a direct effort to rudely wake up anyone who might be sleeping alongside the railway.

Once the train had passed, I was relieved. I realised that, in order to shelter from the wind, the deserts exchange would be to sleep alongside a passing goods train which will endeavour to scare and wake you up at least once during the night.

Back on the road that day and it was into the type of desert cycling I had become used to in the outback of Australia. Everything was about routine.

Wake up, breakfast, cycle, snack, cycle, lunch, cycle, snack, cycle, dinner, camp.

Having a routine made the cycling bearable as there was not much to see and the slow and steady incline prevented me from having the ability to freewheel at any point. I would listen to downloaded podcasts to entertain myself and keep myself from asking the questions about why I was doing this at all. If I could just put my head down and continue, I would be able to continue. I had another three hundred kilometres to go and knew I could cover this in about six days. When I stocked up at the last supply point before Antofagasta, I bought six days' worth of food and carried two days' worth of water, knowing I could replace my water at the roadside shrines across the desert.

All along the road, there is a mix of shrines for the victims of road traffic accidents and the family take care of building and maintaining these shrines to their loved ones. They could range from a simple wooden cross with some photos to a large building of sorts with sofas, pictures, wind proofing even a half drank beer or cigarette left in memoriam. There is also water left, and lots of it. It seems the family likes to ensure the spirit of the dead never goes thirsty and there can be lines of filled plastic water bottles lying around, almost marking an entranceway to the shine. There can be 50-100L of water here and so I decided that if I was to take one I always said thank you to both the dead person and the family for leaving it there. These shrines enabled me to always ensure I was able to have access to water and they never let me down along the desert road and for this, I was super thankful. It also came as a sober warning about the number of road traffic accidents along this lonely road.

Once fully loaded with food and with my water being in good supply I was once again cycling north. Ahead of me lay six days of the road before I would reach Antofagasta where I would be able to re-stock and carry on towards Bolivia. My bike was as heavy as my mind and there was nothing to do but think as I carried on north.

Sandstorms would occasionally blow across the road causing me to stop and cover my mouth and nose. Sand particles whipped up by the unrestricted desert wind turned everything into a golden fog which would sting my face and arms as they charged across the open plains. They would not last longer than a few minutes but each time they brought a welcome change and distraction from the monotony of the desert. I could feel the weight of the journey bearing down on my shoulders and I knew something had to change, either my mood or my journey.

The highlight of my day was at night when I would take shelter next to the train line and make a fire before looking skyward at the millions and millions of stars. It was truly beautiful and much more entertaining than watching TV. Often I would stick my head out of my tent just to check that everything was real and the majestic sight of clear night sky and milky way showing off its beauty was not a dream.

The desert itself was cold in the night. With no cloud cover to keep the heat in and, with ever increasing elevation, it made mornings more and more difficult to get out of bed and get back on the bike. This is also a reflection of where my mood was. My motivation was at rock bottom. Even in the coldest times before this, I had wanted to get a quick breakfast down me and get back onto the bike. I was making slow progress across the Atacama and my slowness was taking its toll on my rations.

Carelessly I had only packed for the six days but with general apathy creeping in and with shorter days due to finding myself hiding in my tent for longer I was starting to run out of food. I knew I would have to reduce my rations in order to get to the next town where I could buy more. My growling tummy was just one more thing bringing my mood down. I had four days left until Antofagasta. I knew that I had to keep pushing on in order to get there and not run out completely.

As I left that morning I began cycling at my slow and steady pace but my headspace was filled with a new and annoying companion. At each turn of the pedal I pushed down, there would be loud and audible click each time the pedals went around. At first, this did not bother me but as I continued it began to grow more and more frustrating. I even found myself stopping and shouting at my pedals as if that would fix it. I tried to apply grease and oil to the pedals but this didn't work so I resolved that I must have some grit within my bottom bracket, the device in which holds the cranks to the bicycle. I did not have the specialised tool in which to fix this problem so each turn of the pedals brought its own little irritation. I solved the problem in the short term by listening to music but I knew soon my batteries would be exhausted and I would have to endure the mild torture.

Click. Click. Click.

I stopped early that day as I tired and had likely been pushing myself too hard, and fell asleep without any dinner. I had now only two days to go to Antofagasta but the road was taking its toll.

That morning my phone ran out of battery and I was back to the curse of listening to the little click get ever louder. At the same time, I was worried about any potential damage I could be doing to the bike in the long term. With all these problems mounting up I decided there and then that if things did not improve then I would get a bus from Antofagasta to Santiago and fly home. I needed a reset and the desert was beating me. Who was I to take on the might of the Atacama?

My resolve was broken and things needed to change. I had two days to go and I had not spoken to a single sole for five days. I had passed neither a checkpoint or gas station and was not due to for another 48 hours. My food was running out and I was looking forward to eating plain pasta and plain oats for the rest of the journey. This was meant to be fun!

I camped that night inside a large shrine, which had doors to protect it from the wind. Lying down inside the small building with pictures of the lost loved ones felt like the right place for me to be that night.

I was safe. I was inside. I was still here.

Thankfully, I wasn't woken that night by any grieving family members and awoke with the fresher resolve to continue. I ate my breakfast outside of the shrine, not wanting to make a mess inside, and packed away before hitting the road again. Thoughts of warm chicken and chocolate biscuits danced through my head.

I was up close to the plateau, therefore the uphill cycling had become much easier and I was able to make a slightly faster pace. Although the sound of the grit inside my bearing was now stabbing my earlobes quicker, the sheer fact that I was going faster made my mood increase. I was not fast but I was steady and the steady cyclist is the happy cyclist.

I was going strong until midday where my belly started to complain of hunger. All I had to eat for lunch was plain spaghetti or plain oats so it was not with any real excitement that I started to look for somewhere out of the wind for to cook my food. When presented with a choice of two plain carbs the joy of stopping is replaced with a feeling of resentment and disappointment.

It was not long until I saw a building on the side of the road and aimed for this for my spaghetti lunch.

As I pulled closer the building looked to be in better condition than I first thought, white walls which were clean, large windows, and even an electricity port on the outside. I immediately saw the potential to charge my phone and therefore drown out the noise my pedals were making.

As I stepped off the bike, I saw a police vehicle parked behind the building meaning someone was in. I approached cautiously and a young Chilean police guard come out and greeted me asking what I wanted. He was a small man in uniform but he did not look happy to see me, a contrast to the usual excited greetings from my previous meetings with the Chilean police. I told him about my bike trip, about my need for somewhere to stop for lunch and asked if I was able to charge my phone. He looks disapproving at me at first and told me to go. In broken Spanish I begged for a few minutes shelter from the sun and wind and he eventually relented, giving me a precious five minutes before he wanted me gone.

I was down-hearted by the experience so I sat in the shade with my phone collecting power from the external plug socket. I was tired but happy just to sit. I wanted to try to maximise my time for rest so I didn't bother to eat anything. I just sat there.

After five minutes the young guard came out, his stony face set. I started to gather my bits together but he motioned me to stay where I was, instead pulling an ice cold bottle of water out from the inside of his jacket. I grinned my thanks. He could obviously see that I was no threat at all. I was just a lonely cyclist resting in the shade of his outbuilding.

We talked briefly before he told me he had to go back inside. Slowly I drank the ice-cool water and felt my body rehydrating. I had been drinking warm and tepid water for the previous six days so this refreshes my body like nothing else. A coolness which radiated my insides with icy joy, it cooled me down instantly and my mouth was thankful for this simple gift.

I had been sitting in the shade for about 15 minutes now when the young guard came out of his air-conditioned building a third time. This time he had a smile across his face. He was holding a small bag and he offered it to me, telling me to take it. I looked down inside the bag to see a treasure trove of delicious food. He had given me what can only be his lunch: a cheese sandwich, a cereal bar, yoghurt and an apple. I protest but he quickly shuts me down telling me he is off shift in an hour and will go to the restaurant in his home town 60km away to get me some more food.

My spirit lifts. My mood lifts. My heart aches for the kindness of humanity and my stomach churns in the expectant joy of varied and delicious food. Everything I had been feeling and struggling with suddenly lifts as I take the first bite into the most amazing cheese sandwich I have ever eaten.

Not only had my palate been starved of taste but my soul had been starved of compassion. The loneliness, isolation and all the negative thought processes started to lift.

The young Chilean guard never knew how happy I was to sit there and eat. It was as if I was in a computer game and my character had just received a power-up. I sat outside the house for half an hour before leaving and felt more refreshed and energised than when I first started cycling in South America. I knocked on his door and thanked the young man with all my heart, he gave me another water and wished me luck, telling me that the next town is only 60km away and recommending me the name of a local hotel.

As I pedalled away I felt the joy of a shared connection. It felt like a happiness radiating through my body. I had not spoken to a single person for five days and had been struggling with thoughts of self-doubt. Deep inside my chest I felt a nagging pull to return home and be with the loved ones to grieve and reminisce.

But as I cycled away, I was smiling. I knew I was on the right track.

To experience pure joy, one must feel sadness first. It's like tasting the world's best cheese sandwich when the only thing on the menu is plain pasta.

Every time I think of the young man I think of a positive experience, not about all the times I struggled through the desert.

I put in my headphones and was able to listen to a podcast rather than the annoying noise. I knew that I could get the bike fixed the following day. I continued cycling, my eyes wondering around the land around me. A majestic desert valley. An empty space of almost nothing. An alien planet of rock and dust. I knew how lucky I was to be out here and to be dwarfed by everything around me.

I thought of my Grandad who did not want me to return home for his funeral. He knew I was living a life very few would ever understand. I believe he was able to understand me. He had seen the world as a young man and was one of the few from his squadron to put his name forward to serve in Malaysia at the end of the second world war. He had wanted to see the world and so did I. I would see it for myself and think of this trip as something which would bond his memory to mine. I wanted to finish this damned bike ride for us both and I was reinvigorated in my intention after experiencing the beauty of humanity served up in cheese sandwich!

The next day I reached the edge of the township of Antofagasta where I stopped in the recommended hotel for just $8 and was able to clean and repair my bike. I replaced the bottom bracket which had sand in-between the bearings which were making the click sound on each pedal rotation. I had an option of dropping down to the port town of Antofagasta but decided I was quite happy in the desert and did not fancy cycling back up the steep road to re-join the road north so I did everything I needed to on the outskirts of the town. I rested for one day before I then continued on the desert road towards the tourist town and gateway to Bolivia called San Pedro De Atacama, another 320km away.

The road was the same, with wind and elevation but my spirit was in a much better place, especially after having a super comfortable stay in the hostel. I had made my decision to carry on for the rest of the trip, a trip that would take me to Reading, USA and another year of cycling. Another year solo but one in which every day would enable for me to see something completely new. No two days would ever be the same.

I would not return for my Grandad's funeral and my mum and dad both agreed with me on the phone that it was for the best. They both told me he would be proud.

It took me another five days of cycling before I reached San Pedro de Atacama and would be finished with the Atacama desert but those five days were so much easier than the previous six. I had faced up to decisions which were as hard and as difficult as it was when I first left the UK some two years previously. I had needed to test my resolve in the world's driest and most arid landscape and I had come through both my feelings of grief and the desert with the sole help of a kind man and a cheese sandwich.

'The doorstep mile' is often called the hardest step in which to take. The first step of any adventure is daunting and frightening but often if you can manage to complete the first mile, to say your goodbyes and begin to see what happens, everything is meant to get easier.

This is not always the case. On longer trips I find that there are many reasons why you needed to be reminded of your decision to say yes in the first place. It can be that you are uncomfortable and have not slept well or perhaps you are missing your home life or maybe you are cycling through a desert with a squeaky bottom bracket dealing with thoughts of grief.

It is important to look back and check your intentions. Why did I begin this trip? Am I still having fun? Do I want to continue? Is there more I want to see and achieve? The ability to say yes is not just when you are starting out but something which you must carry with you at all times. It's that little card you hold in your heart, to look at and check that you are still on the right path. It's there to remind you why you began and what life was like before.

Adventures are not meant to be easy. To cycle or swim or sail repeatedly over great distances is tough and it is important to take time and check your motives and desires. This is, however, much easier when out in the wider world as you quickly realise that the world is a really good place and there are people out there to help you out when you are at your lowest. There are people that offer you something small but something as significant as a cheese sandwich. It might not sound a lot but in those moments it could be the difference between you completing your big adventure or jacking it all in.

Life is good so it is important to remember these things when you are mid-trip.

Dedicated to Grandad Ted.

Email: timcmillikin@gmail.com

Website: www.reading2reading.com

Instagram: @timcmillikin

Chapter 22

Project Mini-Me

by Tracey Bravo

My story is about a different type of adventure. I haven't walked 1000 miles, swam across an ocean or even led adventures around the world, but I did have a dream and I followed that dream until it came true.

Whilst working for London 2012, I had a rare day off, which I spent with my mum. We were walking around our local shopping centre and, out of the blue, she suddenly bought up the subject of freezing my eggs! Excuse me I thought! Not only did I feel a failure for not meeting the man of my dreams by the age of 35 and settling down to start my own family, I interpreted my mum's (probably very rehearsed and took some courage of her own to bring up) words as a jab at me having failed to provide her with another son-in-law and some more grandchildren. "No, I have *not* thought about freezing my eggs!" I said and quickly changed the subject.

Less than six months later, I was on a plane to Sierra Leone. I spent 4 incredible months living in a small town called Makeni, as a volunteer organising the second ever Sierra Leone Marathon for a charity called Street Child.

When I returned, I moved to Brighton after accepting a 12-month contract for the NSPCC. I was in my element, taking advantage of living by the sea with regular sea swimming, boot camps on the seafront, stand up paddle boarding and kayaking, as well as beach volleyball sessions and living a fantastic single life.

Whilst on a work trip to London, I was on the Tube escalators, browsing through the adverts and I stumbled across The Fertility Show. It mentioned egg freezing and I suddenly thought back to the conversation I had with my mum almost 2 years before. I couldn't stop thinking about it so when I got back to Brighton, I phoned a friend, Munch (happily married with 2 kids). She thought it was an amazing idea and was so supportive. She even convinced me to tell my mum that I was thinking of going. I have a close relationship with my mum, although have never felt particularly comfortable talking about boys, let alone creating babies with her so it was terrifying for me. But Munch was right (as she usually is) and my mum was incredibly supportive and offered to come with me. Thank goodness for The Archers, where they had recently had a storyline of a lady having a baby on her own, which I hadn't realised at the time, had already given my mum an insight into this as a possibility.

The Fertility Show was scary. My mum and I felt like rabbits in headlights. It felt like everyone was staring. There were seminars and dozens of stalls from clinics, sperm banks, egg banks, complementary therapies, support or lifestyle programmes, vitamins and supplements and more. They were based in the UK and overseas and we literally had no clue what to say to anyone! We chatted to a lovely lady from the Donor Conception Network who explained she had a donor conceived child and they had some fantastic books that you could read to a donor conceived child explaining where they came from.

Through seminars and speaking to people on the stalls, I learned that IVF was not available on the NHS for single women, co-parenting was a 'thing' and that, like cars, us ladies can have an MOT!

The Fertility Show felt like it was aimed at couples who had fertility problems. I didn't even know at this point if I did have any problems (except the obvious missing ingredient). It was interesting, but I still didn't know what my next steps were...

Before my contract at the NSPCC ended, I started applying for 'proper' (as my mum calls them) jobs. Whilst hunting I found a job in Watford, my hometown. If I did go ahead with Project Mini Me, I would need to consider being close to my family. Both my sister and my parents live in Watford. I couldn't continue living in my perfect pad in Brighton that I shared with three guys in their 30s and 40s – not sure they would appreciate an extra housemate however cute it would be!

So, I applied for the job, thinking that if I get it, it's a sign that Project Mini Me is no longer an idea, but a project I needed to commence! It must have been the most relaxed I have ever been for an interview.

I got the job. I was moving back to Watford, away from my life in Brighton. So before I did, I kept up my side of the bargain, and had my MOT. I was told it all looked good. There was no need to rush into anything, but at my age, things COULD change very rapidly.

But I had to consider the next steps – where to go? I was a bit confused, until I spotted The Alternative Parenting Show in September. This seemed much more aimed towards my situation than The Fertility Show. It was focused much more on LGBT couples or singles that were, like me, missing a vital ingredient!

I was so prepared for this show; I had looked up all the talks I wanted to go to, all the stalls I wanted to visit, I was almost excited. I was going with Emma, another very supportive friend (who I met in Sierra Leone), and I couldn't wait to share this experience with her. The day before, I received a text from Emma. Her flight from Sierra Leone had been cancelled and she wouldn't be able to come. I was devastated as I wasn't sure I could do this alone. I pulled myself together and went on my own. I was so nervous but I have done so many things on my own before, why should this be any different?

It was amazing! Emotional and exciting all rolled into one. By the end of the day, I was content with the whole baby making process not working and having adoption as my backup plan. I had spent time talking to a firm of lawyers in case I used a friend as a donor and what paperwork was required if I followed that route. I spoke to a clinic that stated 30% of their patients were single women (I couldn't believe this was so normal – how did I not know anyone who had done it before?). I was ready – ready to take my next step.

I took Emma along with me to my consultation at the clinic I had chosen. They took blood to test my AMH (Anti-Mullerian Hormone which can assess your ovarian egg reserve and therefore your fertility) levels and also did an internal scan to check out my follicles. Chatting with the consultant made me understand that my only real option was IVF (30% success rate) over IUI (Intrauterine insemination – not hugely different to a turkey baster approach with a mere 5% success rate). The consultant led me to believe it was now or never, even waiting just three months (if I was to use a friend donor whose sperm would need to be in quarantine for that time) would significantly reduce my chances of getting pregnant! Arghhh!

So, still missing a vital ingredient I started to look online at the sperm bank that was connected to the clinic I had chosen. It was a minefield – similar to internet dating without photos. I couldn't decide, I wanted them all for different reasons. A black donor would help me create a beautiful mixed race baby; a ginger one might mean the little one gets cute freckles. Do I pick someone who I could be attracted to if I met in real life? Or would I do the baby a favour and find a donor who had a slim frame, to give a child a better chance of not having the 'fat thoughts' that I had growing up.

I needed help – I couldn't decide!

So, I organised a 'Swimmers Selection Soiree' where I invited some close friends including my mum and sister round for some wine, dinner and more importantly, help! We gathered in my lounge. Andrea, a teacher had handed us all mini whiteboards whilst instructing us to write down characteristics that we thought were the most important and any we felt were least important. All of my guests had decided that having a Caucasian donor was important. It was going to be hard enough bringing a child into the world without the added complication of one that doesn't look much like me. My vision of a mixed race baby was diminishing as I couldn't help but agree. Level of education was quite controversial. Two of my closest friends had left school at 16 and now were hugely successful. A high level of education doesn't mean a good job or guaranteed happiness. Although I still struggled with my own answers, it was interesting listening to the debate, some agreeing whilst others didn't. It was a fun evening and before everyone went home, we had all agreed on an Australian donor.

The week ahead turned into one of the most stressful weeks ever. I realised something wasn't quite right about this Australian donor. My mum's words were ringing in my ears about choosing a donor with allergies when you could just pick one without... So I tore the database apart. I went through it filter by filter, adding each and every donor to a spreadsheet in true Tracey style!

This way I could eliminate one by one. My friend Sheema gave her input from Australia. "Don't pick someone too tall. My brother-in-law is so tall it is a pain. He has to have custom made trousers and even needs a longer bed!"

Then I found donor 187. He seemed perfect. For some reason, I Googled 187. Section 187 of the California Penal Code defines the crime of murder!! I would never forgive myself if my child ended up walking into a school with a gun. I called the sperm bank and asked how they decided on donor numbers. They said it was random. I told them what I discovered and they actually said that 187 was no longer available. Emotions flowed – I couldn't work out if it was a lucky escape or that I should be devastated that I'd missed out on the perfect donor.

Then I discovered a donor I nicknamed 'Wild Card'. He hadn't shown up in the original searches because he described himself as mixed race and not Caucasian. He selected medium as his skin colour, which is how I would describe mine (on a scale of light/fair, medium, olive and dark). So Wild Card became a prime contender.

Days went passed as I stared at my spreadsheet wishing I had more than the 40 donors available to me. I thought it would be like falling in love – when you know, you just know. But it wasn't. I even looked at other sperm banks and I was overwhelmed by the amount of choice out there. Some US based sperm banks share photos, recorded messages and so much more. How on earth was I to choose? I needed more time, and that, I didn't have.

We found 'Jazz Hands' at the Swimmers Selection Soiree and he was a firm favourite of mine and Emma's. He wasn't so popular with the other guests as he was ginger and a performer but I thought he sounded quite fun.

My mum liked the sound of 'Diamond Driller', who claimed diamond drilling was what he did for a living. I'm afraid he did nothing for me, but as my mum was so keen, I thought I should add him to the short list.

'Pen sketches' (I later realised was where a donor writes in their own words about themselves) were available for some of the profiles so I asked for the three shortlisted to be emailed through.

I opened the email on my work computer late on a Friday, and luckily there was no one left in the office but me. I quickly ran to the printer to greet the pen sketches as they were expelled one by one from the machine. I sat down at my desk and read the first one – it happened to be Jazz Hands. I loved it – it felt perfect. It really brought the donor to life, much more than the profile on the website. I packed up at work and virtually skipped home. I had found my donor, I thought.

When I got home, I read the other two pen sketches. Wild Card was amazing too – he seemed such a nice man. Diamond Driller was... just uneventful.

I had previously set up a private Facebook group – 'Project Mini Me'. As I told more people, I invited them to the group. I rarely told people that I hadn't spoken to face to face, I was really concerned how my plan wasn't quite traditional, and it was potentially quite controversial bringing a child into the world without two parents and I wasn't ready to face negative comments. I also still felt a failure having not met Mr. Right – what was wrong with me?

I shared the pen sketches in my secret Facebook group, asking the opinions of my nearest and dearest, to see if they were as awestruck by two of the profiles as I was. Wild Card won the vote hands down. All of a sudden, I was so happy with my choice and I was within the week deadline that I had to order it.

The sperm bank did make a mistake and Wild Card's Bachelor of Science ended up being an HND in Administration but I really didn't care. He sounded lovely, a family man who loves sport and described himself as smiling, warm, adventurous, inquisitive, ambitious and determined. He wrote that he and his wife are unable to have children, and after some reflection, he decided he really wanted to help others. He continued to say his wife is fully supportive of his decision and agreed it would be a wonderful thing to do. WOW!

So – after double-checking with the sperm bank that no other information that they had provided was incorrect, I finally had purchased that missing ingredient with not much change from £1000!

Counselling was included in the price, so I thought I should take advantage. I had no idea what to expect and I found it quite comforting. They explained quite a bit about using a donor – for example he could change his mind right up until an embryo was transferred into me. It rarely happened but I had to know it was his right. And that my future child would find out some non-identifying information about their donor at the age of 16 to ensure they are not dating a sibling. And of course due to the fairly recent change in UK law, any children would have the right to have access to contact details of their donor. The counsellor advised me to join up with the Donor Conception Network and to tell my child about being donor conceived from an early age.

Should I tell my boss? I had figured out that I would need quite a bit of time off work for appointments. I didn't really know how many, but I did get the impression I wouldn't know when they would be in advance. But, if I told him would he hold it against me – I had been in my job for less than a year and I was going through IVF alone – what would he think – that I'm a failure?

In the end I decided to tell him and it was the best possible decision. Despite me getting all emotional and speaking through tears, he admitted that he and his wife went through IVF and he understood the process of what I was about to go through. He said he would help me come up with excuses for the rest of the team so they didn't find out. It was a weight off my mind and it meant I had someone to share my little secret with.

I was eventually ready to call the clinic when my next cycle started. Back to London, another scan, a private prescription for some scary drugs (injections and bum pills I called them), frantically calling round different chemists trying to get the best price.

Suddenly the day arrived where I needed to start the injections. I was hoping my housemate, would be home for some moral support. She wasn't. I sat down on the sofa, got the injection out the fridge and sat for a moment. I couldn't do it!

I texted Debbie, a friend I had known all my life and someone who had gone through IVF with her husband about 7 years before. "Are you around?" I asked.

She was hosting a dinner party – it was Saturday evening after all, but she knew about the journey I was embarking on, so immediately called me back. She was amazing, she sat with me on the phone for about 20 minutes until I eventually looked down and screamed, "Oh my goodness – it's halfway in and I didn't even notice!" Debbie talked me through pushing the needle all the way in and actually injecting the drug. I was full of emotion (as well as new hormones) and so grateful and actually, it really wasn't a big deal.

I had to inject myself for about a week, and that meant doing it in public toilets, as I had to attend a Fashion Show for work, as well as a fundraising quiz. I got quite good at it and it really was only the thought of it that made it so bad. The bum pills however, if I was lucky and got pregnant, I would need to keep up for 3 months!

Several more visits to London, opening my legs for various people to poke surgical implements into my private parts, my body was eventually ready for the egg collection. Dignity became a thing of the past. My mum came with me to London as the clinic specifically said I needed someone to travel home with me. They knocked me out for about half an hour and, as I was coming round, they said they had retrieved 6 eggs. The perfect amount for an egg box I thought. I had no idea if that was good or bad, but it was 6 eggs nonetheless.

The next day the embryologist called to say that four of the six eggs had been fertilised successfully. Day five I was back at the clinic, legs akimbo with my mum present for the conception of her possible future grandchild. Not many grandparents can say that! It was an uncomfortable procedure, similar to a smear, only this lasted about 15 minutes, and on a full bladder. Afterwards, I was presented with my first scan, with a little dot, to show the little embryo sitting comfortably.

In December, I organised a beautiful remembrance event at work.

We were outside on a December evening, including a choir, brass band and carols by candlelight. I walked round touching my tummy, thinking I could be growing my mini me and how precious this was. I really felt like I could be pregnant. I needed to be careful, not carrying heavy things, which is so unnatural to me on event day, but it was beginning to feel quite real.

I ignored the advice of taking the pregnancy test two weeks later. I was impatient and according to the pregnancy test instructions, I could take it earlier than the clinic instructed. I bought a pack of 5 cheap tests. The morning after my event, I tested before work. I ran into my housemate's room and asked her what she thought... She didn't think it was positive, the line wasn't strong enough (why would she know – she has never been pregnant!) so I messaged Munch with a photo. "That's positive!" she said. I promised myself I wouldn't get excited and I would slowly get used to the idea. Every morning for the next 5 days I took another test. Each one said positive. OH MY GOODNESS!

At seven weeks, I went back to the clinic for a scan, this time taking both my mum and my sister. On the screen in front of me was what looked like a caterpillar wearing a Santa hat – it was a couple of days after Christmas so it was totally appropriate. We even heard a heartbeat!

The 12-week scan went well, so traditionally this is the time to tell people. I was not one for posting on Facebook and still only comfortable telling people who I saw face-to-face.

My parents were worried about what/how to tell their friends. Their friends were a different generation to mine, so we were nervous about how it would be received. My mum wanted to email her friends, so she didn't have to face their first reaction, and instead, they could digest it before getting back to her. That made sense so I helped her word an email. She sent it out and we held our breath.

That night she forwarded me some truly lovely responses from her friends. One response said "It's so pleasing to hear of someone going into this having given it the amount of thought that she will have done. So often, I sit in court and hear the expression 'single parent' and so often I'm sitting there thinking, no this is the product of two people just having a bit of fun, and one of them walks away from the responsibility that they have created. In fact, the next time I do a sermon, I might well use it as my subject, it is one of my hobby horses!"

Back in November, I had decided to sign up to 'Strictly Come Hospice', a fundraiser run by the Hospice where I worked. It was seven weeks of dance lessons followed by a grand finale in a theatre. I wanted something to take my mind off things if Project Mini Me wasn't successful - one in five pregnancies don't make it to 12 weeks, so even if this did result in a pregnancy, it didn't mean it would be an actual baby. I figured I would either be throwing my heart and soul into it to take my mind off a failed Project Mini Me, or dancing in a finale, 20 weeks pregnant!!

I remember whispering to Michael, my dance partner, "By the way, I am pregnant! It is really early days so no one knows, but there will be no lifts in our dance."

Michael was a fantastic partner, keeping my secret, and understanding when I needed to take more breaks and eat far more than most dance partners. It was so much fun!

In March, at 20 weeks pregnant, the finale arrived and our salsa version of 'Inspector Gadget' was a hit, we were very excited by our 10/10 from the Senior Vice President and Managing Director of Warner Brothers Studios. The dance judges weren't quite as generous which led me to believe we were better at entertainment than dancing but we were very proud of ourselves!

The pregnancy went well. At 20 weeks, I found out that I was going to have a little boy. I called him Bob the Bump. I pushed myself out of my comfort zone by attending a YesTribe campout (I am not really a camper). Luckily for me, this one was just a 15-minute drive, so I didn't have to lug my bag across London on a train. So I decided to brave it. It was bivy only camp and I had never been in a bivy, but the next thing I knew, I'd said yes and I was arriving in camp. I finally found a use for my jacket having a zip both at the top and the bottom of my coat. I lifted the base of my coat above my bump so I could actually do it up, zipped it to the top followed by unzipping it from the bottom to make room for Bob (leaving me with a cold tummy but warm chest).

It was comedy trying to get into my sleeping bag, and then into a bivy bag with a bump. Luckily there were some super lovely ladies around me willing to give me a hand and I was praying I didn't need to get up in the night to go through the palaver all over again!

Waking up amongst the bluebells was amazing and what an adventure.

Around this time I went into London to YesStories. It was fascinating hearing all about Thomas Hough and how he signed up to doing things, and worked out how to do it after. That evening I vowed to sign up to Yestival. Surely I could do it, with a 2-3 month old baby? (This was the very same Yestival I was too chicken to go on my own six months previously, without a baby!).

Throughout the rest of my pregnancy, I managed a couple more nights of camping, this time in a tent instead of a bivy and also threw in a few local ParkRuns, the last at 35 weeks pregnant. 2016 was a hot summer and the walk home after the ParkRun was one of the biggest challenges. I was used to fitting in quite a lot into a weekend, but realised I had to slow down considerably as my energy levels had taken a hit. Those benches in town centres and parks became so incredibly useful as I had to have a sit down before I could continue some journeys.

On 9th August I woke up and found myself in the very early stages of labour. I messaged Emma, my birth partner, who had made no plans for the last couple of weeks in case she was called in and warned her that I thought today was the day. She was with me by lunchtime, along with my mum, sister and another friend. It was a fun day, watching the Rio Olympics whilst taking breaks to concentrate on my breathing through each contraction.

That evening, we moved to hospital and Emma stayed with me throughout the next stages of labour. I was hoping for it all to be over and done with by morning but I was wrong. After trying out almost all of the different types of pain relief I learnt about in my antenatal group, I was in the birthing pool at 9am. Over 24 hours so far and this little guy was in no hurry to make an appearance. Gas and air brought back memories to my vodka Redbull days!

Later in the afternoon, they moved us to the maternity ward as they were concerned about Bob's heart rate.... At this point I gave in to an epidural. At around 6:30, Emma managed to get the live streaming of YesStories which was happening concurrently. But it wasn't to be as we were then informed that Bob was stuck, and a caesarean was the way forward.

Finally at 9.29pm he arrived.

Decisions on your own are really quite daunting. I wished I had someone to share the burden of naming a human being for life! I eventually settled on Isaac (meaning laughter) Larry (my first mentor, Larrry Estrin, at my first Olympics) Makeni (the village in Sierra Leone I spent time in) Bravo. The dilemma of how to introduce him on social media arrived. How do people who do it on their own introduce their new-born? I still hadn't told a whole bunch of my friends so it was going to be a surprise to many people, especially if I hadn't seen them in the last 9 months. Eventually, a very carefully worded post went out, with no mention of how 'I' or 'we are proud to announce' as I was still ashamed of what people would think. The responses were endless! I did get the odd 'wishing the three of you all the best' which felt bizarre.

Being a new mum was all kinds of emotional and I take my hat off to all mums, both before and after me, who have been through the first few weeks (and beyond) of motherhood. I never fully understood what it involved until I was there myself. I couldn't even stay awake to watch Usain Bolt's 100m race during the Olympics. I watched him start, and missed him finish – seriously this was a race that took less than 10 seconds!

Isaac refused to breastfeed so I added to the challenges of new motherhood by insisting on giving him my milk regardless so for his first year I exclusively expressed for him.

10 weeks after he was born, I made it to Yestival. I chickened out of camping, but we went as day guests all three days. The adventures had begun. I applied for his passport pretty early on, and at 6 months I took him to Canada to meet his 97 year old great, great aunt who was absolutely thrilled to see him. Just a few weeks later we travelled to Australia for 6 weeks to spend time with friends out there.

We are members of the Donor Conception Network and make sure we are surrounded by other donor-conceived children regularly so when Isaac finally understands his story, he will never feel alone. I've even found another solo mum who used the same donor, which makes our children half-brothers. Whilst his mum, Wendy, and I get our heads round the fact that our sons are related, we are planning our next meet. I am able to contact the HFEA in the same way as 'Wild Card' is to see how many donor conceived children have been born as a result of his generosity. Isaac is the oldest, and a year older than Toby. Isaac reaches 18 first so will have the opportunity to contact him then. I hope I bring him up to respect Toby and any other diblings (donor siblings) we may discover along the way if their decision is different to his own.

I would love Isaac to want to contact Wild Card at 18. It would be fantastic to give him and his wife a massive hug and thank them for the opportunity that they gave to me. But I know it is not my decision and I need to respect my little man and the choices he makes. We refer to him as Isaac's donor, not his dad. One day, we may even find a dad for Isaac.

So now, my adventures are different to what they used to be, but they are adventures all the same. Isaac loves trains, buses, aeroplanes, camping, canoeing, scooting, cycling and starting fires.

If you are embarking on an adventure of your own, surround yourself with people who come up with reasons why you *should* do it. Keep your sensible head on to make sure you have considered what could go wrong so you are a little prepared (more so emotionally in my case) as life doesn't always go to plan. And then go, go, go – make some fantastic memories for you and anyone you take with you or meet (or 'make' in my case!) along the way. Finally – tell your story, as it may be just the incentive for someone to live out their dream too.

As I write this, Project Mini Me the sequel has commenced, as I would love to give Isaac a sibling, this time only 3 eggs were collected but all successfully fertilised. The best two were recently transferred and unfortunately didn't work out. Watch this space to see if the final embryo (named Rocky the Runt) makes it. In the meantime, Isaac and I are already planning our next adventures together, including our first bivy together, a trip to Canada for his great, great aunts 100th birthday and getting in/on the water as often as we can.

Tracey Bravo is a full time working solo parent to an almost 3-year-old little man. She has worked in fundraising in the charity sector for over 10 years, which isn't a recommended salary for adventures that cost a lot (like this one).

If you would like to chat about embarking on a similar (or completely different) adventure, or set/encourage the duo on a new adventure then please get in touch. They can often be found hanging out with the Ordinary Superparents (Facebook) or child friendly YesTribe meet ups.

Facebook: TraceyjBravo (avid reader but rarely a poster!)

Instagram: @bravofamilyadventures (trying to learn)

Twitter: @TraceyJBravo (no idea)

Epilogue

Teddington Trust

by Nicola Miller

What could possibly be better than the wonderful The Big Book of Yes? Ah, of course, The *Bigger* Book of Yes!

It`s been so exciting to see this second edition come together with yet more inspiring stories of overcoming adversity, high adventure and living life on your own terms but to us at Teddington Trust this book, much like the first, has an extra layer of wonderfulness.

We are Teddington Trust, the cause behind this epic series, and the sharing of these stories is helping our own community start creating theirs. 100 per cent of the royalties from the sales of this book comes directly to Teddington Trust.

Teddington Trust is a Scottish registered charity with a global reach. We are small yet mighty and our goal is to protect, educate and inspire those affected by the life-limiting rare disease xeroderma pigmentosum.

Xeroderma pigmentosum (XP) affects fewer than 110 patients in the UK and is listed in the ultra-rare disease spectrum with equally low incident rates globally. People with XP lack the DNA mechanism required to repair damage caused by natural and artificial sources of ultra-violet light, rendering them a staggering 10,000 times more susceptible to skin cancer than the general population. They must spend their entire lives 100 per cent shielded from all daylight and most types of artificial lighting to avoid death by aggressive skin cancer. 30 per cent also experience degenerative neurological symptoms often leading to untimely death.

To think about this at the most simple level – please just take a moment to consider your day. How much of it was spent in contact with daylight outside? How long was there light bursting through your window? What portion of your day was spent in the presence of some form of artificial lighting?

Yep – unless you spent the day potholing (which some of our adventurous reader's might well have been doing), chances are your entire waking hours were spent bathed in light of some form.

So you can see how for someone living with XP, having the opportunity to live their own adventure story might be immensely challenging.

Now this is the really great bit! By you purchasing this book, you have personally helped make their lives that little bit more adventurous.

"How so?" I hear you cry…

In 2018, The Big Book of Yes raised over £1,500. This money helped our families start living their own adventure stories.

It helped us fund life-saving protective hats with face shields and UV resistant gloves and clothing. This meant that our children and young adults around the globe could come out of the shadows and step into the light. They now have complete safety from UV and can join and enjoy the world outside!

It helped us fund places for families here in the UK to attend the BIG Teddington Sleepover, where we created a UV safe environment for them to come together and get active. During the weekend they did rock climbing, fencing, team building activities, archery and laser quest - all topped off with a magical night campfire and sing along. Families for whom adventure is normally contained within the pages of adventure books were, many for the first time, living the adventures they had always dreamed of.

And now, thanks to The *Bigger* Book of Yes, we are doing it all again. And just like this book, we are going BIGGER than ever before!

On behalf of everyone at Teddington Trust and our global XP community, thank you for saying YES to buying this book and for being part of our own adventure story. You really are making a difference.

Let the adventures continue...

Keep saying YES!

Nicola Miller

To find out more about xeroderma pigmentosum and the work of Teddington Trust please visit www.teddingtontrust.com and follow us on Facebook and Twitter @TeddingtonTrust.

Please Leave a Review

We really hope you enjoyed reading our stories. If you have a minute it would be absolutely amazing if you could head over to Amazon and leave an honest review. Every review makes this book more visible to the general public so just by tapping a few words and selecting a star rating you are potentially raising even more money for charity. Good on you!

You can use your phone to scan this QR code and it will take you straight to the Amazon page The 'WRITE A CUSTOMER REVIEW' button should be next to the reviews towards the bottom of the page.

Thanks, you wonderful human being!

The Bigger Book of Yes team

So you've finished reading the Bigger Book of Yes. Now what?

Well, maybe you'll go off on your own adventure. Maybe you'll be the next one saying, "Yes!"

In the meantime, if your still looking for more inspiration head over to Amazon right now and buy the predecessor to this book, The Big Book of Yes. Same deal. 100% of royalties go to Teddington Trust.

https://bit.ly/TBBOY1   https://bit.ly/TBBOY3

Printed in Great Britain
by Amazon

45963146R10242